Living the Palio

A Story of Community and Public Life in
Siena, Italy

Thomas W. Paradis

Copyright © 2020 by Thomas W. Paradis

All rights reserved. No part of this publication may be reproduced, distributed or transmitted in any form or by any means, without prior written permission of the publisher, except in the case of brief quotations embodied in critical reviews and certain other noncommercial uses permitted by copyright law.

Thomas W. Paradis has no responsibility for the persistence or accuracy of URLs for external or third-party Internet Websites referred to in this publication and does not guarantee that any content on such Websites is, or will remain, accurate or appropriate.

Published by Thomas W. Paradis
Indianapolis, IN. USA

Includes bibliographic references and notes.
Book Layout © 2017 BookDesignTemplates.com
Typeset in Alegreya
Cover designed by Anna Burrous

All photos (cover and interior) by Thomas W. Paradis
Map of Siena's Contrade provided by David Lown: www.picturesfromitaly.com.

Living the Palio – 3rd ed.
ISBN: 978-1-7334838-2-7 (paperback)
ISBN: 978-1-7334838-3-4 (ebook)

Contents

Foreword 1

Introduction 3

PART I: LEARNING CURVE 5

1. Not Enough Tuscan Sun 7
   Learning from Viterbo 8
   Envisioning a Siena Program 9
   A Traumatic Journey 10
   The Safest City 13

2. Siena from Above 15
   Siena's Three Districts 17
   Via Francigena 18
   The Piazza del Campo 21
   Height Wars 23

3. Discovering the Palio 27
   The Hunger Games on Horseback 29
   Three Laps of Terror 30
   Contrade Relationships 32
   Winning the Palio 35
   Palio Shortcomings 36
   Daddy Monte: Banca Monte dei Paschi 38

4. Life in the Contrade 41
   The Contrada Social Scene 42
   Symbols of Contrada Identity 44
   Caterpillar Rock Stars 45

    Night at the Museum 46
    Contrada Membership 50

5. The Magic of Fontebranda 55
    The Siena Car Scene 57
    Locked Out 59
    Help from the Goose 61

PART II: FEELING AT HOME 65

6. Mixing it Up 67
    Ceramic Shop Friends 67
    A Contrada Resurgence 69
    Social Mixing 72
    The Goose Plate 73
    Exploring the Goose 74
    A Patron Saint of Italy 75

7. Test Pilots 77
    Genius of the European Square 77
    The *Tratta* 79

8. First Contact 89
    A Goose *Fazzoletto* 91
    The Contrada Società 94
    Socializing in Società Trieste 95

9. Building Confidence 99
    The Medici Fort 100
    A Morning Trial 102

10. Prova Generale 107
    The Secret to Adolescent Engagement 109
    Defending Our Turf 115

PART III: PALIO DAY 119

11. A Tough Decision 121

    How to View the Palio 122
    Surviving the Campo 123
    Remote Viewing 124
    The Blessing of the Horse 126
    The *Comparsa* 129

12 Myth of the Republic 131
    The Historical Procession 133
    Contrada Performances at the Duomo 135

13. Underdog (July 2013 Palio) 139
    The Palio Lineup 141
    Ninety Seconds 146
    Victory 149

14. Goose Chase 151
    Celebration at Provenzano 151
    A Chaotic Crossing 154
    Guess Returns Home 156
    The People's *Drappellone* 157
    The Chapel of Saint Catherine 158
    A Contrada Rebirth 161
    The *Drappellone* Returns to the Goose 162
    Ceramic Shop Goodbyes 164

PART IV: CONVERSATIONS 167

15. Midnight Contrada Run 169
    Elusive Contrada Dinner Tickets 171
    Return to Società Due Porte 175

16. Panthers 181
    Arriving at the Dinner 184
    Making New Friends 185
    The Dinner Progresses 190

17. From the Bleachers 197

    Local Economic Challenges 198
    Settling Into Our Seats 201
    Dario's Wish... 204
    Future of the Palio 207

18. Foul Play (July 2015 Palio) **213**
    Lineup of the Horses 213
    The Race Begins... 218
    A New Victor 223
    Buon Viaggio! 226

PART V: STALLOREGGI NIGHTS 229

19. Extraction of the Contrade **231**
    Poor Connections 231
    Unexpected Encounter in the Campo 234
    Meet the Parents.. 241
    A Rewarding Hike 245

20. West Side Story **249**
    A Senese Shortcut.. 250
    Proximate Rivals... 251
    A Pleasant Introduction.. 255

21. A Legendary Race **263**
    Panther Museum Sequel 264
    Contrada Costuming 266
    Sweet Victory... 268
    The Americans are Coming! 271
    Amongst the Panterini... 272

22. Pushing the Envelope **283**
    Assignment of the Horses... 283
    The Eagle has Landed... 285
    Cultural Boundaries 288

23. A Rebirth for the Ages (July 2016 Palio) **291**

    Bombshell 291
    Shower Caps and Wine 292
    Nonna Rising 294
    Cappotto 297
    Parting Reflections 299

Photo Gallery 303

Acknowledgments 329

Glossary 331

Notes 339

Bibliography 343

Author's Note

To protect the trust and identities of individuals mentioned throughout the book, I have replaced their real names with pseudonyms. The exceptions to this are my wife, the jockeys, and any authors or local experts whose books and research are referenced.

Foreword

Siena doesn't celebrate its Palio but lives it as an essential part of the city's existence. As an ancient feast and the city's premier festival, the Palio has remained largely unchanged for centuries, now persisting into the new millennium. The Palio isn't just an evocative event with an aim to attract tourists but exists as a complex plot directly involving Siena's seventeen *contrade* (neighborhoods). It serves as the city's sense of place, a point of reference and identity for the Senesi throughout the year.

It may appear to the visitor that time stopped here in 1555, when Siena's proud people were forced to surrender and open their gates to the invader. Siena's roots are firmly planted in the Middle Ages; the population hasn't increased since then, the city has preserved its character, and its bank—the oldest in the world—remains the city's primary source of support.

Many people tend to associate the Middle Ages with the so-called Dark Ages, but for Siena they really weren't *that* dark—quite the contrary. No one can deny that it was an enlightened era capable of producing an amazing number of geniuses and masterpieces, and that in the tenth century, it could even boast a hospital with public health accessible to all.

The Palio of Siena is as old as the city itself and has accompanied the city's history through the centuries. Understanding the Palio is fundamental for anyone interpreting Siena's culture. To delve into the subject and successfully capture the city's essence, one must acknowledge the contrade. The contrade are like seventeen small micro-states nestled within the walls that envelope the city, each with its own identity, a geographic territory, and an intricate, democratic system to elect its own leaders. The contrade subsist thanks to the voluntary activities of its members, rooted in passion and values that have been handed down through the centuries.

A child in Siena may participate in the contrada to learn the ancient art of tossing a flag, or to beat a drum. A teenager—rather than spending hours on social networks—might simply volunteer to serve and clear tables for any number of contrada social events. As adults, members organize their lives

FOREWORD

around the multi-faceted functions of the Palio and related contrada activities.

What for the Senesi is a day-to-day lifestyle can be a curious anomaly for the visitor. Thus is the paradox. Perhaps the Senesi are the least suitable people to explain the Palio and the contrade system to someone else. Let's face it, Siena may not portray itself as the most welcoming place on earth, and the purpose of the contrade certainly is not to recruit new members.

Because of this, to conceive a book dedicated to the trinity of Siena, Palio, and contrade is not an easy task. One needs an unconditional love for the city to comprehend their inseparability. Above all, one must be armed with patience. Thomas Paradis succeeded because he has managed to catch the symptomatic core of Siena life and—perhaps without even realizing it—conceived of the book by using the same *attesa*, the city's rhythm, which is not the hectic one of our modern times but the one marked by its impressive past.

Dario Castagno

Tuscan expert and author of *Too Much Tuscan Sun, A Day in Tuscany, Too Much Tuscan Wine, An Osteria in Chianti, The District 9 of Chianti, The Miracle of Belpoggio, The Bromide in the Soup, Brunello for Breakfast,* and *The Year of the Chicory.*
www.dariocastagno.com

Introduction

My principal aim with this book—the third and final edition—is to provide an introduction to Siena's fascinating community and its twice-annual Palio horse race. Built around my own humbling adventure stories, the book is informed by a variety of existing scholarship to help readers better comprehend the roles of the Palio within the *Senese* (plural: Senesi) community. Siena's seventeen *contrade* (neighborhoods) serve as veritable extended families and find their roots in the city's medieval glory days. They can be interpreted as miniature city-states, and they provide important lessons about community cohesiveness, urban livability, and civic life—not to mention an incomparable sense of local place identity that many Americans might feel is lacking at home.

This book began as a series of tongue-in-cheek stories about my adventures while leading a study-abroad program in Siena, Italy, during the summer of 2013. Before I knew it, I had typed seventy pages of text following that pivotal first program. Only then did I concern myself with what to do with all the material, eventually deciding to compile and expand the stories to share with others in the form of a book. As of this writing, the book now integrates material and stories from six consecutive summers in Siena, namely 2013 through 2018. The rather personalized tour I share here is roughly sequential, though certain years are emphasized more than others.

To be perfectly clear, I have no intention to contribute directly to the existing volume of academic research about Siena and its signature horse race. Mine is more of a personal journey and compilation of reliable information that already exists. As an educator at heart and a geographer by training, I do bring a spatial perspective, looking at some of the city's social and demographic changes over time. Topics of global influence, economic challenges, pressures of mass tourism, and suburban development are of particular interest here. All communities face a variety of challenges over time, and Siena is no different—despite what some are tempted to view as a nearly utopian society.

INTRODUCTION

Amid my own personal anecdotes, I have provided endnotes for every referenced source to provide appropriate credit. You can view these endnotes as a portal to further reading, or you can simply ignore them to enjoy the story on its own merit. I have done my utmost best to assure accuracy of the referenced material, and I take responsibility for any possible misinterpretations I may have made. Siena and its unique, complex social structure and associated rituals are by no means easy to untangle or represent accurately, so I have paid careful attention to representing the community in a respectful and reliable manner. I am the outsider here, a fact made painfully obvious throughout most of this work.

The lessons to be learned in Siena are potentially endless, which is perhaps the primary reason I have been compelled to produce this book. Beyond that, it was simply a fun thing to do. I hope that comes across.

PART I
LEARNING CURVE

CHAPTER 1

Not Enough Tuscan Sun

MAKING ONE'S WAY TO SIENA REQUIRES A GOOD DEAL OF PERSONAL fortitude. How thousands of visitors manage to show up in Siena during the days of the Palio each summer is beyond me. Since its founding during Etruscan times (prior to the Roman Republic), this Tuscan hilltop community has persisted as a geographical backwater, lacking any major river access, let alone any direct connection to the sea. Even the Romans generally avoided the place, and that wasn't something the Romans did lightly. Some two millennia later, the situation has not improved much, if our first experiences in Siena are any indication.

Siena does not enjoy a main-line rail connection, but it is situated along a minor branch that is still dependent on slower, diesel-powered trains. The nearest larger city, Florence, is more than an hour to the north by car, bus, or train. So one can drive if one dares or take the train or bus, which comes nearly every hour during the day. I personally came to prefer one of the latter options when at all possible.

My own relationship with Siena began when a former dean returned with exciting news after a scouting trip to the city. Given our university's collaboration with the Siena School for Liberal Arts, he not only wanted to see what the fuss was all about but also wondered how our college might become more involved with the Siena School. He liked what he saw. "This is the perfect place for our students to study abroad!" he exclaimed to a few of us department chairs. He reasoned that Siena balanced its somewhat familiar Western social structure with distinctive language and cultural differences. He wasn't kidding about the differences. As global educators would have it, Siena still shocks the sensibilities of students who have spent their lives in or around the suburban tracts of a metropolitan city in the United States. But that would be the point, to nudge them outside their normal comfort zones more than field trips to local places might accomplish.

Learning from Viterbo

From what my wife, Linda, and I had seen on two short visits to Siena, I could not have agreed more. I had recently survived my first study-abroad experience as a visiting professor in Viterbo, Italy, in the fall of 2011, which earned me a spot at this initial meeting with the dean. Viterbo was a perfectly authentic place for some fifty students who convened from numerous universities across the United States. Because in 2011 Viterbo had little tourism and few local English speakers, the study-abroad students had little choice but to experience and interact with a traditional Italian community for an entire semester.

Though most people gape in stunned awe when they learn I taught in Italy, the reality on the ground is a bit different from the mountains of romantic films and books devoted to the Mediterranean realm. It was more like learning enough Italian so the locals would stop staring down the blond-haired fool who was stomping around their damp, chilly, medieval city in November. Then there were the eccentricities: Why did the closest large grocery store close whenever its owners felt like it was a good idea, most predictably when I was in shopping mode? Why did the city literally shut down for three hours in the afternoon—something the locals call *pausa pranzo* (pause for lunch)? Why was getting on a train a risky travel proposition, given that twice the railway employees decided to strike after I was happily seated? How could we get our outdoor clothesline fixed and functioning properly to prevent my limited wardrobe from ending up on the filthy cobblestones below? I'm just getting started here. Romanticized accounts of Tuscany reveal few of these conundrums related to daily living. Whatever the country, the daily planning, communication efforts, and cultural adaptation necessary to succeed in a study-abroad educational program can be described in a lot of colorful—and wonderful—ways. But *romantic* is not one of them.

Even in Italy, we enjoyed few of the modern conveniences of home (clothes dryers, dishwashers, and microwaves, to name a few). If we turned on more than two electric items simultaneously—including the necessary water heater for showers—we would likely blow the entire electrical circuit.

Linda and I lived with this reality for nearly five months within our own medieval-age apartment. Although I tried to strategically shut things off before leaping for another switch or plug, I can't count the number of times I ran outside to flip the one and only circuit breaker. There is a reason why the Italians consume roughly one-third of the energy per capita that we gobble up in America. "Now it's time to suck it up and live like an Italian," I told my students with not a little delight. "You want sustainability? Learn to dry your clothes amid the fresh air and pigeon poop" (which we did). "Your clothes will stand on end, and you will describe them as 'crunchy.'" But we dealt with it. Ultimately, no one denied that the Viterbo experience provided the global education of a lifetime for students, faculty, and spouses. Simply put, the experience changed lives—and from what I can tell—for the better. Still, I personally won't miss running outside a few times a week to throw the circuit breaker.

Envisioning a Siena Program

Recalling the reality that was Viterbo, part of me thought better of jumping at the possibility of the dean's newfound Siena project. In less than two seconds, however, I naturally found myself asking, "How can I help?" My inner voice was strongly urging that I make a return voyage to Italy. After all, I had struggled for some two years to learn basic Italian. That part hadn't been easy either. Why not take advantage of the learning curve? So several of us faculty members began to recruit students from a number of social science disciplines within our college, plunging ahead into planning mode for an eight-week summer program focused on sustainable agriculture, livable cities, public spaces, and walkable urban design.

Oh, and our early summer schedule would apparently coincide with something called the Palio. "We'll need to find out more about that, but it sounds like a neat opportunity," I told the others. "Let's build that into the end of our program, to finish with the proverbial bang." At the time, we had no idea what kind of bang this event would actually produce. All we knew was that there was some kind of maddening horse race in the city square on July 2 and that it would most likely provide yet another educational opportunity for all of us. Little did we know.

Regardless of all this adventure behind me, my small inner voice insisted that I had not yet absorbed enough Tuscan sun (whether technically in the region of Tuscany or elsewhere). We would provide a fresh set of students with a unique opportunity to experience the reality of living in a foreign place—discomfort and all—albeit amid some of the most timeless and inspiring Tuscan landscapes.

But first, we would all have to get there—something easier said than done.

A Traumatic Journey

It's May 2013. The students of our Siena cohort are flying separately into the regional airport hub outside Florence. We hope that our academic hosts at the Siena School for Liberal Arts will collect us when we eventually show up on their home turf. As the first to arrive for our eight-week adventure, Linda and I survive customs and spill out the one-way airport security doors. We immediately look for signs indicating shuttle buses. Our students will follow in our footsteps in the next day or two—or they will at least take a good stab at it. I review my carefully prepared notes from the meticulous Siena School staff. *Okay, the instructions look innocent enough*, I think—except for the fact that the Italians seem to purposely hide certain services, such as transportation, in unsuspecting places and provide mystifying signage that seems to lead you around in circles. It takes three attempts with my beginner Italian to determine exactly where airport management has placed the shuttle boarding area. It turns out that we must exit the far end of the airport, skirt through various hedgerows, and jaywalk across airport access roads. I am already wondering how our unsuspecting students are going to find this on their own.

Once happily on board, our shuttle coach delivers us to the train station in Florence, the impressive Stazione di Santa Maria Novella. The driver is apparently stopping adjacent to the station's imposing modernist facade and has little interest in continuing to the regional bus terminal, where we hope to find the bus to Siena. Since we are familiar with the train station from previous visits, we presume the bus terminal can't be far away. Logically, it may even be attached to this transportation hub.

LIVING THE PALIO

The first mistake here is to rely on logic—at least my logic. Some twenty minutes of sniffing around the station area yields nothing: no buses, no signs. We finally grab our bags and start asking employees staged at the entrances. Each time the apparent answer is the same, given my less-than-adequate listening skills in Italian. The respondent grumbles something and points. I repeat this process five or six times, bouncing from one guide to the next like someone on a scavenger hunt. Linda drags the additional bags behind.

Encouragingly, everyone I ask keeps pointing in the same direction, so we move another fifty feet and find someone else when the trail disappears. At the far end of the station, we run out of guides and now must turn to regular civilians. I think, *It's time to play the tourist role. Sometimes we have to do this.* Half the population of Florence seems to wander past us at some point, and we randomly ask directions from unlucky passersby. These responders end up pointing in different directions, however, and I begin to think a conspiracy is afoot. There is no sign of any bus station, let alone any bold, blinking signage or distinct architectural facade. Then it dawns on me to "do as the Romans do."

Linda and I start spying the buses themselves. Getting wiser but more desperate, we wonder, *Where are they going?* It's like following hornets back to their hive. Then I see it, a motor coach in better shape than most city buses, turning off a major street and disappearing into a five-story commercial building! *Aha!* I am puzzled and emboldened at the same time. We hike down the street and find a subtle garage-door entrance in the facade of a much larger structure, blending easily into the urban streetscape. The bus had entered this unadvertised hole and disappeared. We peak through the entrance and discover our goal—a fully functioning and rather massive bus terminal, completely hidden from public view. Buses enter through one building wall and exit through the opposite side. *These crafty Italians!* (To be fair, this architectural practice does have historical precedence in the design of interior cloisters and courtyards to provide light and open space). *But how are students ever going to find this place?* We will discover within the next forty-eight hours that they simply won't.

Fortunately, the bus to Siena is where it is supposed to be, and we quickly find the ticket counter. A little more than an hour later we survive a teeth-shattering ride along a pot-holed freeway (recently repaved), arriving miraculously in one piece at Siena's Piazza Gramsci. Somehow, we locate a friendly staff member of the Siena School, who takes charge and leads us through the maze of medieval streets and squares—a route that becomes familiar over the next eight weeks.

Although we have now accessed our new home, my stress level remains high. Our students are expected in at different times, coming from who knows where, and will hopefully arrive on the same regional bus that just deposited us. Later I make multiple hikes to Siena's bus terminal at Gramsci to await the hourly bus from Florence. With my Kindle in hand, I wait a total of several hours, but no students arrive—ever. I eventually give up, with no idea what my colleague is up to either. He was supposed to arrive from Rome, but I have not seen or heard from him; I presume his phone isn't working.

Certainly my own iPhone is useless. I now refer to it as iWon't. Regardless of promises made by confident Verizon staff back home, the phone does not recognize the Italian cell phone system, nor will it do so for the entire eight weeks we are in Siena. Having just bought the phone to launch me into the smartphone era, I am skittish about buying a new SIM card for Italy that, with my luck, would instantly erase my settings for back home. As it happens, nobody else's iPhones are working either, so we are all forced to flash back to the 1980s. Only Linda's Droid phone works, but nobody has Linda's phone number except me.

Ultimately, the students are forced to discover their own persistence and inner courage. After many a tear shed, they eventually discover the train system and avoid the buses altogether. Like a parent, I am relieved after the last student accesses her apartment sometime after midnight a full day later. A nice Italian family across the hall from the student's apartment had taken the late arrival in, as none of the other students were there to open the door. At this point Linda and I come to a quick decision about how to repeat this adventure in the future: group flight. Although the start of our walkable adventure is not ideal, the students pass their first test just getting to Siena. Within three weeks they would master the bus and train system, ultimately venturing out on their own and successfully returning without a hitch. Later, they would look back and laugh at themselves, wondering why they had fretted so much over the complexity of travel in Italy. One of the clear personal changes that student experience on study-abroad programs is increased self-confidence and problem-solving skills. Not just incidentally, the same can be said for the faculty. At least there is a silver lining to all of this.

The Safest City

It does help the chaperoning experience that Siena has the reputation of being the safest city in Tuscany and one of the safest in Europe. This statistic becomes an ongoing study theme for our young American scholars. They discover that there were no homicides during the past few decades and that the city boasts an exceptionally low crime rate overall. Teenage delinquency is also amazingly low. There are no gangs as we think of them, and graffiti within the city is rare, quite unlike many Italian counterparts. Granted, since 2000 the local perception of safety has declined marginally, with more locals viewing their city as only "quite safe" rather than "very safe" as they had perceived years earlier. Despite this perceptual change, the scholar Wolfgang Drechsler still describes the city as "almost ridiculously safe."[1]

This situation makes me wonder, *What have the Senesi learned about building a strong, vibrant community? How do they keep their teenagers from succumbing to slothful boredom and questionable temptations?* Among many other topics of study, our group will try to find some conclusive answers to these perplexing questions while we are here. I personally suspect that the city's relative ease of walkability and compact neighborhoods have something to do with it. A clustered and people-friendly environment does not necessarily cause vibrant community interaction, but it certainly can encourage and enable it. Shall we take this particular *walking city* for a spin?

✺ CHAPTER 2 ✺

Siena from Above

DESPITE THE MONSOON-TYPE RAINS THAT HAVE BEEN DUMPING ON US, I AM taking advantage of this fine Saturday morning to enjoy Siena from above. As I enter the expansive public square Piazza del Campo, or simply the Campo as I will refer to it henceforth, the sun is still casting shadows. I scan upward at one of the city's most dominant and beloved landmarks—the Torre del Mangia, a bell tower. It is attached to the monumental city hall itself, the Palazzo Pubblico. Completed in 1348, this massive brick tower was clearly built for maximum height and longevity. Job well done! Knowing next to nothing about how one gets to the top—other than paying a modest entrance fee—I am embarking today on an exploratory mission to see if I can obtain what many geographers covet: aerial photographs of the urban scene.

After I purchase my ticket, the saleswoman points me toward the back corner of the Palazzo courtyard, where apparently there is an entry to the tower stairs. *Is it just a straight shot up from here or something more complicated?* I ask myself. I eventually uncover the nondescript hole in the wall used for the entryway, and I double back to look at the sign that lists all the things I am not allowed to do in the tower or take with me. *Wow, looks like backpacks and water bottles are out. This could get dicey if they're confiscating water bottles. But where?* There's a set of stairs but no "tower police." Then I hear a male voice behind me. "I guess my backpack might be a problem here," a tall, lanky man muses. Knowing English when I hear it, I return the sentiment immediately. "Well, looks like my water bottle may not make it either, but there's no one here to take anything." He replies with my own thought: "Let's press on and see what happens." Indeed.

We enter and take the first set of stairs, heading up a few flights, not knowing how far or when the situation will change. *A friendly guy and clearly*

American, I conclude. We introduce ourselves by our first names—Doug is my new companion of chance. Shooting up ahead of me, he asks, "What brings you to Siena?" This is a standard greeting with strangers here. I tell him briefly about leading a student group for eight weeks to study topics of community and urban livability. Intrigued, he responds, "Cool. I'm leading an art history program from Kentucky, and we're here for six days." It turns out that my new companion is an art history and humanities professor, and his program is taking some forty-five students on a multicity expedition. I can't help but ask myself, *How on earth do they manage forty-five students?*

We hike up a few flights and suddenly find ourselves in a small receiving room with a few other people, including two police officers (or the equivalents of tower guards). Before we can open our mouths to ask anything, one of them is indicating that my water bottle and Doug's backpack need to go. There are lockers on the side wall, so I grab one with a key and stash the bottle. He does the same. This is also where they collect the entry tickets. As expected, I receive a ripped version of mine to keep as a souvenir. I wonder if I will need to buy the obligatory T-shirt as well, proudly announcing that "I survived the Torre del Mangia."

Cleared to press onward, we find another few flights of stairs ahead of us, and we pass the time by sharing more about our respective programs. Doug is clearly intrigued about our group's plan to build our schedule around the Palio, wanting to learn more about our educational approach. Soon we find ourselves spit outside again, essentially on part of the Palazzo roof. I liken this to a fun-house experience of my youth—at an amusement park where you step outside briefly to gather your wits before diving back into the little shop of horrors.

Phase three of our climb is beginning. The path upward becomes narrower and more unpredictable with the timeworn unevenness of stone stairs, occasionally replaced with timber ones. We are finally inside the actual tower, wrapping our way around to the top. "It's an ingenious design for the fourteenth century," I comment to Doug, delighted that it still seems to work for us today. After all, this is a load-bearing structure that has been required to support its own towering walls for seven hundred years now. The stairway is actually built into a series of spiraling, vaulted arches that most likely double as internal stabilizers. Chatting about Doug's educational program in Rome, Greece, and elsewhere helps to pass the time quite handily. Soon we are once again outside—this time on the observation deck behind the prominent stone crenellations, or battlements, of the tower platform. *That wasn't so bad*, I conclude, mildly impressed that our mission to get to the top didn't kill us.

Thankfully, we arrive at the right time. There are few other people around, providing fairly unblocked access to the openings between the alternating crenellations. I wonder if the architects realized that this defensive platform would become quite convenient for the future peacetime activities of curious tourists—Siena's most recent and successful invaders. Once on the platform, we continue our conversation, checking on whom we might mutually know at various universities and other related chatter. I'm thrilled I've made a new friend and one who does not require periodic apologies for my poor Italian. But it's game on now. Signage around the viewing area makes it quite clear that there's a fifteen-minute viewing limit, and I've become conscious of this precious window slipping away. Back in geographer mode, I make my way from perch to perch and collect my digital prizes—shooting nearly every conceivable angle, zoomed in and out, of the urban scene below us. *I've got just enough battery to conserve for the final viewshed down below*, I calculate, relaxing a bit.

Siena's Three Districts

Then Doug asks, "Do you know how the city is laid out? It doesn't seem quite circular." Doug and I find a perch to share, and I start to explain a few things. "Siena grew piecemeal over time during the medieval period, mostly between AD 900 and 1350, until it occupied three separate ridges. In Siena they refer to them as *terzi* or 'districts.'" I point Doug to the north and west across the Campo in front of us, the easiest directions to see with the sun to our backs. "The Duomo, or cathedral, was strategically placed at one of the highest ridges of today's Siena, and the oldest part of the city surrounds it. The district on the western ridge is the Terzo di Città." I continue with a quick anecdote: "The other day, a guide from the Siena School asked the students a great question: 'Which buildings around the Campo are the oldest?' They quickly identified the dark-brown, almost dirty-looking exteriors on the western side." I point below to the wall of buildings to our left. "Our guide then asked why the buildings curve away from us and explained that those facades once served as the outer wall of the older city. I hadn't known that either."

Pointing north again, I show Doug how the city extends quite a distance away, almost vanishing at one point. "This is another of the three *terzi*, the Terzo di Camollia. At the far end is the city gate on the historic route to Florence." Finally, we shift to the other side of the tower. The late morning sun is now pounding down, making it difficult to pick out much detail to the south. "The third of the districts is the Terzo di San Martino, with its city gate serving as the way to Rome. No surprise, it's called Porta Romana. All in all, Siena's three *terzi* form the rough shape of a Y, and they all intersect right here at the Piazza del Campo. So the irregular city shape is determined quite heavily by the physical terrain on which it sits."

Doug then starts thinking logically about the growth of Siena and asks, "So how did this place grow to such an extent? It seems more difficult to get here than other places where we're taking our students—Rome, Florence, Venice." *Good, I can answer that question*, I think. I am feeling a bit more confident up here. I glance at my watch to see how much time remains, after which I decide to explain a few things: "It's true that Siena isn't really in an ideal geographic location. It's not built along a prominent waterway—any water, actually. But what early Siena did have going for it was its location along a very important overland route—the Via Francigena."

Via Francigena

I explain a bit about the road's significance to Siena and the region. The ancient route actually began in the cathedral city of Canterbury, England, though it is more commonly known for its starting point in France. The Italians therefore refer to it as the Via Francigena, "the road that comes from France." Siena served as an important trade and way station for the route, together with its hospital, which assisted sick and infirm travelers. The road also provided a lifeline to boost Siena's struggling economy, usually following the devastating Plague episodes such as that of 1348.

"This was the US Route 66 of its day," I explain, which is what I also tell the students to help them relate to the Via Francigena. Although we're standing here a thousand years later, the same geographic rules of centrality and connections still apply. Just like small towns in the American West that benefitted economically from their position along Route 66, numerous small towns and cities here in Europe did likewise, thanks to their location along transcontinental routes. In its day, Siena essentially was providing the food, gas, and lodging for travelers of the fourteenth century headed to and from Rome.

Not only did the road guide pilgrims into and through the city, but it also encouraged Siena's banking entrepreneurs to discover new markets elsewhere in Europe. Already by the beginning of the twelfth century, Senese bankers were working abroad and returning home with new fashion trends, architectural and artistic approaches, poetry, and other foreign cultural ideas that helped this rather isolated city to connect more globally. Geographers refer to this regional exchange of ideas and innovations as *cultural diffusion*. Soon Siena was minting its own coinage, thanks to the silver mines nearby, and the city became known far and wide as a regional hub for banking. Today, the legacies of prominent Senese banking families and firms reveal themselves in the place names of streets, squares, and palaces here—those of Piccolomini, Salimbeni, Tolomei, and Buonsignori, to name but a few. Two of the three main streets are even named for the city's banking heritage—Via Banchi di Sotto and Via Banchi di Sopra (the banks of the lower and upper roads, respectively). Perhaps one pair of authors, Giuliano Catoni and Gabriella Piccinni, summed it up the best: "Siena was born from the road."[2]

In another parallel between then and now, I explain that this route is becoming a popular tourist destination in its own right. Like Route 66, the Via Francigena may not be what it once was, guiding pilgrims on months-long journeys through Europe, but more people from around the world are returning once again to hike parts or all of it. This popularity has not been lost on Italy's local and national governing bodies. The Italians have been intent on recovering the route and highlighting it once again, a project the region of Tuscany initiated in 2009. In 2004, the Council of Europe declared Via Francigena a "Major Cultural Route."

After the brief lesson, Doug's patience is still holding out, to his credit. I then use our aerial perch to point out the route. "Look to the north, back to Porta Camollia," I instruct. "That was the northern entrance into town from the Via Francigena. Like in twentieth-century America, businesses and housing clustered along well-traveled routes. Today, you can barely make out from here the main road winding its way through Terzo di Camollia and through the sea of red-tile roofs, down to the back side of the Campo. The main intersection between the three *terzi* and the Via Francigena is right there behind the Campo. If there's a dominant medieval intersection here in Siena, that's it—where Via di Città, Banchi di Sotto, and Banchi di Sopra come together at a three-way intersection."

Pointing behind us to the east and south, I continue, "The Via Francigena continues as the spine through Terzo di San Martino and out the gate of Porta Romana. From there the pilgrims would continue their journey to the Holy Land of Rome." To drive home my geography lesson, I conclude, "So this city would not have grown to the extent that it did, nor would it have likely become a regional power, had it not been for its fortunate location along that major banking and pilgrimage route."

Now Doug starts to query about specific buildings, and I feel my confidence dropping as quickly as if we had jumped off the tower. "What's this huge Renaissance facade down here?" He motions just below us to the east. *Okay, I can answer that one.* Being an art historian and humanities expert, Doug is naturally gravitating to the churches now. Had he pointed to any number of other church bell towers peaking up on the horizon, he wouldn't have received much information from me. "That's the Church of Santa Maria di Provenzano," I answer, "a late Renaissance structure completed in the early 1600s. I think it's a great Renaissance gem found in the midst of its older, medieval district." I can't help but pull in the Palio, of course. "And that's where the winning *contrada* [neighborhood] celebrates its Palio victory after the July 2 horse race. There are two races each summer, and the July 2 event is dedicated to the Madonna of Provenzano." I then point back to the Duomo commanding the hilltop of Terzo di Città. "The August 16 race is celebrated at the cathedral instead. The Senesi also race in honor of the Virgin Mary on that day, but the intent there is to celebrate the Assumption."

Doug looks a bit perplexed. He says, "There's only one Virgin Mary that I know about." He chuckles. "But there are two races?" I can tell I've got him hooked now on the Palio. Our conversation turns to horse racing rather than his interest in art history. "In one sense, the Senesi celebrate two versions of the Madonna. They have raced the July 2 Palio in honor of the Madonna of Provenzano going back at least to the 1600s. Even before that, they were using different animals and running through the city streets. However, the August 16 race in honor of the Assumption is perceived as a completely different event, albeit with the same rules and approach. An unsuspecting visitor would not notice a difference. The August race is the younger of the two races. It was held in fits and starts through the 1700s, but it was not regularized until the early 1800s."

The Piazza del Campo

We're both keeping an eye on the time now, though I'm starting to suspect that nobody in an authoritative role is paying much attention. It's not too busy yet, and we are enjoying this gorgeous Saturday morning. At some point the fifteen-minute time limit comes and goes. *Maybe they care more about time when there are crowds of people in line downstairs? Or, more likely, maybe the time limit is more like the Italian approach to road signs and traffic controls, which are generally interpreted as suggestions.* Regardless, I start to notice small surveillance cameras subtly placed at strategic locations, but I see no loudspeakers that might blast a warning at us to "Come down, now!" At this point I'm concentrating on the most central and visual focus of the city: the main public square, the Piazza del Campo directly below us. At some point I notice that Doug has disappeared. So I spend some precious reflective moments scanning the populated scene below. Most amusing is the elongated shadow of our tower being cast across the Campo, inside which some 90 percent of the lingering population is crunched to avoid the sun. *There is hope for human rational thinking after all*, I think amusedly.

As I mentioned earlier, Siena grew and prospered during the medieval period, commonly known as the Middle Ages, due to its activities along the Via Francigena. At one time the city was as large as Paris. Amazingly, much of the irregular urban layout and massive architecture from that period survives to this day. The integrity of this densely packed urban scene has earned Siena recognition as a UNESCO World Heritage Site—just one external acknowledgment of the historic resources found here.[3] The locals are also quite proud of their variably successful republican governments throughout the city's history, and they are still somewhat nostalgic for the days of their once-independent city-state. The heyday for Siena was roughly AD 900–1350, symbolized most prominently by the impressive, Gothic-style city hall, Palazzo Pubblico, and its commanding bell tower, the Torre del Mangia, on which I am now perched. The tower's curious name, incidentally, came from a nickname given to a tower bell ringer known to the Senesi as Mangiaguadagni or, more literally, "profit eater" for his lavish spending habits. Numerous variations of this story seem to exist, but that fact is the one rather consistent part of the legend.

In a way, Siena's off-the-beaten-path location has helped the historic city resist urban development over the centuries, saving itself through what historic preservationists call *benign neglect*. In a nutshell, there wasn't much pressure for constant economic development after the 1400s, and so the older city fabric was saved by simply leaving it alone. Still, the Senesi regret the final fall of their independent republic, which ceased permanently when the city-state fell to Florence's Medici overlords around 1555. Since then, Siena has been governed by outsiders. By 1861 the city-state style of government was long gone, with the peninsula more or less united—forcefully or otherwise—into the new Kingdom of Italy.[4] Nonetheless, Siena faithful can still be heard shouting, "Remember Montaperti!" during soccer matches with rival Florence or at related events. They are referring to none other than the defining battle for the city's independence when the Senesi clobbered the Florentines on September 4, 1260—yes, that's right—1260. Try to get your head around that; I dare you.

No doubt, the most prominent and much-admired feature in Siena is the spacious Piazza del Campo, which is sprawled out below me. It is laid out in the shape of a scallop shell, and it is considered to be one of the more beautifully proportioned public spaces in Europe. Countless academics, historians, poets, and random visitors have written about this very place and enjoyed its aesthetic and social qualities. Prior to the twelfth century, the Campo had been divided into two separate areas, already serving as a marketplace at the junction of Siena's main thoroughfares along the Via Francigena. In an impressive bout of medieval urban planning, the communal government at the end of the 1100s had the two sectors united into the semicircular open space that graces the city to this day.

But these early planners weren't done. A series of local ordinances was also adopted to regulate the architectural styles and building forms around the Campo and surrounding streets. They essentially mandated the continued practice of designing Gothic-style facades to unify the appearance of structures around the central piazza. For instance, in 1346 the city council insisted that it redounds to the beauty of the city of Siena and to the satisfaction of almost all people of the same city that any edifices that are to be made anew anywhere along the public thoroughfares ... proceed in line with the existing buildings, and one building not stand out beyond another, but they shall be disposed and arranged equally so as to be of greatest beauty for the city.[5]

Today, we still see some of this original architecture with the distinctive twin-arched or triple-arched Gothic windows that are quintessentially Senese. Known collectively as multilancet windows with their pointed arches and slender columns, they provided the central focus for the new building regulations after the Palazzo was built. That is, all buildings facing the Campo would need to be designed with the same style of windows, to portray appropriate architectural uniformity around this important public space.[6] As one might imagine, much of the architecture has changed here since those heady days of the republic, with the Campo now sporting a diverse mixture of Gothic and later Renaissance styles—the latter with their brighter, more horizontal facades and massive window openings.

Still, Siena remains known as the Gothic City for its faithful adoption of Gothic architecture at the end of the Middle Ages. As a local example of cultural diffusion, many of the prominent families here looked to the Palazzo Pubblico for inspiration, thereby repeating its Gothic, pointed-arch forms in their own architecture. Almost unbelievably, many of these palazzi remain with us today, providing a physical connection to centuries past. Even the unique, slender style of the Torre del Mangia has since diffused around the world, providing the model for replicas in unsuspecting places like the train station in Waterbury, Connecticut, and the Pilgrim Monument in Provincetown, Massachusetts—both of which I personally recall from my upbringing nearby.

Height Wars

Suddenly, Doug reappears and asks me excitedly, "Did you go up to the top?" I reply that I thought I was already there. "No, no, those stairs in the center keep going upward to another viewing area! I got to see them preparing to ring the bell." Now I know where he disappeared.

"That's cool," I say, "but I'm happy seeing the city from here." I think that going another fifty feet higher isn't going to provide me with any new award-winning views, and I remember my claustrophobic trip to the cathedral dome in Florence. I ask, "Have you and your group been up inside the cathedral dome in Florence?" In fact, Doug tells me, they had completed that harrowing tour just recently. He adds that he had loved it and that he made it all the way to the top of the dome. I respond, "Well, I don't usually mind closed or tight spaces, but I eventually went so far up inside the dome that my brain told me to retreat back down immediately," I recount, chuckling. I had reached my height limit on that one. Like here, I didn't feel the need to prove that I can go the extreme distance. Hanging out is just fine with me. I got my photos, and it's not raining for a change. I couldn't be more contented at this moment.

We then reflect on the urban and political significance of this very tower and the massive structure attached to it below. Today, historic urban landscapes like Siena are replete with symbols of early attempts at communal government, not the least being massive city halls like Siena's Palazzo Pubblico. Their bell towers—this one a strong case in point—are likewise clear indicators that a new central authority had arrived by the 1200s, following centuries of uncontested power by the Catholic Church. In Florence, for instance, church towers and domes continue to visually compete with their rival city government buildings for attention, each clearly trying to outdo the other.[7]

The same is true in Siena, with a height war still persisting between this very Torre del Mangia and the Duomo, which provides its own commanding view of the older city below. When communal governments were formed during the Late Middle Ages, the loyalists and protectors of government-by-the-people were determined to resist further subordination to religion. As one might imagine, the Catholic Church and the new civic governments did not always get along. When construction on Siena's bell tower began intently by 1338, city leaders ensured that it would reach the precise height of the cathedral, despite the tower's disadvantaged location at the bottom of the sloped Campo.[8] In this way, the city government would demonstrate its authoritative local equality with the church. Tower designers probably weren't so concerned with the aesthetic view we enjoy now, although for defensive purposes it must have come in handy.

Just before we descend to the terra firma below, Doug and I steal a few last glances between the humungous stone crenellations. Noticing the most recent urban landscape on the edge of town, I explain that little was built beyond the city walls until after World War II, a practice typical for much of Italy. Instead of Gothic architecture and red-tiled roofs, the landscape changes immediately to clusters of multistory apartment flats with little in the way of architectural ornamentation. This is the Italian version of suburbs, with clusters of modernist apartment blocks for Siena's various waves of immigrants, most of whom arrived within the past century and particularly in the past fifty years. Thus, Siena is geographically a tale of two cities. As of 2013, the entire city might boast of some fifty-three thousand residents, but more than half the population lives outside the city walls. For now, I concentrate foremost on arriving at the bottom of this tower in one piece, as more people are now inching their way upward and crunching in around Doug and me. This must rank as one of my best-used—not to mention longest—fifteen-minute time periods.

CHAPTER 3

Discovering the Palio

THROUGH CENTURIES OF SUCCESSIVE GOVERNMENTS AND EXTERNAL influences, Siena's prized annual horse race, the Palio, has continued largely uninterrupted. This ferocious ninety-second race seems to flow through the blood of the Siena faithful, providing the central theme for their city and for this narrative.

The Palio attracts many thousands of people to Siena twice each year for the aforementioned days of the Palio. These include the races on July 2 and August 16 and the three days leading up to each race. Despite the ever-larger hordes of visitors like us, the Palio is not directly promoted for outside consumption. Instead, the event and its associated rituals are found at the center of Siena's own identity and sense of place, both of which run incredibly deep in Senese culture. The excitement of the Palio race forms the most visible tip of a very complex social system. More understanding of this system will shed light on the safest-city question and why the Palio is run in the first place.

To understand the Palio race, one should become acquainted to some extent with Siena's seventeen distinct neighborhoods, known as *contrade* (plural form of *contrada*). Without the contrade, the Palio would simply vanish or, perhaps even more horrific, devolve into a mere reenactment for outsiders. The Palio and contrade operate hand in hand, each mutually dependent upon the other. The map below provides the names and locations of all seventeen contrade in Siena, with the Piazza del Campo located near the center. Siena's three districts, or *terzi*, are also labled.

DISCOVERING THE PALIO

Map of Siena's seventeen contrade and the city's three districts (terzi). (Source: https://www.picturesfromitaly.com/tuscany)

As indicated on the map, each contrada occupies its own geographic *rione* (territory) within the city walls. Further, each enjoys its own local government, elected officials, flag, constitution, and political jurisdiction within its geographic boundaries. Put another way, each neighborhood comprises a miniature city-state, and each revolves intently around the annual cycle of the Palio.[9] For this reason alone, visitors struggle to find meaning in the race, not really having a good reason to cheer for one particular contrada's horse over that of another. Without an emotional attachment to a particular contrada—in the way one might identify with certain sports teams—one's decision to cheer on, say the Porcupine contrada's horse over that of the Snail, would be just as random as choosing a gelato flavor while blindfolded.

At the beginning of our stay, I was curious to see if that *outsider ambivalence*, as I call it, would actually last for us after living in Siena for two months. Would we end up supporting a particular horse and jockey representing a specific contrada?

The Hunger Games on Horseback

I eventually make a humorous, if not disturbing, comparison between the Palio and contrade and Suzanne Collins's apocalyptic *Hunger Games* series. This trilogy has been at the forefront of my mind lately, as some colleagues and I have started to prepare for a conference on the topic for students within our college. *Let's see if I understand this correctly*, I contemplate during our first week. All seventeen neighborhoods (districts, in the Hunger Games) show up at the town square for the *extraction* (reaping) to determine by lottery which neighborhoods will enter the Palio (games) that summer. Each neighborhood chooses a hired jockey (tribute) who must stay alive on his horse until the finish line, risking injury to limbs and, worse, life. The winning district gains a year's worth of fame and bragging rights. Occasional victory tours transpire after the win, where the winning contrada parades the Palio banner, or *drappellone*, through the streets of other contrade, pretty much shoving it in their faces.

Continuing the *Hunger Games* analogy, the winning jockey is guaranteed a hefty payoff as well. Losing jockeys go home disappointed and sometimes injured, though still paid for their troubles. More-unfortunate jockeys have been known to desperately climb up the bleachers onto building ledges to avoid the wrath of contrada members suspecting a betrayal. Should they happen to fall off their horse in enemy territory, they risk secondary injuries from emotional *contradaioli* (contrada members) seeking their vengeance. In fact, the jockey doesn't matter that much in the Palio, as he doesn't always finish the race atop his steed. All that matters is that the contrada's horse wins. Welcome to the city's public stage (the arena)—the Piazza del Campo—where the race is run.

Romans. Palio. *The Hunger Games*. Aside from my rather tongue-in-cheek comparison, there is some historical truth that ties these three entities together. All three are focused on the notion of providing bread and circuses (food and games) to the delight of the masses. It is no coincidence that Suzanne Collins named her mythical, messed-up country Panem (bread). *Panem et Circenses* is Latin for "bread and circuses," providing an appropriately symbolic setting for the now-famous Katniss and her dystopian world.[10] Siena's rulers encouraged the locals to entertain themselves with food and games after the fall of the republic, just as the Roman Empire had done with its own arenas, gladiators, and related distractions. Keep the population satisfied with cheap food and entertainment, the theory goes, and they are less likely to demand strong participation in civil society or to instigate uprisings.

This same rationale was used by the Florentine Medici overlords when they conquered Siena in the 1550s but still encouraged the continuation of the Palio and other games.[11] Chances of rebellion against the Medici were theoretically reduced if the contrade stayed focused on their own entertainment and fierce competition among themselves. The locals would also be less likely to demand a return to their nostalgic republican, city-state ways. For *Hunger Games* enthusiasts, this divide-and-conquer approach may seem all too familiar.

From the perspective of outside rulers intent on maintaining local peace, the contrade formed "a seventeen-way division of class interests."[12] As Wolfgang Drechsler directly asserts, "The *contrade* system does, to some degree, provide *panem et circenses*"—now as well as centuries ago.[13] As for us, we admittedly were looking forward to this unique mix of bread and circuses in upcoming weeks.

Three Laps of Terror

Let's look at the structure of the Palio as a way of laying the groundwork for later stories. First, the race itself lasts no longer than approximately ninety seconds, more or less—about the time required to complete three full laps around the Campo. The brief duration of the race shocks unknowing visitors right off the bat, as an entire year of community rituals is built around this precious minute and a half. Twice each summer, the otherwise picturesque and touristy Campo is almost instantly transformed into a dirt racetrack around its perimeter. About a week before each event, wooden barriers are installed, and a special blend of dirt is compacted with steamrollers to form the track. A two-story balcony known as the *palco dei giudici* (judges' stand) is installed at the main entrance for city officials and contrada captains to view the excitement.

Out of Siena's seventeen contrade, only ten are allowed to race, due to the hazardous track conditions. That means that for any given Palio, seven contrade do not directly participate in the race. Those not racing are then guaranteed a spot in the next year's Palio (keeping in mind that the July and August races are considered separate annual events). The final three contenders are determined by an *extraction*, or lottery, about a month prior to the race.

Aside from the steep slopes of the track, there are two horrendous turns. The most dangerous is the curve of San Martino. According to one study that tracked Palio accidents over a two-decade span, 57 percent of all Palio accidents occurred at this turn.[14] This is a ninety-five-degree turn that launches the horses into the main straightaway. The challenge is twofold here. First, the competitors must get around the steep downhill turn in one piece—or actually two pieces: horse and jockey. Then, the riders must avoid the worrisome Cappella di Piazza, a monumental marble chapel that juts out into the track. An impressive piece of architecture in its own right, it was built following the devastating 1348 Black Death (Plague), as a token of appreciation for the sixteen-thousand-some-odd citizens who managed to survive.

The next most likely place for Palio accidents is the turn at the Casato, which is also hazardous but uphill. This is at the track's southwest corner where the street, Casato di Sotto, intersects with the Campo. Some 37 percent of Palio accidents occur here. The risk is reduced a bit, given that the horses tend to be more separated from one another by the time they reach the Casato—but not always. All in all, the Palio is a harrowing race on a dangerous track.

Experienced horse-racing fans will notice something else: the Palio horses travel clockwise around the track, unlike in all other major Western races, in which they travel counterclockwise. Because the horses lack both saddle and stirrups, it is rather common for jockeys to get thrown off, usually at one of the turns, with the unperturbed horse simply continuing on without a driver. A horse with no jockey is known as *scosso* (shaken). And a horse without a jockey occasionally wins, as long as its head ornament remains attached to its forehead. Known as a *spennacchiera*, this symbolic piece generally consists of a small mirror and plumes that include the contrada colors. In 1989, for instance, an empty horse won both races in July and August, for the She-Wolf and Dragon contrade, respectively. The Giraffe contrada also managed that type of win in July 2004.[15]

If you have deduced that the horse is much more precious than the jockey, then you are right. The horse can still win the Palio, whether or not its fearless jockey remains attached. As for the jockeys, or *fantini*, they are basically hired mercenaries, often from other parts of Italy. Each contrada can negotiate with potential jockeys until the morning of the Palio, after which the jockey cannot be changed. The contrade are often in contact with prospective jockeys throughout the year. Each contrada pays to secure a jockey, and the payout for a winning jockey is even larger.

Contrade Relationships

Further, each contrada has its own allies and usually its own longtime rival or enemy. There are actually four types of relationships possible between the contrade: alliance, friendship, no relationship, and enmity.[16] The relationships can change over time, for instance from no relationship to friendship—as when one contrada assists another in realizing a Palio victory. Five of the contrade are not currently part of a reciprocal enmity pair, those of the Wave, Dragon, Forest, Caterpillar, and Giraffe. The traditional rivalry between the Giraffe and Caterpillar contrade was annulled through a "peace treaty" in 1996. Is there any doubt that these communities view themselves as miniature city-states?

Certain contrade might harbor ill feelings toward others, but those feelings of enmity are not necessarily official. The Wave, for instance, seems to harbor ill feelings for the Tower next door, although the Tower apparently reserves its energies for the despised Goose rather than waste time on its smaller neighbor. Contemporary online lists of the paired contrada enemies, however, tend to list both the Goose and Wave as enemies of the Tower. In any case, there is some bad blood there. The following list details the traditional contrada enemies:

- Tower—Goose
- Porcupine—She-Wolf
- Snail—Turtle
- Shell—Ram
- Caterpillar—Giraffe (annulled with a peace treaty in 1996)
- Eagle—Panther
- Owl—Unicorn

It stands to reason that the potential for hostility and contentiousness intensifies when more pairs of rivalries face off during a given Palio. Following the extraction for "our" Palio, we hear gossip that this race will indeed be one of those cases. Four rival pairs will compete in the July 2013 edition of the Palio, providing a relatively high number of contrade desperate to deny victory to one another.

Like the Palio itself, contrada members consider their traditional enemies with varying degrees of seriousness, given the wide range of responses I received throughout our sojourn. Speaking to my colleague, one male landlord in the Owl made it clear that the sense of animosity toward their archrival, the Unicorn, ramps up to "hatred" levels only around Palio time. At most other times rival contrada members get along just fine, more or less. In fact, one popular butcher from the Unicorn maintains his shop in the Owl and regularly provides meat for them, employing dangerous butcher knives and all.

I gained a similar perspective regarding the Panther-Eagle rivalry from a proud grandfather in the Panther. He corrected my use of the word *enemy*. From his perspective, he quietly reflected, "The word *enemy* is too strong. It's more like having an adversary. Yes, *enemy* is too strong." Our friend Viola from our favorite ceramic shop (we'll meet Viola again later) agrees. She explained in Italian that, during the Palio, the Goose and Tower contradaioli pretty much hate each other but are fine together at most other times of the year.

Given that we are all well past the Middle Ages, I suppose it's refreshing to see that even rival contradaioli can take their traditional enemy relationships with a grain of salt. Still, sentiments for their neighborhood rivals seem to consistently lurk beneath the surface. I asked a female Panther contradaiola at a mixer dinner, "What's your recommended pizza on this menu?" Each of the seventeen pizza offerings had been creatively named for a different contrada. After showing me her favorite, she ended quietly with, "The Aquila [Eagle] pizza is the worst."

Throughout the year, contrada leaders are expected to make secretive, backroom agreements that will either hurt their enemy's chances of winning or help their allies. The contrada *capitano* (captain) is elected by his constituents as a veritable commander in charge of the Palio efforts, including having carte blanche to secure such deals. Although considered illegal within the Palio's official regulations, it seems that everyone knows and expects that such agreements will be made. Known as *partiti*, such clandestine arrangements occur throughout the days of the Palio, but they intensify greatly on the day of the race. This practice is enabled by the walkable nature of the city, as spokesmen for each contrada will often choose a public space or nearby private home to hold hastily scheduled meetings, rather than risk a bugged phone or an imposter making the call.[17] I suppose a walking city can consequently help satisfy pangs of paranoia.

A contrada considers it a moral victory if its ally wins or, in turn, if its rival loses. Payoffs from one contrada to another have reached into the quarter-million-euro range to secure such *partiti*. While these backroom deals seem antithetical to American ethics, it is important to keep in mind the cultural and historical contexts in which this whole system operates. We cannot think of this in terms of American sporting events, as we are rooted in a different cultural system. "The *Palio* simply would not be the *Palio* without *partiti!*" argue Alan Dundes and Alessandro Falassi, because the *partiti* represent "man's attempt to control his fate through skillful diplomacy and manipulation."[18] This may not be so surprising when one is reminded that each contrada behaves as a miniature republic desiring to maintain some semblance of local control and sovereignty.

A few other traditions are also quite different from US sporting events. The only payout for a victorious contrada is a cloth banner known as the *drappellone* or *palio*. The word *palio* actually holds a dual meaning here—for the entire race event itself, and as another name for the victory banner or *drappellone*. *Palio* is actually derived from the Latin word *pallium* or piece of cloth.[19] The Palio banner is designed and hand-painted for each new race by a carefully selected artist. The current practice is to commission a local Senese artist to design the July banner, whereas the August version is designed by someone from outside the city. Its very design remains a mystery until about a week prior to the race when it is presented at a public press conference in the *cortile*, or inner courtyard of Palazzo Pubblico.

Winning the Palio

For some contrade, the odds of winning have not been in their favor as of late. The Caterpillar went without a win for forty-one years (between 1955 and 1996). This scrappy contrada is making up for lost time, however, bringing home the *drappellone* three times so far in the twenty-first century. The Panther, in contrast, has won only once since 1994, and the Shell hasn't pulled off a win since August 1998. In such cases, an entire generation of young people might not experience a victory in their memorable lifetimes.

During a dinner with a family of twentysomethings from the Panther, we asked them about the last time their contrada won and what they remembered. The Panther's last victory was in 2006, and they were only about twelve years old then. "When you're twelve, the experience is very different because you are supervised by your parents," explained one young woman. "So we didn't really see much of it. Before that, we were less than two years old, so of course we don't remember anything." Her best friend of the same age added, "It's best to enjoy a Palio win between ages eighteen and twenty-eight when you are independent of your parents and probably not married with a family yet." We all had a good chuckle over that comment. I personally can't image what it would be like to be emotionally invested in a favorite sports team and not be able to enjoy a victory in a decade or more.

Winning is a big deal, make no mistake. On the flip side, a victory is incredibly expensive for the contrada that wins, necessitating numerous celebrations throughout the year and, of course, the handsome payoff for the jockey and to other contrade that agreed to assist. Each win is strictly a cultural and emotional victory based on the community's strong attachment to place. It is, therefore, not economically advantageous to win. That approach would never work with American college or pro football, for instance. The team would simply be out of business. I can imagine contrada leaders secretly cringing when they win almost back to back, wondering how they will dig out thousands of euros once again to pay for it all—and, likely, to pay off their allies as well. The Wave, for instance, won the July 2 Palio in 2012 and would win the August 16 race a year later. The contrade encourage pledges from their own citizens in advance of each race, in the rare chance that they pull off a victory and need to pay out. Some of these pledges can run upwards of €5,000 (about $8,000) or more from the most devoted contradaioli.

The pledges serve as conditional promises to pay a certain amount to the contrada should it win the Palio. Wisely, members generally wait to pledge until they see what horse has been extracted. A particularly good horse can stimulate substantial last-minute pledges.[20] If a contrada has not won for some time, it likely has amassed a sizable treasury. The contrada that has suffered the longest without a win (referred to as the *nonna*, or grandmother) is likely going to inflate the *partiti* that occur before the Palio. The *nonna* will likely spare no expense to win, encouraging its enemies to spend more in turn to keep the *nonna* from winning. Other contrade will then raise the bar and spend in kind, attempting to pay off this or that contrada if it assists in some way. For the July 2 Palio during our visit, the *nonna* (She-Wolf) is indeed running, in addition to the four sworn rivalry pairs. There seems to be a lot at stake in this particular race.

Palio Shortcomings

Not everyone is enthralled with the Palio and its virtual lock on Siena's social life. Those less enthusiastic, however, tend to have relocated to Siena from elsewhere, if our small informal sample is any indication. Even a UPS store employee in Siena had little interest in the Palio despite working in the midst of it for years. When asked about it, he frankly explained that he's not a Senese native and therefore does not get emotionally involved. Other non-native residents, including one acquaintence who moved from the United States, have simply decided to remain neutral by not joining any contrada. His own network of friends includes a mix of contradaioli and others who remain unaffiliated like him.

More globally, outside interest groups have even called for the discontinuation of the Palio, given sustained accusations of abuses to the horses. If there is an ugly side to this centuries-old tradition, this is it—at least from an outsider's perspective not rooted in local heritage. Despite the extreme pampering of the horses while in the custody of all the contrade, numerous participating steeds have been drugged, injured, or killed over the years, either during or after the harrowing race and its trials. Recent and heart-wrenching deaths in 2004 and 2011 brought renewed calls from animal rights groups to ban the race altogether. Though horse deaths have been drastically reduced, some forty-eight animals have met this fate since 1970 according to a prominent animal rights group.[21] Italy's own tourism minister has decried the race, and in 2011 the Palio was pulled from possible contention as a UNESCO World Heritage event. A portion of Palio videos on YouTube reflects this controversy, with lists of comments that can often be vitriolic and emotional in support of one side or the other.

This outside attention has clearly led to improvements, if not the permanent end of the event sought by some. To its credit, the city has taken some serious measures to better protect and care for horses and jockeys alike. Horses need to pass strict antidoping tests, and they need to be at least four years old (I'm not sure how the steeds feel about being carded and then being subjected to regular urine tests). Further, only crossbred horses are allowed to race, as they are considered to be stronger than purebreds and are therefore less prone to injuries. The entire list of extensive regulations is found in the annually updated *Protocollo Equino* on Siena's municipal web site, which includes a set of detailed instructions and rules related to the training of the horses. More visible at the curve of San Martino is a series of mattresses installed against the building walls. Injuries have been reduced but not eliminated.

In addition, the city of Siena takes pride in a veritable retirement home for Palio horses. Known as the *Pensionario*, the facilty is located west of Siena near the village of Radicondoli and is the product of a creative agreement signed in 1991 between Siena and the State Forestry Corps. The expansive outdoor estate allows Palio horses to live out the remainder of their lives with full vetinary services and related amenities. The Pensionario will adopt horses from owners who no longer wish to care for them, along with those injured during Palio events. More than 20 horses have become residents since the facility's inception.

Making safety improvements for the Palio may be the least of Siena's challenges right now. Perhaps unfortunately for us, we have coincidentally arrived during one of the most—perhaps *the* most—tumultuous community crises since World War II. There has even been talk of cancelling the race itself this July 2013, something unheard of since it was actually suspended between the war years of 1940 and 1944. Given our hard-earned intent to build our program around this particular race, it would be dumb bad luck indeed if we showed up to an empty Campo for our grand finale.

Daddy Monte: Banca Monte dei Paschi

The current, ongoing crisis for Siena centers on what many locals fondly call "Babbo [Daddy] Monte," considered the oldest continuously operating bank in the world, which prides itself on its founding in 1472. To put this timeframe in perspective, Native American tribes had yet to be inflicted with Columbus and his successors when the Senesi were already starting a five-century-plus relationship with Daddy Monte or, more accurately today, the MPS, Banca Monte dei Paschi di Siena.

To say the bank is intricately linked with Siena and its Palio-contrada system is an understatement. According to Sydel Silverman, "The relationship between the bank and the city and its festival is complex and reciprocal."[22] To understand Siena and the financial underwriting of the Palio, one must not ignore the MPS. Aside from its financial importance as Italy's third-largest bank in 2013, MPS and its lucrative foundation are responsible for the lion's share of Siena's employment, general wealth, and many of its cultural resources and activities—not the least being the Palio.

More jaw-dropping is the total amount of donations to local organizations since the bank's *Fondazione* (Foundation) was formed in 1995—some €400 million. In 2010 alone, the Foundation's last full year of activity, €80 million was given to local institutions and organizations, according to a 2013 Bloomberg news report.[23] In case it's not obvious, we're talking about a lot of money here, signifying an incredible dependence on the bank. In return, the Palio and all the business it attracted helped contribute to the bank's expansion. Both MPS and the city of Siena have mutually benefitted one another, in turn enabling the financial sustenance of the Palio.[24] Then the bottom dropped out.

The bank's recent and ongoing troubles are too complicated to unfold here with any clarity. But in brief, the economic crisis in Europe contributed to the MPS losing some $4.7 billion in 2011, and by September 2012, the net losses had already reached another $1.7 billion. MPS was seeking government bailouts. A most unsettling response to the economic crisis was the bank's decision in 2013 to cut some 8,000 jobs and close 550 branches.[25]

As indicated above, the codependence of MPS and Siena is incredibly complex and interwoven. Giovanni Grottanelli de' Santi probably embodies this unique relationship more than anyone. A former dean of the University of Siena Law School, he served as MPS president from 1993–2000. At the time, he was perceived by Siena's citizenry to be the city's most important person, beating out the mayor, university rector, and the archbishop.[26] During his tenure, the bank had underwritten a sizeable portion of Palio costs as direct grants to the city and its seventeen contrade. With nearly twenty-seven thousand employees by the early 2000s, the MPS and its foundation spent an astounding half of its annual profits on culture and heritage within Siena.[27] By 2015 this regular and expected philanthropy had become a thing of the past.

With or without the financial support of MPS, the twice-annual Palio remains the central identity for Siena's citizens and the emotional source of their collective passion. Scholars who have studied the equestrian event confirm that this sense of local identity is only becoming stronger. Warner claims that the Palio has undergone a revitalization especially since the 1970s.[28] By the end of the twentieth century, the Palio had become particularly strong, for citizens and outsiders alike. Unfortunately for the Senesi, MPS is no longer locally owned and consequently will not play the significant role it once did.

❖ CHAPTER 4 ❖

Life in the Contrade

LURKING BENEATH THE SPECTACLE OF THE PALIO IS THE FASCINATING IF MIND-numbingly intricate contrada social system with roots going back to medieval times. Each of the seventeen contrade is a legal entity that operates like a nongovernmental organization (NGO).²⁹ And each is distinctly territorial, with fixed geographic boundaries inside the walled city. Thus, contrada memberships have been determined for centuries based simply on where a person was born. Prior to the advent of modern-day hospitals, the actual location of the birth is what determined a baby's contrada membership. To say that someone is "born into the contrada" today, however, refers more generally to the location of the family's home within the contrada's territory.

Take, for instance, a baby girl "born into" the Giraffe. Even if she moved across town or to another country later in life, she would remain a Giraffe. In other words, to be born in a contrada is essentially the gold standard of community membership. That person has a special place—a home—and a dizzying array of extended family members for life, no questions asked.

Like *Giraffe*, most of the contrada names are based on totemic figures, usually an animal, which is not unlike the totems of various North American indigenous tribes. Contrada names can elicit a few respectful smiles: Eagle, Unicorn, She-Wolf, Snail, Porcupine, and so forth. The Tower, Wave, and Forest contrade are also associated with animals, although they do not tend to use their names—elephant, dolphin, and rhinoceros, respectively. Some of us were hoping that the Chiocciola (Snail) contrada referred to a chocolate specialty, but we had no luck there.

Overall, the contrade are loosely tied to specialized, medieval trades and crafts, although today it is nearly impossible to find any lingering connection.

For example, the Caterpillar represented silk workers, while the Goose signified wool dyers. Members of the Shell contrada were potters, the Panthers were apothecaries, and the She-Wolf represented bakers. The Eagle was associated with lawyers or notaries. The contrada boundaries have shifted over the centuries, but overall they have remained impressively consistent since 1729.

That's when Siena's governess, Violante Beatrice of Bavaria, decided to lock them in place. Her goal was to consolidate the more numerous contrade down to a manageable seventeen, thereby distributing the local population more evenly and solving numerous border disputes. Six contrade were instantly dissolved, namely the Lion, Rooster, Oak, Strong Sword, Viper, and Bear. I can't imagine the fuss it must have caused when members of these unlucky neighborhoods woke up one morning to find themselves in another contrada, with—for starters—a new flag and new songs to learn. As for the surviving contrade, their legacies go back even further, at least to the 1540s. By that time all their current names were appearing in various legal documents.[30] These names, therefore, provide a modern-day connection to the days of the Siena republic.

The Contrada Social Scene

Returning to current times, each contrada owns and manages a *società*, essentially the contrada social headquarters, which typically includes a clubhouse of some sort. The clubhouse often comes complete with a substantial interior space for large gatherings, a bar with discounted prices for contrada members, an outdoor patio, contrada trophy displays, volunteer sign-up sheets for various functions, and other amenities. Unlike an exclusive American country club, however, everyone in the contrada is welcome regardless of age, gender, or socioeconomic status. Members just show up, and they are treated like family.

The fact that contrada membership cuts across all socioeconomic class divisions—welcoming all members into its social sphere regardless of their wealth or status—is one of the more remarkable characteristics of the contrade. This social equality is referred to as *interclassismo*.[31]

In other words, when contradaioli attend contrada-sponsored functions, they are considered equals regardless of their stature within the larger community. Thus, the contrada is a social leveler to some extent, discouraging the homogeneity often experienced in US suburban neighborhoods, where people earning similar incomes are buying similar-priced houses. One friend from the Panther contrada confirmed that "the contrada is like a big family, and everyone looks out for one another." The contrada even serves as a mutual-aid organization to take care of its less fortunate residents.

Without prompting, our friend added, "This is the main reason why the crime rate is so low here." Isn't this a basic premise of a strong community? Perhaps if one feels a deep sense of belonging, one is less likely to destroy or deface it.

Each contrada's social activities occur largely in its own neighborhood, especially in such hubs as around the contrada chapel, società, and horse stable during the Palio. Like most Italians, the Senesi are largely outdoorsy people. The street is to be celebrated as the focus for informal community interaction and social activities. In fact, most, if not all, contrade identify strongly with a specific street or other public space as the center of their communities. In American lingo, this might represent the Main Street of the contrada, where adults enjoy socializing and kids learn how to interact respectfully with their peers and elders in public.

If there is no central street for gathering, certain contrade identify with other types of public spaces, such as a courtyard (Owl) or small piazza (Giraffe). The center of community life for the Giraffe is found in the Piazza del Provenzano, to which we will return later. Each contrada further identifies a specific entrance or unmarked gateway into its *rione* (territory), typically oriented inward toward the center of the city—sometimes directly from the Campo itself. Thus, one enters the contrada's main public space from within Siena rather than from separate gateways on the periphery. Clearly, the geography of public space is of utmost importance to these people, as is their symbolic relationship with the city as a whole.

Streetscapes are even more festive around Palio time, when each contrada installs specially designed sconces and colorful contrada flags on its building facades. The wall sconces used after dark are particularly brilliant fixtures, considering both their contrada-specific color schemes and bundles of uncovered lightbulbs that, together, are likely visible from space.

LIFE IN THE CONTRADE

Symbols of Contrada Identity

Another understated but significant focus of identity is the contrada fountain. Seventeen of these various-sized water features are found distributed throughout the city, not always in obvious locations. Some are tucked away below raised streets (Caterpillar) or built into the facades of otherwise uninspiring buildings (Turtle and Unicorn). The Goose enjoys its own covered fountain, literally a centuries-old Gothic stone structure around which the water—and Goose contradaioli—regularly flow. The fountain is known as Fontebranda, and the Goose identity with this ancient landmark is strong enough for Goose loyalists to call themselves the "people of Fontebranda." That's the description the local media uses as well when writing or speaking of the neighborhood.

It seems that visitors in the twenty-first century enjoy mapping Siena's fountains, tracking them down and, of course, taking the requisite photos; the experience is not unlike a scavenger hunt. To the members of each contrada, however, the fountain remains the most special of places, where baptisms into the contrada are held and where youthful members practice their drumming or flag-waving skills. If geographically possible, contrada dinners tend to be focused near these water features. Tourists can easily mistake a contrada fountain for a civic piece of art. In other words, although tourists may indeed find them, the unknowing visitor to Siena would only see these spaces as part of the normal urban fabric, unaware of the deeply rooted meanings these public places hold for hundreds or thousands of contrada members.

The strongest direct symbol of personal contrada identity is the contrada scarf, or *fazzoletto*, which is typically worn around one's neck. Today, as in the past, the authentic *fazzoletto* is made of 100 percent silk and is given to someone born and baptized into the contrada. Ideally, contradaioli receive their *fazzoletti* (plural) when they are born and keep them for life. Still, as globalization and demographic changes continue to influence the contrade, it is now possible to be born or to marry outside the contrada and still receive a silk *fazzoletto*. There are other exceptions as well, as we would discover later in our stay.

While the Goose and Panther would gradually creep into our hearts, our earlier attention was focused intently on the Bruco (Caterpillar) contrada or, as the community is officially known, the Noble Contrada of the Caterpillar. Months prior to our summer adventure, I had consumed Robert Rodi's book *Seven Seasons in Siena*, ultimately praising it to family and colleagues.[32] Rodi provides a rather fun and painless entry into contrada and Palio life. The book tells of Rodi's personal attempt to integrate socially into the Caterpillar. As a lighthearted introduction to contrada society, it was a natural choice to put on our students' required reading list.

Caterpillar Rock Stars

Before our arrival, we could not have possibly imagined the book's future influence on our educational program. By our first week in Siena, students and faculty alike had been completely won over by Robert Rodi's beloved Caterpillar. At the center of our discussion was an ongoing debate over the merits of Rodi's attempt to somehow become socially accepted by its rather private community. Gaining social acceptance is of particular concern to nearly everyone on the planet, it seems, no matter the community's size or location. Rodi chose quite a challenge, to say the least. He took on one of the more extreme transitions from urban Chicago to a closely guarded Italian neighborhood—a whopper of a shift if I ever did see one.

Rodi's personal tale provides wonderful lessons surrounding local-versus-outsider dynamics and community cohesiveness. But was he realistic in his expectations for social acceptance? How does a person know when he or she is accepted? And who makes the determination? What does it take to be accepted as a local in any community, let alone a Siena contrada? The book spawned numerous discussions around these very questions.

One of Rodi's main characters throughout the book is Dario Castagno, a local writer who has gained a following through his many publications. In fact, Castagno has become a bit of a celebrity outside of Siena with his popular books about Tuscan culture, especially his uproarious observations of tourists. Two of his better-known books are *Too Much Tuscan Sun* and its follow-up, *Too Much Tuscan Wine*.[33] First and foremost, Castagno is a proud member of the Caterpillar contrada. After absorbing Rodi's book, some of our students sought out Castagno's works as well.

Now within a few weeks of our arrival, both authors are obtaining the status of veritable rock stars in the students' eyes. Overall, our students are displaying an enthusiasm for reading and discussion that I had not previously witnessed during my nearly twenty years of teaching. Occasionally, our discussions last well past our allotted time. If students are impatiently checking their watches or smartphones, we do not see it. The people of the Caterpillar, known as Brucaioli, are clearly on the students' minds.

More than once I catch our students exchanging Castagno's books. Even Linda is participating in this reading adventure. This gradually snowballing interest in all things Castagno and Rodi could not have been more strategically planned had we tried. After all, an Italian history museum is in our students' future. Museums are not typically found on the top-ten destination list of visiting students. Still, this one—the Caterpillar museum—would prove to become an unforgettable highlight of their eight-week stay. Seeing students count down the days to a museum visit is a rare sight indeed.

I had learned an important lesson about visiting museums while teaching in Viterbo two years earlier: mixing historical museums and college students was not one of humanity's smartest ideas. Add interior summer temperatures of 80° F or higher, and the combination is lethal. One instructor insisted on stuffing his students in this or that museum for hours at a time, moving methodically from one display to another. While this was a valiant effort to instill a sense of history and culture within young minds, these visits did little more than drive them nuts. As wonderful as these places are for enriching our societies and cultures, museums present a teaching challenge because they often lack a cultural context to link all the bits of information together in a meaningful way—especially if presented in a foreign language. Of course, much depends on the audience. For those interested in Etruscan culture or Italian art, museums can be educationally fundamental. For business or science majors, however, such visits can test their patience. As the oft-quoted proverb states, you can lead a horse to water ...

Night at the Museum

The anticipated night finally arrives, and we manage to find the obscure Caterpillar fountain hidden below and off to one side of Via dei Rossi, where we are to meet Dario Castagno. With our class waiting patiently near the Caterpillar neighborhood, Castagno shuffles in and introduces himself in his rather subdued manner. He's not over the top like some tour guides, with a false sense of enthusiasm; instead, he is down to earth and conversational.

Our first stop is the Caterpillar headquarters, Società l'Alba. "*Alba* stands for 'dawn' or 'sunrise,'" Castagno explains near its nondescript entrance. "When the organization was founded, contrada leaders met to determine the name of the società. They argued through the night and couldn't agree on a new name, until the sun finally started to come up. Noticing this, someone suggested naming it for the dawn, and they finally agreed." We follow Castagno back to an immaculately manicured garden patio and lawn area—a place rarely seen by tourists or even other Senesi. The class lets out a collective gasp at the grotto-type green space, with one adding, "This is where the natural vegetation is hiding!" The students had noticed a distinct lack of greenery inside the city walls—from an American perspective—and wondered how the Senese locals handle such a dense urban environment. "The green space is often managed by the contrade, aside from the city-managed public parks and market areas," explains Castagno.

This is essentially the collective backyard of an extended family with some 2,500 members—and growing. Numerous Caterpillar contrada social events take place here, along with practice sessions for promising Caterpillar flag throwers, known as *alfieri*, preparing for the next Palio. Much to our delight, Castagno has arranged for two *alfieri* to show their flag-throwing moves. Looking around, I sense that more than one of us is trying to imagine the Palio-eve dinners that Robert Rodi attended in this very space, which he had so humorously described. Once back inside the società hallways, Castagno quickly motions to a wall with massive sign-up sheets hanging side by side. One of them is reserved for young people who can sign up to volunteer at an upcoming Caterpillar dinner event. The sheet is packed with names. *Did their parents make them sign up?* I suspiciously wonder. No, Castagno confirms that young people are more than eager to help, if it means being a part of their larger extended family.

Moving past the designated sign-up wall, we discover an obscure, backstage entrance to the contrada chapel, where the horse is blessed when the Brucoioli are running in the Palio. The students were more than a little disappointed when they discovered that the Caterpillar contrada would be sitting this particular Palio out. The Baroque-era chapel is a visually busy place, with little wall space left unadorned. The rather modest chapel area consists of a fascinating blend of religious and contrada imagery, revealing how these two ritualistic traditions have complemented each other through the centuries.

Castagno points to several medallions on the wall, each with a contrada symbol painted in the center. The Caterpillar medallion is appropriately placed above the other three, which include images of the Porcupine, Tower, and Shell contrade. These are the Caterpillar's alliances or friendships; as I mentioned earlier, the Caterpillar contrada no longer has an official enemy. It is rare for traditional enemies to change relationships, but Castagno indicates that his contrada has accomplished precisely that. Its long-time enemy, the Giraffe, agreed to downscale that status to one of no relationship following the Caterpillar's Palio victory of 1996. "A good job we did," adds Castagno, given that the Giraffe won both the July and August races the following year! Had the peace treaty not been signed, the Caterpillar would have considered both events the equivalent of serious losses.

The final highlight of the tour is a surprisingly modern, antiseptic museum that carefully preserves and displays contrada parade outfits, medieval-style armor, trophies, and, of course, all the Palio banners won since the early 1700s. Rather than seeking a hidden exit to make an early escape, the group is content to remain as long as Castagno allows. Some students eventually make the connection between this museum and one of Rodi's stories, where he becomes unwittingly caught inside one night, stumbling around in the dark to find his way out. "Yes, this is where Robert was trapped," confirms our grinning guide.

I marvel that we are in the midst of the contrada's most precious heritage with all its meaningful collectibles. The evening ends with an invitation to a well-placed table staged with Castagno's books for sale and a polyester version of the Caterpillar *fazzoletto*. He cautions, "If you attend our contrada dinner as our guests the night before the Palio, be sure to wear these and not the cheap knockoffs from the tourist shops—the designs are not the same, and we can tell immediately which one you are wearing." In other words, if you're going to join them as their guest, don't look like a tourist.

I can't resist asking a question that I had already asked others, for comparison: "Is it acceptable for us to wear the *fazzoletto* around the contrada during Palio time?" Without hesitation, he replies, "Sure, it's not a problem." His response throws me a bit, because it contradicts what I have heard elsewhere regarding the contrada's most important symbol of identity. I had received a different answer from a Siena School acquaintance who is a proud member of the Eagle contrada. She cautioned that it would be in bad taste to "pretend" you are a contradaiolo by wearing the *fazzoletto*. She continued, "The true contrada members can tell immediately who the visitors are, and so it's actually more appropriate to not disguise your status as a visitor and just come dressed to reflect who you really are." There was an exception, however, in the case of a victory. "If the contrada wins and is celebrating, they won't mind anyone wearing the *fazzoletto*. They'll accept anybody during that joyous time," she chuckled.

Given these responses and other sources, I admittedly remain quite confused about if or when it is acceptable for a visitor to wear the *fazzoletto*. It seems to be a question of whether one has been invited to the pre-Palio dinner, whether the contrada is accustomed to hosting a lot of visitors (the Caterpillar seems to attract many such visitors), the perspective of the person answering the question, and the general sentiment of the contrada population both before and after the race. Though perhaps mildly frustrating to this outsider, it should not be surprising that definitive answers about complex social customs such as these are hard to come by.

Regardless, for now we have a chance to purchase the Caterpillar scarves, and all proceeds from these sales are earmarked for the contrada. Even Linda and I jump at the chance to buy the cherished green-and-yellow scarf—in fact, we'll take two please: one for my office and one for home. A final group photo with Castagno closes off a perfect evening. Now *that* is the way to visit an Italian museum!

In my estimation, the students' bewildering enthusiasm for the Caterpillar facilities was due to their earlier readings and discussions surrounding Castagno and Rodi. They had already learned to appreciate the context and connections but had not yet gained access to the physical relics. In other words, we essentially flipped around the common approach to visiting museums by focusing on context first, whetting their appetite, throwing in a minor rock star, and then—as one student said after the magical evening with Castagno—"making the book come alive." It worked, though I humbly admit that it was mostly due to serendipity.

Contrada Membership

Because local-versus-outsider issues are an ongoing theme of our studies, we are still wondering just how challenging it is for an outsider to become an accepted contrada member. Typically, official contrada membership occurs after an individual of any age is baptized during a secular ceremony, once a year during the contrada's patron saint celebration known as the *festa titolare*. We found that it does not happen often for foreigners—including non-Senese Italians—even though the contrada social system is starting to open up more than it once did. Today some two-thirds of Senesi live outside the city walls in what we would consider suburban neighborhoods—what some locals dub the "neutral zone" (sounds seriously *Star Trek*-ish if you ask me). The suburbs are "neutral" because territory outside the city walls is not controlled by any particular contrada. Unlike in the United States, however, the Senese suburbs are generally clustered around the historic city, with most residents living in modernist, multistory flats. Although still close by, this suburban shift has brought a myriad of challenges to the traditional approaches for contrada membership.

Continued suburbanization has necessitated that contrada membership be expanded to include individuals from outside the traditional contrada *rione* (territory). In the 1990s a young woman from the Wave provided a wonderful explanation of how one can become a contrada member, during a personal interview with anthropologist Arthur Figliola, who was researching the inner workings and social dynamics of the contrade at the close of the twentieth century. I don't expect that her answer would change much two decades later, as she was already noting the realities of expanding membership to include people from outside the *rione*, a trend that continues at a slow pace. In part, she explained:

> It's not by chance that the rule should be that one is a *contradaiolo* because one is born in a *contrada*, in a certain territory ... even if, today, naturally, we pass the *contrada* on to one another as we have children, since it happens less and less frequently that a child is born within the walls, no? So one takes the *contrada* of the father or the mother, it's a bit like "citizenship" ... or, one becomes a *contradaiolo* through passion, as, for example, people who are not

from Siena or who may even be foreigners ... they're struck by lightning, they fall in love, they catch the Siena sickness and become *contradaioli*. And if they approach the *contrada* with the right spirit: if they're willing to listen, to be available, to be open, then they'll succeed at integrating themselves into the *contrada* ... if you're capable of giving to the *contrada* ... not to the people (of the *contrada*), but to the *contrada* itself![34]

I interpret Robert Rodi's own lovesickness as one case in point, with his determined efforts to prove his worthiness to the Caterpillar. At one level, this is no different than integrating into any close-knit community. To earn respect, one needs to be more or less present, participate in some way, and give of oneself to a larger community cause. This all makes a good deal of sense and, therefore, does not come as a monumental surprise. In some ways, the contrada may not differ all that much from our own communities where participation and dedication are of foremost importance. As Rodi discovered, however, this is no American bowling league. You have to want it badly, and after that, the jury may still be out for quite some time.

Some contrade have grown in population and membership due in part to their geographic proximity to a city gate. This has led to uneven memberships in today's contrade. Given that suburban residents tend to gravitate to the nearest contrada, it stands to reason that the Caterpillar, Shell, Snail, and Porcupine have swelled, as has the Goose due in part to its gate proximity and its popular local landmarks. Incidentally, the Goose apparently maintains the largest population still living within its original *rione*. In contrast, the populations of landlocked, interior contrade that have no city-gate suburban access remain smaller, namely the Eagle, Panther, Owl, and Unicorn.[35] Although territory outside the walls is technically considered a neutral zone, each contrada adjoining a city *porta* (gate) tends to lay unofficial claim to the area immediately outside its jurisdiction. When one interviewer asked an elementary school student where he lived, for instance, the kid mentioned a street outside of Porta Pispini, the city gate providing access to the Nicchio (Shell). His teacher corrected, "You really do live more in *Nicchio*."[36]

In addition, increased global influence has encouraged the proliferation of family networks and marriages extending well beyond the contrada walls and beyond Siena as a whole. Thus, the gold standard for contrada membership may still very well be one's birth and upbringing within its actual boundaries, but increasingly the contrade are opening up on some level to include nonresidents among their ranks. Still, no one should be under the illusion that membership is a walk in the park. One young woman from the Panther responded in this way to my question about membership:

> I think it's tough to join later, as we all know each other, have been around each other since we were kids. The group is hard to join; it takes time. Especially teenagers, coming in new, as we already have our groups. It can take a year to become a member, and you have to be here to participate, and you should know something [about the contrada].

Thus, despite their slightly more global approach, it is still not realistic for someone without familial ties to be accepted fully as a local here. A rather direct, if amusing, indicator of this fact is one online source that provides frequently asked questions about the contrade. To the question, "How does one become a contradaiolo?" the response is laser-sharp: "One *belongs* to a contrada; you cannot just be a fan of it."[37] True membership is still determined, the answer continues, by right of birth or, if outside the city walls, by parental affiliation. The answer then becomes fuzzier after those initial proclamations, perhaps a half-baked recognition of alternative approaches to membership that may occur once in a blue moon.

Our students now know of two Americans who have tried to integrate themselves into the Caterpillar in recent decades. Although I have no actual data on how many others have attempted or succeeded, this is a very short list and a well-advertised one. This tells me that it's still quite a big deal to even think about contrada membership as an outsider.

One successful American was Roy Moskovitz, a professor in New York, who happened to walk past the Caterpillar chapel in the 1960s at the time the contradaioli were blessing their horse for the Palio. What are the chances of that? According to Castagno, the professor became enthralled with the curious ritual of a horse being blessed inside the chapel, and he decided to stay in town longer than he had planned, to learn more about the Caterpillar. After finding that their level of community engagement remained high even after the Palio, he eventually made Siena his second home. The fellow was apparently well-loved by the contrada and by Siena as a whole, and he became accepted as a member of their close-knit extended family. He ultimately included the Caterpillar in his will, and now there is a meeting room above the museum dedicated to his contributions and membership.

The second American known to us is Robert Rodi, the Chicago author himself. I will leave it up to future readers to consider his ultimate level of success. There is no end to the debate on this question within our own group. Perhaps that was his intent? Rodi also refers quite often to someone he called Rachel who, from his descriptions, may have enjoyed some, if not more, success with becoming affiliated with the Caterpillar contrada.

As far as our own cohort is concerned, in some ways we are already starting to feel like locals. Having ventured away from Siena several times already, our students are already catching themselves saying that they "look forward to going home" near the end of such regional excursions. Humorously, they are not referring to the United States. Everyone may have laughed when one student caught herself referring to Siena as "home," but they also readily agreed that Siena was starting to feel like a "home away from home". Still, a veritable wall is emerging beyond which we cannot easily tackle the language divide. This had proven frustrating in Viterbo for both students and faculty—just as it is doing now in Siena. Still, for Linda and me, it is time to become better acquainted with the contrada just outside our window, to see what Rodi's fuss with contrada life is all about.

❋ CHAPTER 5 ❋

The Magic of Fontebranda

AT FIRST GLANCE, OUR DREADFULLY STEEP STREET, VIA DI FONTEBRANDA, appears to be just another winding medieval funnel, mostly for cars and the miniature Route 54 city bus. It's not a fun place to walk, although pedestrian traffic actually mingles well with the occasional gas-powered vehicle. Our calves get a workout tramping up or down, as do our ears, listening for the inevitable revving of car or bus engines. More often it's the obnoxious whine of scooters and motorcycles. Though we cringe at their high-pitched motors, we are impressed by the number of scooters in Italian cities. They are one of the more practical and economic ways to move about the city. In residential Siena and other cities, they are parked along the streets nearly everywhere they will fit. This is definitely not SUV territory, if you actually want to get somewhere. Next door to our apartment is a full-service mechanic's shop devoted to all things scooter, a trade which I imagine enjoys high job security around here. We wave to the owner daily on our way in or out, though he is nearly always busy with customers.

Our humble abode is just outside the tourist realm. Nearly all day-trippers are content to remain at the top of the steep incline along Via di Città, one of Siena's main spines. At the intersection, curious visitors gaze through the arch where our street begins, and they quickly note that it drops off precipitously like an urban black-diamond ski run. This is a natural deterrent for most visitors, who quickly calculate the slim chance they would make it back up the hill in time for their group dinner—if at all. Thus, most visitors scurry past, while others notice a picturesque photo opportunity when they see one. They won't risk skipping down our street for fear of never returning, but they will certainly photograph it from the top. The view could almost be

THE MAGIC OF FONTEBRANDA

found in an Italian painting, with its winding medieval structures and, in the background, the majestic Basilica of San Domenico.

Linda and I have also discovered another favored perch for visitors—sometimes legions of them in large group tours—atop a commanding overpass near our apartment. From that vantage point, they enjoy a breathtaking view of San Domenico, the valley, the medieval neighborhood of the Goose contrada far below—and of Linda and me, regularly trudging up and down the street. It becomes a bit unnerving, if amusing, to see these folks spying on us from above. We come to understand a little better how locals can feel objectified, essentially becoming a spectacle on their own street. Occasionally, we hold up our own cameras from below and return the favor, just for fun. I often wonder if they can tell immediately that I'm not Italian, given my typical combination of baseball cap, university jacket or, later, crewneck shirt—not to mention rather blond hair and fair skin. I am not likely contributing to their idealistic Italian scene. I most certainly ruin many a promising photo as my baseball cap or deep-red Università di Siena sweatshirt steals the show while I lumber up the hill.

Our street, therefore, serves more local Senesi than visitors. The locals are usually on a daily commute into or out of the city, mostly by scooter but occasionally by bus or on foot. The use of multiple modes of transportation here is noteworthy, despite the narrowness of our street. There is only a short dedicated sidewalk for part of the distance. The wayward visitors who choose to park outside the walls will pay the price with the extended incline. As mentioned in chapter 2, Siena's urban layout is roughly in the shape of a Y, nestled along three intersecting ridges. Dare to stray from the main streets along the ridges, and you briskly head downhill into one of the valleys. Once I remarked to Linda, "This is the only place I know where the fastest route is not a straight line." The more efficient, speedy route is along the ridges of Siena's three *terzi* (districts), carefully avoiding the valleys. Not to be outdone, she remarked with some exasperation, "Every direction in Siena is uphill!"

By parking below, unwitting visitors find that Linda's assessment is accurate. They puff up our hill, muttering expletives or other facetious statements as they walk past. We found one group recently walking backward up the hill, to even out the muscle work. "Half way there," another man yells back to his family, to which they sigh and press onward to their prize, the tourist-centered medieval core. I've cheered such people on more than once, convincing them that they don't have much farther to go. Usually they're satisfied when they hit the flatter and less arduous Via di Città near the Campo. Actually, so are we.

Occasional Goose dinners provide yet another level of activity along our street. Although the contradaioli may take some warming up to accept outside members into their contrade, they sure do embrace American pop culture. This seems to be true in much of Italy. I find the sheer volume of American pop music consumed by Italians remarkable, which suggests a full-on globalization of the dominant US music industry. Some Italian radio stations regularly play the stuff—from Madonna to Katy Perry. Linda and I regularly sing along with the outdoor soundtracks backing up various Goose events, usually opening our apartment window to enhance our vicarious enjoyment. "Is that what I think they're singing in Italian?" I check with Linda during one such event. "Yup, 'You were on my mind.'" I can't help but wonder aloud, "Do any Senesi actually comprehend the English lyrics, when they are not dubbed in Italian?" Not likely, but it doesn't seem to stop them from singing the likes of "California Gurls" and "I Gotta Feeling" at the top of their lungs until one in the morning. Not to mention Goose karaoke nights, when it becomes clear that the Senesi have, on average, no better singing abilities than Americans at such events. Linda pleads with me well past midnight during one such event, "Make it stop!" Just when you think you're back in the States, however, the soundtrack shifts to traditional songs and Goose-specific versions of the beloved Senese melody, "Il Canto della Verbena" (see chapter 10). This restores my hope that Italians haven't completely abandoned their musical roots.

The Siena Car Scene

As for the car traffic along Via di Fontebranda, it never fails to amaze me what humans will do to bring their vehicles as close to home as possible. For all my fawning over Italian street life, these people are not entirely immune to coveting popular four-wheeled vehicles. Along Via di Fontebranda, this means converting street-level storage areas beneath buildings into garages where no cars were ever meant to fit. The automobile bug has clearly infected the Senesi and many other Italians as well. Nearly every day we watch residents work tirelessly to stuff Toyotas or Fiats into storage areas under their five-hundred-year-old buildings. Never mind that they are doing it from a narrow street with a steep slope and no shoulder space for wiggle room. Consequently, they rely on a five-point or seven-point turn. A friend helps the driver back in, or alternatively, drivers struggle on their own to avoid touching the scraped-up stone walls with flimsy side mirrors. (They seem to have little success, based on countless dinged-up stone corners and cracked mirrors.) I did a double-take with one such garage on our street, which was cleverly retrofitted with a two-tiered platform to store one car above the other—a vertical two-car garage.

With many Senesi needing to commute somewhere by car, not everyone is enamored with the city's decision to eradicate traffic from the city center. Traffic and parking weigh heavily on locals now—just as these same issues continue to do so back in the United States. One woman interviewed in the 1990s was less than sympathetic with the banning of automobiles *in centro* (downtown):

> Until a few years ago, you could bring the car into the center. Now it's no longer permitted, because they've closed off the *centro storico*; and even if you are able to bring the car close to the center, there are difficulties trying to find a place to park, either because there are no parking places, or else, they're very expensive and therefore eat into your salary. So I've been forced to buy a scooter. I now have to take a longer route to work, using up more time. With the car, I bring my kids to school, then return home, leave the car there, and go to work on the scooter.[38]

Such issues with commuting, parking, and juggling family responsibilities should strike a familiar chord with many Americans, especially kid-toting parents. Although the local geography here may be rather unfamiliar to most of us, with its thousand-year-old walled, medieval center and all, it is sometimes uncanny how much we have in common with people around the world.

Locked Out

As readers have likely deduced by now, our tiny apartment is within close earshot of Goose Central just around the corner. The contrada's official title is the Nobile Contrada dell'Oca. A bit farther down from our apartment is one of the city's remaining medieval public water sources, that of Fontebranda. This is one landmark along our street worth remembering and visiting, and it does provide a respite to tourists as they make their way up or down to the city gate. It is said that Ocaioli women washed their clothes in the fountain through World War II and beyond until an amazing invention called the washing machine forever made the laundry ritual at Fontebranda obsolete. Nonetheless, Fontebranda remains a landmark for the Goose contrada and for Siena as a whole, although it is now relegated to simply being a picturesque water feature. In fact, unsuspecting passersby would have no way of knowing that it is the hub of the Goose contrada's identity. Beneath the dense stack of rooftops across from our apartment, thousands of loyal contrada residents go about their daily routines and occasionally attend contrada dinners and other events.

The Goose contrada's close-knit network came to our attention in a humorous and much appreciated way during our first week in Siena. Moving into a foreign city is no small task. There is simply no time to enjoy some form of hyper-romanticized Tuscan sun. In fact, I typically make diligent efforts to avoid the sun with sunscreen and other measures, lest all that romanticism burn my fair skin right off my body. Our first full week in Siena had been usurped by an unending litany of arrival logistics, delayed student flights, cell phone connection problems, Internet concerns, grocery shopping mysteries, apartment furnishing, floor scrubbing, and only Saint Catherine (patron saint of Italy) knows what else. I was fairly well fit to be tied as we struggled through the second week, when I nonchalantly mentioned to Linda, "It would be wonderful if we could have a chance to see the city."

And so it was that, after several orientation meetings and our first class, Amy from the Siena School heavily promoted a promising Thursday night social event known as *aperitivo*. Our class was instructed to meet Amy in the Campo near the Torre del Mangia around dusk. She would then lead our group to an outdoor garden space to enjoy good company and refreshments.

THE MAGIC OF FONTEBRANDA

It appeared that we would finally be able to relax a bit with our group and maybe even meet some new friends. Fate would end up stymieing that plan.

Earlier that day another Siena School staff member had arranged for a repair of our apartment's entry door and lock. We thus prepared to have a fix-it person make the necessary improvements sometime during the day. Before setting out for the Campo that evening, Linda and I headed back to our new home on Via di Fontebranda to trade off a few clothes and prepare for the evening out. I stuck my key into the door as usual, expecting it to unlock. But something was wrong. I presumed that the locksmith must have changed the mechanism earlier in the day. I tried again, but entry was denied. There was no sign of wiggling or fussing inside the lock. We were locked out. Resignation set in, and I logically assumed that the landlord had changed the lock as part of the maintenance effort. *If this is the case, why didn't anyone tell us or give us a new set of keys?* I thought. My earlier patience transitioned into frustration and concern that we might be homeless by nightfall.

The only short-term safety net we had was our impending rendezvous with Amy at the Campo. We would be rather late due to this newest development, but going there would allow us to corner Amy if we could get there in time. I was never as overjoyed as when I saw Amy chatting with our group precisely where she said they would be waiting. After hastily acknowledging the group, I dove for Amy and immediately pulled her aside with a tone of urgency. I offered my own theory as to why we were currently homeless. "We don't have Linda's set of keys for some reason," I explained, "and mine show no signs of wanting to work, probably because someone changed the lock." Amy had already demonstrated her devotion to making our collective lives easier while we transitioned into this foreign place, as had the entire Siena School staff. In one sense, we were at their mercy, and I was hesitant to bring up more problems.

Regardless of my concerns, she immediately launched into problem-solving mode and hatched a plan. She would walk our group to the *aperitivo* event and introduce them to the scene. Then she would double back with me to assess the situation for herself. Once again, the benefits of a walkable city were becoming evident. None of this back-and-forth would require a car. That being said, our plan ended up requiring quite a hike—essentially two round-trips to and from the *aperitivo* site near the edge of town, about twenty minutes each way.

While the remainder of our crew settled in for light fare and socializing, I waved good-bye to Linda and walked a beeline with Amy to the apartment. In my typical style, I treated this opportunity as an impromptu interview. Amy told me about her own discovery of Siena, her past schooling, and why she absolutely loves living in this Tuscan town. We encountered several of her friends in the street, making it clear that she had already crafted an impressive social network. She joked, "I have to plan an extra ten minutes for my walking commute if I'm going somewhere to account for the time chatting with friends I see in the street." I chuckle at the thought of padding a schedule to account for likely encounters with friends. This doesn't happen often in the States, even within our own neighborhood.

When we arrived at our apartment, our entry attempts began anew, this time with Amy leading the charge. No luck. My hopefulness deflated by the minute as Amy seemed genuinely stymied. Up to this point, Amy had been invincible, solving any problem we threw her way: acquiring cell phones, setting up Internet service access, purchasing lightbulbs—you name it. Still, the lock would not budge. I asked Amy if she could call the landlord. Her phone, I learned, included all sorts of useful contacts—her friends, the school staff, and likely a third of Siena's local population. *Which phone-a-friend option will she use?* I wondered. I finally dropped my sweater on a stair railing and took a seat while Amy made a flurry of calls. Although American by upbringing, Amy was nearly fluent in Italian. Ultimately, the landlord's son turned out to be the most productive choice. "Giulio will head over here shortly to see what he can do," Amy announced.

Help from the Goose

The remainder of this story unfolded like a Hollywood script. We headed back outside to await Giulio, who showed up in good cheer on his scooter. However, his attempts at entry failed as well. Amy and Giulio exchanged a rapid conversation in Italian, which I conveniently ignored, hoping there was a successful strategy at the end of it. To my disturbing shock, they asked me which window was ours. Fortunately, I vaguely recalled that it was the farthest window on the up-slope side of the building. Giulio surveyed the window from the street and was satisfied that we had apparently left the window unlocked. So the open window became his new strategy. I was not

THE MAGIC OF FONTEBRANDA

amused, as the window was rather high off the street, and in any case, I wondered, *Don't these people simply have the new key to the lock? Is this a magic trick of some kind?*

I felt helpless, so I stepped aside and allowed my two companions to take the helm. Giulio soon boarded his scooter and coasted down Via di Fontebranda, with me more perplexed than ever. Amy then brought me up to speed. "Giulio is going to find a ladder and try to climb through the window," she said. *No way. This is the plan? How long will it take to find a ladder? How is he going to get it here? Will it be tall enough? Am I thinking too much?* (The answer to this last question would come later in our visit.)

Then I learned an important factor in this plan: Giulio was a proud member of the Goose contrada. At this point I had no idea where the various contrada buildings or secret storage areas were located, but Amy expressed confidence that Giulio would be right back. True to her word, Giulio returned to save the day with a ladder attached somehow vertically onto the back of his scooter. *How did he do that? This can't be good*, I thought, especially after he assembled the ladder behind a parked scooter and gingerly ascended, with Amy trying to steady him. Even I saw from afar that there was a good six-foot gap beyond the top ladder rung and the window. Giulio did confirm that the window was open, however, which turned out to be our saving grace.

Amy and Giulio admitted temporary defeat, and he headed off back down from whence he came. In the meantime, Amy explained how he had gotten the equipment so quickly. Giulio and his family were Ocaioli, or Goose contrada residents. Confirming what Robert Rodi and acquaintances here have explained, the contrada behaves like a giant extended family, and it may indeed be one of our planet's most impressive social networks. Contradaioli look out for each other—even after nonfamily members. Not one to give up, Giulio finally returned with a longer ladder, similarly borrowed from a contrada storage space somewhere in the neighborhood. This time, I was satisfied that the ladder was apparently tall enough to access the window.

The remaining problem was the uneven street. We had to find a way to balance the legs of the ladder, which were not at the same height. Giulio shifted the scooter around while Amy and I moved the ladder. *I am hoping to at least present an outward appearance of being useful*, I thought. Climbing up, Giulio somehow launched off the ladder and through our window. I tried to remember what we had placed on the other side of the window where he would inevitably land. *I think it's the clothes drying rack.* It was a stroke of good Ocaioli luck, I suppose, that our window was the closest to the road, given its steep slope. It provided the necessary elevation for the primitive ladder approach to be effective. Once inside, opening our door was a piece of cake. Giulio soon appeared outside the building with Linda's set of keys.

Amy and I were curious about what he found. It turns out that, as I have often discovered in this country, my logical presumption was inaccurate. Linda's key was still inserted inside the lock, preventing my key from working! We had neglected to remove her key from the inside of the door when we left! This was embarrassing, as I was already blaming the mystery landlord for changing the lock without telling us. Instead, we had already gotten into the habit of leaving a set of keys inside the lock at night, as suggested by another acquaintance. As Amy winced, I explained that the logic was to insert a key into the lock at night to prevent any unwanted Senesi from entering. True enough, no Senesi had interloped, but the plan had now backfired. Had that window not been open, I imagine we would have had to use heavy mechanical equipment or sledgehammers. (We learned much later that Giulio's wife had been less than pleased that he simply didn't call the fire department.) Consequently, Linda and I decided that we would no longer leave any keys inside the lock. And why should we need to do so anyway? Siena was one of Europe's safest cities. I supposed Americans like us aren't often that trusting.

I thanked Giulio, using my best Italian expressions of appreciation. *"Di niente,"* ("It is nothing") he replied, and to his credit, he seemed to be sincere. We had asked him to help on a moment's notice, taking him away from whatever he was doing, which no doubt was certainly better than this. He was kind and patient, however, throughout the process. Moreover, the Goose contrada had just saved us. A strong social network provided our landlord's son with access to whatever he needed, somewhere only a few hundred feet away. From this point on, I could not help being impressed with the Goose and the contrada system as a whole.

PART II

FEELING AT HOME

❈ CHAPTER 6 ❈

Mixing it Up

As I walk to school on an otherwise normal day, I notice a ceramic shop, one of many, along my usual route. Like all such places, this one includes displays of the artist's work on the outside wall, with the primary aim of attracting people like me to enter on impulse. Also in character for Siena and much of Italy is the modest, single-door entry with little indication that this is a business.

Ceramic Shop Friends

What makes me wander into this place today, I do not know. There are seemingly hundreds of ceramic shops like this one—perhaps outnumbering pizza joints and gelaterias combined. Apparently, the demand is through the roof for decorative ceramic products. I start to browse the intricate designs of the plates and many other ceramic knickknacks, a behavior which predictably ends up attracting the attention of a grandmotherly woman, with a genuinely warm smile and very gray hair. Someone else with curly, equally gray hair, presumably her husband, is slumped over a plate that he is painting in a separate room behind the counter. *They look like a friendly couple*, I surmise. This ends up to be an accurate assessment. I provide my standard greeting in Italian and say a few extra words to indicate that I'm not an ordinary weekend visitor—not that there's anything wrong with that. With this greeting I have apparently earned a detailed tour of their shop, which is divided into three sections: contrada plates and accessories, Renaissance-era designs from Siena (not Florence, she corrects me quickly), and replicas of the now-popular floor art found in the Duomo. After a small while, I gravitate to the contrada plates, still fascinated with their traditionally distinctive colors, symbols, and designs. I hone in on a dinner-sized Goose plate, perched on a top shelf.

MIXING IT UP

The fun is just beginning—along with the awkwardness of my limited Italian speaking abilities. The woman asks me why I'm interested in the Goose plate, although I really can't quite tell what she is saying. I speak well enough with the Italian that I know, but when it comes to understanding someone else, it's a never-ending bout with frustration. I can ask questions quite competently, but the fun stops when I actually have to comprehend the answers. After they hear me speak a little of their native language, however, they invariably presume I am fluent and therefore unleash themselves and chatter on as if I'm a family member. Then comes my blank stare and empty look in return and a regretful "I'm sorry" or "I don't understand" because "I only speak a little Italian, and I'm really just another American imposter." This does slow the Italians down, often but not always, and they happily help me understand what they are saying.

Fortunately, this woman is particularly patient with me from the beginning, and she seems impressed that I at least know a little Italian. I would like to imagine this is refreshing for her after laboring year-round on one of the busier tourist thoroughfares. So I open up the conversation with something I can say: "I am a professor in Siena for eight weeks, teaching American students, and we live on Via di Fontebranda." I have nearly mastered these connected phrases, which provide a lot of information in an efficient manner. I don't know what she finds most intriguing, although the professor thing seems to make a difference. Not everyone here is that fond of the University of Siena or its students because they have taken over a portion of the city's official population. But she really lights up when I say Fontebranda, which leads to a flurry of arm waving. She excitedly tries to tell me that she and her husband are members of the Goose contrada themselves! *No way!* Way. As we fumble through some simple Italian, I convey that I am indeed aware that we live in the Goose and that we are enjoying the Fontebranda neighborhood very much. And just like that, I now have new friends from the Goose contrada.

I become equally enthusiastic at this news, and I ask her if they are natives, born into the contrada. Not quite. Her husband may be a pure Ocaiolo, from what I gather—someone born into the Goose. However, her family is from Sicily, and they moved here quite some time ago. She therefore became a contradaiola through marriage, and they currently live in a small town outside of Siena. Then the conversation starts going south, so to speak.

I have reached and clearly moved beyond the limits of my language skills, fumbling for words and grasping for time to think. I finally admit that I don't understand everything she's saying, but to her credit she remains patient and is seemingly willing to put up with me.

I decide to leave this poor couple alone for a while, as other customers are now browsing. I somehow convey that I will return with my wife, who will enjoy looking at the pottery and plates. We exchange names. She is Viola, and her husband is Riccardo. I joke that my name is *Tomasso* in Italian, having learned recently that most people here have some issues with comprehending the simple "Tom." She starts calling me *il professore*, and we exchange pleasant good-byes.

Recovering outside, I realize I have just made my first social acquaintance with Goose contradaioli, and it did not involve being rescued and certainly not where I expected. Throughout our stay, this mixing of contrada residents with businesses around town, landlords and renters, and so forth makes it clear that the social dynamics of the contrade are anything but simple. Yes, there are physical street boundaries that delineate the edges of each contrada or *rione*—the physical neighborhood—marked discreetly with small colored tiles inserted high up on the buildings. But like all cities and political boundaries, the social geography is more complex. People living in one contrada commonly work in another, and landlords from one contrada own property elsewhere. All this activity further bleeds into the suburbs outside the walls and with the mixing of families and relatives well beyond city limits.

A Contrada Resurgence

The contrada's importance in Siena's social life and history has actually increased since roughly the 1950s. Prior to that time, this social structure in Siena had remained relatively insignificant. Now it was being used to preserve a traditional way of life in the face of change. As someone's birth within the city walls has become less significant, the importance of contrada membership to one's identity has only grown. Basically, as more individuals and families live outside the walls today—due in part to higher rents, the influx of thousands of students, and the increasing growth of mass tourism—association with the contrade has intensified while social activity within the rione has diminished. Fewer families now live within the historic center of the city, and therefore fewer and fewer Senese actually treat their contrada's rione as home. This concern has continued to show up in local media and community conversations for decades. Hamish Park uncovered two quotes to this effect from local newspapers in the 1980s: "I hope that our children do not have to use a map like the tourists when they come to Siena," and from another, "The *rione* hardly exists any longer."[39]

Park found that by the early 1990s most contradaioli felt that changes were occurring for the worse. What these Senesi remembered nostalgically was how the *rione* brought community members together on a regular basis, with or without the Palio as a driver. And just as in pre–World War II communities and smaller towns in the United States, people felt that everyone knew everybody else. This changed with the suburban age and the great dispersal of the population. Likewise in Siena, people moved out of the *rione* for more spacious and modern housing, and community activity within the *rione* and its associated società diminished. The result, still apparently continuing, is that while the contrada has quite successfully attracted greater membership, fewer Senesi identify closely with their respective *rione*.

By the 1990s, the number of paying subscribers to the contrade had never been higher. In stark contrast, Park estimated that only some 10 percent of the contrada membership actually belonged to a women's group or the società.[40] The exact opposite had been true earlier in the century: while the *rione* and its società boomed, the contrada itself played a much less significant role than it does today.

The younger generations of the past several decades have consequently made their friends and other acquaintances from outside the traditional *rione*, even if they still remain somehow identified with a specific contrada. Their friends from school and elsewhere are perhaps more globally aware and view life beyond the *rione*. In fact, the vast majority of the younger Senese generation have never even lived in Siena, but they make the trip into the historic city and perhaps their contrada neighborhood during the days of the Palio. This explains why one can easily see groups of teenagers hanging out in town during the days of the Palio, often with each one sporting a different *fazzoletto*. In other words, they are more than willing to hang with friends from outside their contrada, even at Palio time. I have caught myself doing double-takes when spying rival teens from the Panther and Eagle laughing it up with one another, thereby blurring the contrada boundaries even further.

What suffers, regrettably, for those remembering the heyday of their neighborhoods, is the community cohesiveness once found within the *rione* and its social connections. That being said, as an American, I view all of this as being relative. Despite these immense demographic changes and the suburbanization of the local population, Americans like me marvel at the relatively strong community cohesion of the Senesi and their support for one another. While the Palio and its preceding events may certainly drive more of the annual cycle of social activity, I have yet to see anything like the Senesi cohesiveness elsewhere. From our perspective, the historic buildings are still largely occupied by locals—at least deep within each *rione*—and their active street life (both day and night) still remains impressive.

This is confirmed by a new friend of mine from the Panther contrada, who—despite his desire to see more citywide activities—believes the contrada still provides a strong sense of family and belonging:

> The contrada is not only a big family; it is also a sort of vigilance. Indeed, Siena doesn't have a high percentage of criminality like in Rome or Milan. The members of a contrada are tight because they've had a special feeling for the neighborhood where they live and for the city of Siena too. Everyone is a part of the contrada: young men, older people, newborns, and teenagers.

When being interviewed by a journalist, Senio Sensi reported that a similar resurgence in contrada members was continuing through the mid-2000s. At that time, Sensi led an intercontrada consortium responsible for organizing the Palio.[41] Though fewer teenagers may be rooted within a particular *rione*, Sensi noted a "rekindling of *Palio* fanfare" among the younger Senesi. They are even more eager to join a contrada. If they are sixteen years old or older, they can persevere through a communion-type ritual to do so. Sensi further attributes this youthful resurgence as an effective antidote for various "social ills" that tempt their young counterparts elsewhere. I guess the relatively low crime rate here is not a coincidence after all. Young and old residents alike identify strongly with something greater than themselves—

the contrada; consequently, they care for it and maintain a personal stake in its success.

Social Mixing

Aside from the perplexity of seeing groups of friends sporting different *fazzoletti*, we have encountered numerous examples of social mixing across traditional boundaries. For example, my colleague shared with much amusement that his apartment, entrenched within the Unicorn contrada, is actually decorated in blue and white, the colors of the Wave. Another unexpected experience took place at a *trattoria* (family dining restaurant) that was a favorite of ours. Called the Trattoria di L'Aquila (Restaurant of the Eagle), it is named for its location within the Eagle contrada. While enjoying a leisurely meal at the trattoria one evening, the sound in an adjacent room was ramping up. This finally erupted into male voices singing in unison. "Those must be the officials from the Eagle," we agreed, chuckling with appreciation. On our way out we mustered the courage to peak around the corner to find some twenty middle-aged or older men singing and laughing it up. When we questioned an employee, however, our presumptions were turned head over heels. The group actually hailed from the Tower contrada. The men were apparently provided with a friendly place to congregate by the restaurant's sympathetic owner, likewise from the Tower.

Making the situation even more complex are the restaurant's employees, who come from any number of contrade. The staff member with whom we spoke at L'Aquila actually lived in the Goose for some six years at that time. While he did not seem to identify strongly with his residence near Fontebranda, he was still working for someone representing the arch enemy of the Goose. This type of social mixing must drive the Senesi nuts, but overall, everyone seems to accept reality without much ado. They're not tearing out each other's flags or discriminating against their traditional enemies within the restaurants. All seem to be friends on the surface and accept the fact that there are seventeen contrade and that somehow they all have to get along. They may not be best friends, especially around Palio time, but their work and lives, which are intertwined in this dense, medieval city, are impressively civil. They are all Senesi, after all, even if many still identify strongly with their own contrada.

The Goose Plate

After making the acquaintance of Viola and Riccardo in their ceramic shop, I return with Linda as promised, and we both decide we want to make a purchase to show our appreciation for their friendliness. Linda quickly warms up to Viola. They are both vigorous arm wavers and quite social by nature. As I stand by to watch their lively dialogue, Linda receives the requisite tour of their shop. Based on my earlier prodding, Linda has already agreed to purchase the coveted Goose dinner plate. While certainly not the eye-catching design of other contrade such as the Shell, Panther, or Dragon (the Shell is apparently the hottest seller due to its deep-blue background), this graceful bird represents our home away from home. There is no better or meaningful souvenir that I can imagine.

Gravitating toward the plate, Viola quickly notes our interest and conveys that it is the last one in their shop. "No more Goose!" she finally establishes through broken English. The message is clear: *Palio time is coming. Get it now. We don't know when we will make another one.* Looking around, I see that her statement seems to be accurate. Aside from some smaller Goose items, this is the last large plate. I want to whisper to Linda that there are probably dozens of these things in the back room, but I decide to simply trust Viola. We can see that these plates are designed and made from scratch, made all the more obvious with Riccardo bending over his workstation, which is placed strategically within sight of the displays.

As the tallest person in the room, I naturally move toward the Goose plate on the top shelf and reach for it. This triggers a quick, defensive move on Viola's part. She pushes me aside and grabs the plate herself. Though possibly a polite gesture to save me the effort, her primary intent is probably to signal that she isn't quite ready to trust this gangly customer with her handmade merchandise. I understand. So with her short body and arms she struggles to reach the plate, which is perched precariously in a plastic display holder. As she reaches for it, the plastic holder slides out from underneath the plate and nearly falls to the floor. I immediately envision the last Goose plate turning quickly into a thousand little Goose pieces. As the plate wavers, I lunge to the rescue, cautiously grabbing the plate's side to provide stability while still allowing Viola to be in charge. Crisis resolved, Viola wraps the plate and sinks it into a protective canvas sac.

Although it is pricey, it will serve as a cherished souvenir. At this point in our stay, I have not strongly identified with any one contrada—at least not to the point of decorating our home with its memorabilia. We are certainly making some meaningful acquaintances in various contrade—the Panther and Caterpillar to name a couple. But the Goose is likely as close as we will get to an attachment to place. And quite frankly, remaining completely ambivalent toward all seventeen contrade will not prove nearly as much fun when Palio time comes around. After all, we have an excuse beyond the pretty designs: We live there. We are, for a short time, two of the people of Fontebranda.

Exploring the Goose

Soon thereafter I decide to start winding through the Goose streets to find the elusive Via di Santa Caterina, which Viola says is the place to be for all things Goose—the geographical heart of their *rione*. Indeed, this is the contrada's main street. Coincidentally, I choose a quiet afternoon after shopping for some groceries, traveling the route that can easily dump me into the narrow Goose streets. Having previously not wandered around this area, I am now on a mission. I unleash my imaginary antennae and start paying close attention to the narrow streets and their intersections. I marvel that somehow residents manage to live and commute on these streets, despite the fact that none of them are level. Even four-way intersections are connected to streets that go steeply up or down. *American traffic engineers would be beside themselves with this situation, and even San Francisco has nothing on this place*, I think. After skulking around a bit (one might recall skulking from *Four Weddings and a Funeral*), I soon discover the social center of Goose life, although it is virtually unmarked. Without the neon signage and promotional banners one might expect in the United States, this neighborhood is the precise opposite of flashy.

After stumbling down part of the famed Via di Santa Caterina, I scan for signs of contrada offices and the like. On one corner, a subtle storefront with some plate glass comes into view. It is labeled in green letters for the *Segretaria dell'Oca* (Goose Secretary). *Bingo. That was too easy.* One corner of the narrow storefront displays some memorabilia, apparently not for sale but to demonstrate contrada pride. This practice vaguely reminds me of university bookstores or the homes of superfans who publicly display memorabilia of their favorite sports teams. I fail to catch the business hours, but all appears to be quiet here on this afternoon during *pausa pranzo*, the standard three-hour Italian "pause for lunch" between one and four o'clock. After this, Italian shopkeepers tend to return to work until seven or eight in the evening, before heading to dinner. I continue along and quickly encounter a modest church facade with no flamboyant pretensions, built into the continuous row of medieval and Renaissance-era buildings. Only its distinct Renaissance-style pediment above the entry and the equally subdued bell tower distinguish this as a church. It also has—rather humorously—two 3-D models of white geese attached to the walls on both sides of the entry. It seems that I have discovered the official Goose contrada chapel, or *oratorio*. Eyeballing the geese, I chuckle under my breath. *Only here can people get away with geese decorating a chapel entrance.*

A Patron Saint of Italy

To make a very long story much shorter, the Goose's most famous resident was St. Catherine, or Santa Caterina in Italian. Her real name was Caterina Benincasa, and she likely had no idea as a child that she would go on to assume religious stardom within Siena and all of Italy. Born into a wool dyer's family along Vicolo (Alley) del Tiratoio in 1347, she experienced visions at an early age and decided to live a secluded life within her own home. Her reputation grew as a holy woman, and eventually popes and kings corresponded with her. Towns and city leaders sent for her to solve various disputes. She was the veritable Dr. Phil of her day. Her grandest accomplishment, it seems, was to convince Pope Gregory XI to relocate the papacy back to Rome after it had moved to Avignon, France. (She likely closed the deal by asking, "How's the France thing working for you?") Her clout won the day, and Caterina returned to Rome with the papacy. She died there at the young age of thirty-three, having already amassed impressive accomplishments.[42]

In 1460 Caterina was canonized, and during the nineteenth century, she was declared co-patron saint of Italy (along with St. Francis). Needless to say, the people of Fontebranda are extremely proud of her, and her house and attached wool dyer's workshop are now preserved as a shrine—the Santuario e Casa di Santa Caterina (the Sanctuary and House of St. Catherine). The rooms within her home have been converted into chapels, and the adjacent oratory now serves as the Goose chapel. Because the official contrada stable is across the street from the chapel, the resident horse need not tire itself as it makes its way to the chapel for the traditional Palio blessing. I head home with the happy news that I have completed my quest, having found the trifecta of società, chapel, and stable. Gradually, we are learning more about our new home, and our particular locale is only becoming more intriguing.

CHAPTER 7

Test Pilots

I ARRIVE AT PIAZZA DEL CAMPO AT 8:30 A.M., WITH THE SUN STILL CASTING LONG shadows on this gorgeous morning. June 29 has arrived. It has taken a week to transform Siena's premier public space into a veritable arena complete with dirt track and *palchi* (bleachers). The so-called days of the Palio have begun. Actually, there are probably 365 such days; in some ways the Palio cycle never ends. Still, there are four consecutive days when this cycle reaches its climax in intensity and activity, and today is the first.

When I scoped out this place a few days ago, I found the outer rim of the Campo magically developed into a dirt track, on top of which the unending café chairs and tables came marching back. From that day forth, these establishments have competed for space and turf around the Campo with the temporary wooden bleachers fanning out into the eating areas. The preparation for the Palio apparently exerts little impact on the daily ritual of setting up chairs, tables, and umbrellas. I wondered if these items would sink unevenly into the turf, creating a landscape of drunken cafés. There was no chance of this happening, however, given the success of twenty-first-century steamrollers. The earthen material spread across the Campo perimeter might as well have been pavement, for how packed it is. Once horses gallop across it, however, they still make quite an impact on the turf. It must be soft enough for racing.

Genius of the European Square

Back in the Campo once again, I feel as though I am standing in the midst of European greatness, perhaps even genius, if Henry and Suzanne Lennard have anything to say about it. In their book *Genius of the European Square* they explore the social and cultural benefits of central public spaces like this one, claiming Siena's type of city square is a distinctly European invention. "The square is the essence of the European city," they expound, "epitomizing the community's heritage and symbolizing its identity."[43] The Campo is undoubtedly one of Europe's gems—one of the most impressive and highly studied public spaces on the continent.

This particular city square happens to be shell-shaped, due to its physical slope, historical development patterns, and arguably ingenious human intervention during, yes, the Middle Ages. Topography played a role, providing a type of natural outdoor amphitheater. Siena's local geography and urban pattern actually mirrors that of Rome and numerous other cities on the peninsula. Like Rome, Siena developed on a series of adjacent hills or ridges, its initial Etruscan residents having made smart and strategic use of such defensive strongholds. Likewise, readers may be familiar with the Seven Hills of Rome, upon which at least three of Rome's initial settlements were placed. The Roman Forum, the very setting for the infamous Julius Caesar and friends, was logically developed in the low-lying valley between these hills. So too in Siena, where the Campo serves as a central public space in the low saddle of land at the junction of its three hilltop *terzi* (districts).[44] In this way, the historical geography of Siena and Rome strategically developed under similar conditions.

By definition, a true public space welcomes everyone and is in no way exclusive. All are welcome to hang out, socialize, meet, chat, sit, walk, play with the kids, and otherwise enjoy the setting. In its ideal form, the square serves as a safe and inviting place like an *outdoor room*, as community planners like to call them. And the Campo is one serious community living room, capable of hosting the bulk of Siena's medieval population, give or take, and most of today's residents as well. There are concerns about the future of such public spaces. The Lennards have noticed some serious demographic and social changes as of late. Although most European cities have wisely taken back these precious places from the automobile parking lots they had become, continuous pressures of tourism and suburbanization are taking their toll.

In Siena the pressures are similar. Development took a serious turn in 2003 when the city made numerous apartments within the historic center available to visitors for the first time.[45] The Senesi, perhaps not surprisingly, continue to move into more spacious and inexpensive accommodations outside the city walls. But Henry and Suzanne Lennard are concerned about the social future of the Campo in particular. They wonder, *If children are not being brought up in public places like this, will they identify with such urban squares in the future?* While the contrade and their memberships are stronger than ever, the traditional social life on the streets is lagging and may continue moving in this direction.

That being said, from our perspective, it is a challenge to find significant social problems here. Americans like us arrive in Siena and can't help but gape in awe at the strong sense of community displayed daily and nightly. Back home, many of us drive into our garages and shut ourselves in for the night. Pedestrians are few and far between, with those venturing outside usually dragged along by a canine companion or two. By comparison, Siena's main streets are teaming with social life, especially in the evenings after the tour groups retreat for the day. And now, within sight of the Palio, street life is off the charts. One does wonder, however, to what extent Italians, and the Senesi in particular, will allow the American-style car culture to alter their lifestyles.

The *Tratta*

Aside from the hopeless romantics eating outdoors, the turf is about to get its first true workout. Today is the *tratta*, which will precede six *prove* (trials) for the Palio horses and jockeys. As it turns out, the *tratta* and successive trials are just as useful for the spectators, like me, who remain quite clueless about what will actually transpire here. During this morning's *tratta*, approximately thirty-five horses are tested on the track, under nearly precise Palio conditions—save for the speed of the actual race. Groups of six to seven horses will be tested at a time, each group allowed three complete laps to mimic the final race three days later. Some horses are veterans, even winners of past races. Others are novices, having never raced in the Campo before.

Still, the horses have been trained prior to today on a mock Campo and related tracks outside Siena, designed to simulate this one. The local media outlets provide weekly updates on the status of this training. The thirty-plus horses appearing before us today are actually the semifinalists from a larger pool of around ninety horses whose owners offered their potential service for the Palio. Today's *tratta*, therefore, is only the latest of a rather drawn-out phase of testing horses and weeding them out. Following the *tratta* later this morning, the ten *capitani* (captains) of the competing contrade will choose the final pool of ten horses to compete in the Palio three days later. Once chosen and assigned through a highly emotional lottery, or *estrazione* (extraction), the horses will be tested further during the six trials.

Today's *tratta* provides a critical opportunity for jockeys and horses alike to run the track. Like taking a plane out for a test flight, jockeys will sometimes open the throttle to test a horse for speed and confidence, but often they are working with the horse on any number of other variables. Contrada faithful may even chastise an ambitious jockey for taking too many chances with the horse during the trials. Some horses have been injured in these presumably innocuous events, thereby disqualifying the contrada from racing. Thus, bursting to the front of the pack each time is not going to win a jockey much applause.

Having arrived early for the *tratta*, I make my way into one of the shady corners of the Campo, which happens to be the turn at the Casato. I screen my surroundings with the eyes of a newcomer, the early crowd mingling socially and not yet densely packed. I can walk right up to the inside corner of the track, with the exception of a fenced box that occupies what seems to be an eight-by-eight-foot space. Some people are inside the box, leaning up against the track fence. It seems to be a sacred space of some kind, however, so I stay clear. Instead, I find an easy perch on the track fence just outside the box, with an uncanny view of the entire straightaway in front of the Palazzo Pubblico. With no better idea of where to go, this is where I decide to camp.

Beyond my camera and iPhone, I came prepared for the outdoors. Sunscreen is already applied on my face and neck. I am wearing a long-sleeve shirt and pants for even more sun and wind protection. It's still a bit chilly in the shade, so there is no need to shiver with short sleeves. Most important, a bottle of water is sunk into my cavernous pants pocket. This is a reason why guys love khakis like the ones I am wearing: They serve as a virtual man-purse. My pockets are loaded down with survival gear, which gives my hands the freedom to fumble with two camera options. I come further armed with a bag of cookies. These will allow me to last for hours here if necessary.

Standing next to me is a gentle-looking, middle-aged man with his hands draped over the barrier. He is waiting patiently for the action to start. He has friends here, as he occasionally converses with one or more individuals around him. I would not be so intrigued by him were it not for a nondescript rectangular card that he holds in his hands, with pencil at the

LIVING THE PALIO

ready. I wonder if this guy is someone of significance, perhaps someone who is strategically placed to keep track of the horses. When he looks just bored enough, I let my guard down and ask him in Italian about the card. *Big mistake.* Like a champion *Jeopardy!* player, I can master the questions but lose quickly when it comes to comprehending the answers. He points to the card, waves around a bit, and instructs me about his involvement in the tone of a pleasant schoolteacher. I thank him profusely, still having little idea about his role or why he is keeping track of the horses.

Actually, I did pick up enough to understand that he will judge the horses to be run in the *tratta* this morning. Later I discover that one can acquire a copy of the card from a local newspaper to participate in the *tratta* from the sidelines. Even more helpful are little pocket guides with the names and owners of all the horses. Enthusiasts can later match the chosen horses with each contrada and jockey, thereby keeping a running log of who is competing in the race. Today, the card in this gentleman's hands is titled *Le Batterie di Selezione*, and it will eventually be filled with his own judgments of the best and worst horses. He may or may not agree with the decisions of the captains later, which I suspect is all part of the fun.

It is close to 9:00 a.m., when the *tratta* is scheduled to start, and yet hordes of people are still milling around on the track. Many of them are lingering near the curve of San Martino. The constant din of the crowd reflects the social nature of this event, basically with locals enjoying each other's company inside their primary public space. *What's up with that? Cutting it a bit close,* I surmise. *Do the locals somehow magically know when to leave the track? How do they*—Kaboom! A shock wave that sounds like a cannon blast cuts across the Campo. Instinctively, I drop my head and look in the direction of the explosion. Others around me do the same. We're all alive and in one piece, we assess, looking around to express our mutual surprise. There seem to be a lot of visitors around me, clearly as clueless as I am. I do recall now that a faint drumroll preceded the cannon. *This must be the official call to arms signaling the beginning of the tratta.* No, I decide, *it must be more akin to dimming the lights on and off in advance of a theater production to signal the crowd to sit down.* This happens to be precisely the case. Taking the form of an unassuming black box perched atop a tall pole near the *mossa* (starting line), the *mortaretto* (small mortar) provides the signal that it's time to clear the track. *Some sound system!*

TEST PILOTS

A single line of blue-costumed police officers—otherwise normal men and women smiling and saying hi to friends—slowly processes toward us from the Palazzo entrance. Forming a human chain as if pushing back a riot, they walk slowly forward and literally sweep the track of humans lingering ahead of them. This is known here as *far pulito*, or "making clean" the track. Bystanders are forced ever so slowly and calmly into their bleacher seats on the opposite side of the track or into the center of the Campo where I am rooted. I recall that the Palio race itself lasts only ninety seconds or so, given that the horses run at breakneck speeds. Try that with a lumbering lineup of police like this, however, and the same romp around the track takes seemingly forever. This is all enthralling, however, and I find myself trying to make sense of the whole thing as it unfolds around me. Gradually, an empty dirt path opens up behind the police. There are no violations behind them that I can see.

More amusing is a small army of men and women with city-issued work clothes who are making their way not far behind the police line. With authentic straw brooms, they perform their own dance as they sweep up not humans but the trash the humans have produced. Their synchronous motions magically collect the trash into the center of the track. Not to be outdone, a separate trash collection detail moves methodically among the sweepers and shovels it into a mobile trash cart. When they pass our crowd, we stare them down, and fans like me take dozens of photos. But nobody claps or cheers, which I find curious. In the United States I have seen high-spirited crowds or audiences clap and cheer, somewhat sarcastically but all in good fun, to acknowledge various stagehands or other staff who are not really part of the show. I suppress my urge to do the same, as I would be the only one doing so and would likely get stared down myself.

The officers have their work cut out for them at San Martino on the opposite side of the Campo. Hordes of people are hanging out, doing who knows what. *There's a race to run. Get out of the way,* I silently command. But I am the novice here, and I simply watch the process with a sense of amazement. Without much fanfare or disorder, the crowd slowly parts and disperses. At this point I realize two things. First, I am now stuck in the middle of the Campo, as the authorities have subtly but definitively closed off all access from outside streets. Police officers have been stationed strategically to prevent spectators from crossing the track, which now behaves like a moat to keep us penned inside. Second, they are preventing people from entering the Campo as well, with the main entrance opposite us blocked with an eight-foot wall and an equally solid line of police officers. Nobody is leaving or entering at this point, and that's a bit unnerving, if equally exciting.

When time and weather allow, Linda and I sometimes sit in the piazza in the evening to watch people until the urge for a gelato or a stroll gets the better of us. Not now. I'm inside, and that's that. I am confident with my survival gear, however. Consequently, beyond a mild sense of alarm, all is well. The track is finally empty of humans and their trash, but everyone penned inside the Campo is giddy with anticipation. In the United States, this would be called stalling or boredom. Not here. There is something intoxicating and magical about seeing the empty track and awaiting what comes next. The adrenaline rush from the first *mortaretto* blast alone is something I will not soon forget.

But now a distinct set of well-groomed humans is emerging, once again from the Palazzo's front entrance. This is home base, I conclude. Everything seems to emerge from there. It is quickly obvious that these humans are special, wearing suits, ties, and dress shoes much too expensive for the dirt track. They are walking in small groups of three to seven people, mostly men, with one or two wearing a *fazzoletto*. Are they going to walk around the track as well? *Break out the cookies*, I think. *We're in for the long haul.* I lose sight of them up near the main Campo entrance over which the judges' stand has been temporarily installed. The city officials and contrada captains exit the track here and take turns shuffling up a tightly wound spiral staircase to access the observation platforms above. They will watch the show from there. Interestingly, the contrada presidents (*priore*) are located elsewhere, elevated on their own balcony overlooking the curve of San Martino. This separate, if smaller perch is appropriately known as the *palco dei priore*.

By this time I have made the acquaintance of some folks around me, including two middle-aged couples traveling together from Minnesota. They are here for the weekend and hit it lucky to actually see some kind of festival in Siena, of which they know next to nothing. *They don't know what's about to hit them*, I think, as they unwittingly get stuck in the Campo for several hours, watching the Senesi prepare for the mother of all races. Still, they come armed with a pair of oversized cameras and zoom lenses, which are ready for

TEST PILOTS

whatever action may ensue. I turn on my teaching role for a little while and volunteer some information about the Palio.

They seem intrigued, so I end up giving them the PAL 101 version of the contrada system and the Palio itself: "Do you see those flags lined up on the wall of the Palazzo?" I ask. "There are seven on top and ten below, representing the seventeen contrade or "neighborhoods" of Siena. Only ten contrade are allowed to race in each Palio, so the ten lower flags represent those running on July 2. The seven above are those that are sitting this one out. Next July, however, the seven not running this time are guaranteed to race, with three more competitors chosen by a lottery or *extraction*."

That's about all I can explain before the *mortaretto* booms again. We are thrown off our guard as everyone's adrenaline goes sky high, including mine. Out of the Palazzo Pubblico emerges the first set of seven horses, with jockeys wearing identical outfits and caps. It's showtime. The outfits are designed simply with alternating black and white stripes—the colors of Siena and its elegantly simple shield or herald. The jockeys this morning have likely been chosen by the owners of the horses or assigned by the city of Siena, given that the horses have not yet been selected to race or assigned to specific contrade.

The horses may not even be the fastest or strongest, which may once again run counter to American logic. The job of the captains is to assure that all horses enjoy at least a chance to win. For statistics fans, we're talking about the middle of the bell curve here. The playing field is therefore evened out to some extent, with horses at both ends of the continuum—strong and weak—removed from contention.[46] To say it another way, the horse variable is minimized. Despite all this, the gossip in Siena for days to come will be centered on which contrade landed the strongest and weakest horses. Sometimes this gossip comes down to which horses are veterans (presumed to be the most desirable) or novices to this particular racetrack (the least desirable).

I continue to liken the jockeys to test pilots, as each is courageously taking on an unfamiliar horse and seeing how it responds to the track and conditions. Hopefully they can come in for a graceful landing without incident. As if on cue, they reach the *mossa* (start) and circle behind it before lining up at the *canape* (rope). At this point, the horses all have numbers on their hindquarters, allowing judges—official or otherwise—to identify them during the *tratta*. Local media sources and the handouts mentioned earlier provide the names of all the horses that have made it to the *tratta*, with their respectively assigned numbers.

Although the final ten horses have not yet been selected by the contrada captains, a whole lot of preparation has already led up to this day. Captains or their delegates have likely scouted these horses on their home stomping grounds, and some horses are already known from past Palio or other horse races, returning now for an encore. Further, the city veterinarian has already evaluated the horses, assuring that, following the *tratta*, no contrada is assigned a sick or injured steed.[47] One might imagine the ensuing disappointment of contrada members should their horse emerge with the flu.

The horses and their jockeys line up one by one, and with little warning, the first group bolts off the *mossa*. Within seconds, they accelerate and descend toward the notorious curve of San Martino. They seem too eager, running faster than my gut says is necessary. Some of the horses clearly want to run, essentially dragging their jockeys along with them. These guys are racing—at least that is the outward appearance. I tell the couples from Minnesota with a tone of surprise that they're moving much faster than I expected.

Today San Martino takes its first victims. We know something is up when a collective gasp of surprise rumbles across the Campo. The mood is replaced shortly with a mix of laughter and disbelief. At the first turn, two of the test pilots are ejected onto the track, reminding me of the real dangers here. One is carried off in a stretcher after an initial flurry of treatment under the Cappella di Piazza. His ultimate fate is unknown. The other recovers to ride later, the dark brown mark of track dirt providing evidence of his initial mistake. A collective gasp from the crowd starts to grow, as one white and one brown horse make it clear that they really do not want anything on their backs. In the Palio, jockeys ride bareback—no saddle, no stirrups. All they have is a rein for driving. But ditching jockeys is a rare occurrence during the *tratta*, when horses have not yet been selected.

Statistics don't matter today, as two horses are running amok, and they are not stopping of their own accord. The scene becomes humorous, almost jovial, among those of us processing the unfolding events. Cameras are racing through their digital ammunition. The horses aren't stopping, but one is following the other at breakneck speed around the track. Lap 5. Lap 6. Lap 7. (It reminds me of the comical film *Airplane*: "By the way, is there anyone on

TEST PILOTS

board who knows how to fly a plane?") They are proving their stamina if nothing else. The other jockeys have since cleared their horses from the track. Every thirty seconds or so, the determined steeds blow past our spot. After a few such passes, small crews of courageous men jump into the track, waving towels and then escaping quickly.

Following several attempts at this distraction, the horses' steam runs out, and they lumber more than race up the hill toward the Casato. One horse is grabbed by the reins and pulled to the side. The other horse takes another lap and finally relents to facing the same fate. In this way the first set of the *tratta* concludes. I don't know about the captains, but I think they found two of their top picks! No doubt this will be the feature topic for Palio gossip around Siena today. Five sets of the *tratta* remain, and they all proceed without incident.

As the city staff sets us loose from the Campo, I say my parting words to the Minnesota couples, accepting their thanks for the Palio lesson. I leave with a total feeling of intrigue and a sense of wonder for what I just witnessed. Having never thought much about horses or horse races, I am now hooked, looking forward to the actual trials. I shuffle my way out of the Campo with an energized crowd. I squirm my way back to the Goose to tell Linda about the experience. I imagine she will want to join me for one of the next trials.

Our students end up witnessing the extraction of horses in the Campo, directly following the *tratta*. I end up missing this emotional event, a mistake I vow to not make in the future. The captains of the ten competing contrade have chosen the final horses that will run the Palio. These finalists are then assigned by lottery to each contrada—to the ecstasy or agony of those paying attention to the stronger or weaker horses. A simple if protracted drawing determines the final match between horse and contrada. One student relates later, "The Ram got really excited, and we think the She-Wolf as well." Indeed, according to local gossip, the Ram has extracted perhaps the best horse. For its part, the She-Wolf has extracted a veteran, a horse named Indianos, and is quite pleased. There is no word on the luck of the Goose at this point.

With horses matched to the ten contrade just after noontime, the crowds finally disperse, and the horses are led back to their respective stables, pampered like royalty. The pace of this process is nothing short of impressive. Only this morning the final ten horses were chosen quickly from a rather sizable pool. By 1:00 p.m., they were assigned to the contrade, and this evening they will be led back to the Campo with much fanfare for their first real trial. *How do they pull this off so quickly?* I ask myself. Tonight we move one step closer to full Palio conditions. The current jockeys will don their contrada colors for the first time and lead their precious animals into the arena.

CHAPTER 8

First Contact

Later that afternoon, I make my return to Goose headquarters to scan the activity there. I am more mentally prepared to encounter local Ocaioli should the occasion present itself. Somehow I even welcome the opportunity. Arriving at what I call the chapel-stable complex, I see activity I had not witnessed on my prior visit. A few people are stationed lazily around the simple wooden barricade that signifies the stable, and—oh wow, the stable door is open! A few others are quietly conversing while leaning against the opposite building. I peak over the barricade, and there he is! A bit of hero worship sweeps over me, in this case for an unsuspecting animal that is already winning the hearts and minds of the locals.

Across the street against the building is a friendly-looking Senese fellow who is enjoying the view of the stable from afar. In a rare moment of boldness, I abandon my sense of caution when it comes to approaching or bothering strangers—let alone Italian ones. Having learned the horse's name earlier from Viola—she had written and pronounced it for me (like "Gwess")—I approach the fellow and begin in Italian, "Good evening, is this Guess?" Leave it to a horse or a football team to open a conversation. *Of course it's Guess; it sure as heck isn't Seabiscuit*, I think, but this question enables a couple of things to happen. It shows that I've been paying a bit of attention to the affairs of the contrada. Beyond that, the fellow sees that I can speak a little Italian, which usually doesn't hurt.

He warms right up, with a kind smile and nonchalant attitude. His name is Antonio, and I quickly provide my canned, if honest, introduction of living along Via di Fontebranda for eight weeks while teaching American students. Guess provides an immediate topic for conversation. I then ask if Guess is a strong horse. Antonio's response is candid enough, if not a bit modest. I keep

FIRST CONTACT

in mind that bragging about a strong horse can lead to bad luck during the Palio, according to the more superstitious Senesi. Predictably, he gestures that Guess is so-so, probably middle of the pack in terms of desirable horses for the Palio. The odds are apparently not in the Goose's favor, as the contrada did not extract the most coveted animal. Superstition or not, this indirectly confirms what the students had related to me after the extraction—the favored horses went to the Ram and She-Wolf. Expectations for this Palio are clearly downplayed for the Goose faithful, but they seem to be okay with it. Really, do they have a choice?

Regardless of the racing quality of the horse, every contrada still enjoys a shot at victory. Each designated steed is treated as veritable royalty. Above anything else, the horse represents the contrada and its strong place identity, and so the horse's strength is of little concern when it comes to protecting the four-legged Palio star. I depart without extending my stay too long, eager to tell Linda that I have just made first contact with a Goose stranger on the contrada's main street, right there at the stable. Note to self: Don't expect the Goose to win. Several informants now point to the Ram for that distinction.

Later, Linda and I return to the site of first contact so I can show off my findings. "There's Guess." I proudly point out. This remark is followed by a quick outdoor tour past the chapel and up to the *segretaria* office. It is open. Although the door is unlocked, the entry is less than welcoming—unlike the one on the front side that is more spacious and includes a small doorway. Someone is at a desk just inside, and it seems that the open door we discovered is a little-used entry to the street. A few staff members are scurrying around the compact space, and the furniture and wall cabinets are tightly packed. The entire office might only be about fifteen-feet deep from the street. Linda motions for us to go in. Not the boldest of visitors, I naturally balk, wondering why we would want to bother these fine people. Never mind that we are standing at the hub of official contrada business. I see where this is going—well, where Linda is going, anyway. History tells me that resistance is futile (okay, another *Star Trek* reference). I quickly pull together some combination of Italian phrases before bursting in on these unsuspecting folks. *Didn't Linda see the sign?* I think. *"No tourists or American blond-haired geeks allowed."*

We actually would like to inquire about the mysterious pre-Palio dinner we've been learning about in piecemeal fashion. That seems to be our initial rationale for stopping by. Viola claimed that we could buy tickets for the Goose dinner here. Linda and I both remain uncertain about our own level of interest, especially at the steep price of thirty-five euros per person. Yet the whole idea is intriguing: an actual contrada dinner is just a ticket purchase away. And this is not just any contrada dinner but the granddaddy of them all—the *Cena della Prova Generale* (literally the Dinner of the General Trial), commonly interpreted as the dress rehearsal dinner. All ten contrade participating in the Palio hold their own outdoor event for hundreds, if not thousands, of their own contradaioli. The contrada officials and the jockey sit at the head table, typically providing uplifting speeches when appropriate. Outsiders are generally allowed to attend, although tickets must be purchased from contrada offices or equivalent venues at least several days beforehand.

Linda bursts in and says, "*Buona sera*" (Good evening) to the nearest staff member. I have only one choice now—to play along. We have entered the building, and all bets are off as to how this will transpire. Getting kicked back to the street with a mad Italian woman chasing us back down to Fontebranda is one possible outcome. Somehow Linda asks about dinner tickets to confirm what we have been told, and I follow up with some Italian. I quickly unload my canned introductory speech. As predicted, their interest perks up, and I feel that we have earned at least a brief welcome. All joking aside, these Goose contradaioli could not be kinder people. They confirm that the dinner tickets are indeed thirty-five euros each. We look at each other and quickly dismiss the idea of buying them and kindly say, "No, thank you." Aside from the cost, we would be highly uncomfortable attending alone with nobody to socialize with, let alone speak to in our own language. The dinner would have to wait for another time.

A Goose *Fazzoletto*

Then our boldness kicks in, and we ask about the prized contrada *fazzoletto* (scarf). Linda begins in English, and I quickly follow up in Italian. *My gosh*, I think to myself, *we're asking about the scarves. How will this go?* As it turns out, quite pleasantly with a happy surprise. The young lady paying most attention to us maneuvers around the tight space and opens a metal cabinet against the wall. She indicates that they are for sale as well. After some confirmation with her colleague—a rather humorous exchange to determine which scarves are

FIRST CONTACT

silk and which are polyester—she removes an example of each and displays them for our inspection. Wow. The real silk *fazzoletto* is right here in front of me. I ask how much the scarf costs. Thirty-five euros for the cheaper polyester model and fifty euros for the upgraded silk Cadillac. For me the decision is instant, though I look to Linda for confirmation. She is considering options as well. The bottom line is that we've found a contrada official who is willing to sell the silk version to a couple of eight-week Goose inhabitants. We've got some cash. "We'll take the silk *fazzoletto*, please," I say. At this point I am containing my amazement as the transaction takes place. This trumps even the Goose plate as our most significant memento to take home. Part of me wants the cheaper one as well, but I decline, thinking that I can get a polyester version at nearly any shop in town for only eight euros. Eventually I do just that, even though the design of the tourist knockoff is subtly different from those sold by the contrada.

With the silk *fazzoletto* now in our possession, I feel that I have to ask the big question. I stumble through it in Italian but am ultimately successful with communicating my point: "Can we wear the scarf here?" I follow up with an unsure expression on my face, though she is already indicating yes. I add, "This is only for real contrada members, yes?" She understands, quickly responding, "No, no, it's okay ..." She has thus given us definitive permission to wear a silk *fazzoletto*—the very kind that people are given when they are born into the contrada and wear for life—here in this very Goose neighborhood.

As if to confirm her permission, she asks in Italian if Linda wants help putting it on. At this point my cautious instincts fly out the door, replaced with my phone camera to record personal history. It's like being hooded at graduation. The young woman places it around Linda's neck and ties two corners together in front. After some final adjustments, Linda is now a Goose contradaiola—at least as close as we are willing and able to become on this eight-week escapade. Although certainly not a Caterpillar baptism like that experienced by Robert Rodi, it is a significant moment for us nonetheless.

This experience is an example of a more global approach to contrada policy and practice, indicating that contrade are taking one more step to extend their welcome to visitors not born in their locale. For a donation to the contrada, officials are willing to part with some tradition. Are they recognizing that they can garner more contrada support if they open themselves to outsiders? Does this represent the first step toward the commodification of contrada traditions—that is, basically you can buy your way in? On a more positive note, perhaps the sale indicated a greater recognition of reality, that the city and local populations are becoming more heavily influenced from the outside. Traditions like the Palio will continue to change, but they still don't die. There is clearly plenty of tradition to go around and amazingly strong community cohesion. My geography training pops in as well, and I realize that we are actually willing participants in the ongoing globalization of Siena and the contrada system, for better or worse.

Beyond the delight I feel at being this close to contrada life, my concern now—I always seem to have at least one—is this: Sure, we received permission from the *segretaria* office, but I wonder if the policy of selling to outsiders is universally accepted throughout the contrada. Are the more traditionalist members scoffing at the office's decision to sell themselves out? If we walk along the streets of the Goose proudly supporting the contrada, nobody else will know that we actually live around the corner, even for a short time. We will be perceived like all other tourists, here for only a few days and likely not understanding their complex social traditions, let alone the meaning of the *fazzoletto*. Italian locals can read people like a book. If I had a choice, there would be an additional statement on my back stating "*Segretaria* Approved" or something with a local map and arrow that says *Abitiamo qui* ("We live here").

To Linda's credit, she enjoys her *fazzoletto*, and I will likely ask to borrow it in upcoming days. I am glad we made the purchase. I silently reflect that it's good she's wearing it and having fun, rather than keeping it hidden under glass to protect it from reality. We might as well wrinkle it up, get some sweat on it, and display its use over the short period we are here. This philosophy is similar to a geographer taking personal pride in a well-used atlas that gets beaten up and faded over time—almost like a badge of honor. (Well, actually, Linda's protective defenses kick in later when some spilled carbonated water gets too close for comfort. And when a student twirls it above her head near an open window, Linda nearly lunges for the student and grabs it back. Note to self: Careful with the *fazzoletto* or be afraid.)

With Linda now decorated as a Goose, we wander along Via di Santa Caterina and end up conveniently at the contrada's social hub, which is buzzing with all kinds of activities today. It is Palio weekend, and the place is swarming with young and old alike, all of whom seem to have some sort of purpose to their movements. Welcome to the Società Trieste, a few modest doors up from the chapel. I can't help but wonder about the importance of this venue for present-day contrada faithful.

The Contrada Società

Local residents from across Siena have confirmed the significance of the società to their own contrade. As with any community, of course, some people frequent the place often, while others show up only sporadically to meet someone or only during the days of the Palio. Contrada members who show up only during the days of the Palio are sometimes referred to as *quattrogiornisti* (four-dayers).[48] One young adult from the Shell, interviewed by anthropologist Arthur Figliola in the 1990s, summed up her perception of how often people attend the contrada, by which she probably meant the società:

> You see, there are two types [of contradaioli]: those who are active every day, or not every day, but, for better or for worse, find their way to the contrada at least once a week; and then, there are those who remain a little more distant. Within this second group there are some who prefer not to be a part of the contrada, which does not, by the way, mean that they don't live the Palio. This is something else.[49]

According to others interviewed by Figliola, a portion of contradaioli treat their società like a second home, showing up there to play cards or other games and to eat and drink with friends at least several times a week.[50] The obligations of daily life can and do get in the way of regular patronage, however. Now that most contradaioli live in the suburbs, locals lament the loss of activity in these places, as noted in an earlier chapter.

Another interesting trend regarding these places is how their primary community role has shifted over the decades. Each società once served more to organize mutual aid for contrada members willing and able to donate to those less fortunate. This role was fundamentally important after World War II, prior to the return of widespread wealth to the city. Now they provide primarily a social outlet through food and drink, according to one resident, a member of the Shell, interviewed by Figliola. This resident's grandfather had helped form their società in 1947. After its founding, the resident remembered, "The contrada and the società were two separate entities." The società was formed by his grandfather and others who were "very poor," primarily as a "mutual aid society, to help each other out." He continued, "Over time, this idea of mutual aid disappeared."[51] The società transformed into more of the social venue it is today and actually more for exclusive use by only contradaioli. This generally describes the trend experienced throughout all the contrade.

The function of the società bar, however, still supports the notion of *interclassismo*, where anyone who shows up there is treated more or less equally. The way these bars function is nearly universal across all contrade. They tend to open at 9:00 p.m. and serve drinks and food at slightly reduced prices than at other city establishments. Contrada members from all walks of life volunteer for bar service once or twice a month—even the occasional university professors from Siena who are, happily for me, apparently held in rather high esteem.[52]

Socializing in Società Trieste

With our Goose *fazzoletto* decorating Linda's neck, we wonder if we should venture inside the social hub of the Goose. Linda is once again the instigator, which I truly appreciate. While I tend to shy away from being intrusive, she is ready to chat it up with the locals. This has been true since before we were married, when she played the role of "advance team," warming up local businesspeople before I hit them with interview questions for my dissertation. Things haven't changed much, except that my confidence level has improved greatly over the years. Linda is in the door and dodging busy Ocaioli before I can think more about it, so I simply enter behind her and take the plunge. This is Società Trieste, revived after World War I and continuing the traditions of its predecessor formed in 1904. Like others, its purpose was mutual aid and recreation for its members. *Let's take this fazzoletto for a test-drive*, I think. I happily find a familiar face in Antonio, who hasn't gone far since the first time we met. I introduce Linda, and we suddenly have a new acquaintance in the Goose. He is friendly, a character trait that I believe does a lot to boost our confidence when communicating with the locals. A kind,

FIRST CONTACT

patient soul is a great confidence builder, not unlike Viola and her husband across town.

It is true that first impressions mean everything, and Antonio unwittingly becomes the gateway into the Goose social net. He is representing his contrada well, from my perspective. Then things get a little dicey—for me, at least—as I'm not quite sure what to do next as a bumbling outsider who wandered in with a *fazzoletto*-draped wife. At least I've talked with Antonio beforehand, so we are not total strangers (think *Forrest Gump*). He takes us through the hallowed entry halls, basically a series of wide rooms lined with contrada trophies for soccer and other honors. A few kids are playing that very game *inside* the halls. We laugh and accept this behavior because it's cute and because the adults don't seem to care.

Sports teams are relatively recent additions to social life in all contrade, hence the trophies and photos of teams that the Goose has fielded in the past. Each contrada will sponsor one or more sports, especially soccer, basketball, or volleyball, for teenagers and young adults. Even the women participate now in organized sports, although this is somewhat of a novelty for some contrade. Nonetheless, such activities now play an important community role, as stated by another one of Figliola's interviewees: "Every società has its sport groups, and they work well at keeping the people together."[53]

The Goose società is a true community center, we quickly observe, with all ages mixing socially and accepting one another, most donning their white, red, and green quite proudly. Heading toward the back of the società building, the second great room empties into an exterior courtyard that is well groomed with grass and shrubs and plenty of space to hang around and socialize—clearly the chosen activity at this hour. We further discover the barbecue grills on the patio, a topic of some amusement at times while walking down Via di Fontebranda back to our apartment. While we can't see the barbecue grills themselves from our street, we certainly see the giant plume of white smoke reaching for the sky. Now back inside, others are preparing for Palio-related events and dinners, buzzing around with food, materials, and other implements that will come together later that evening down at the fountain.

Antonio introduces us to an older, distinguished-looking gentleman named Fabio, who I imagine is someone of significance to the contrada, although we are not there long enough to engage in such a complicated conversation. I use my best Italian to repeat who we are and why we are there. You know the story. It works. We are having an actual conversation with two busy contradaioli at the heart of their social network, and they are actually paying attention to us and expressing interest. This is impressive. We discuss the *fazzoletto* a bit, trying to explain how we acquired it. They don't seem to mind. Fabio asks us what we want to drink. *Oh, crud.* This is not the best question for me to answer quickly. *Fanta perhaps?* Though I normally don't mind ordering soft drinks to throw others off their guard, I sense that this is not the place to play this game. Antonio rattles off a variety of common Italian drinks, including grappa, prosecco, and others I don't quite recognize. Trying not to act like the ignorant American that I am, I briefly look at Linda and answer quickly, "We will have prosecco." After all, Robert Rodi had continuously prattled on about this rather innocuous drink throughout his own book. It's probably my safest bet to avoid full embarrassment; even I can drink some of it without needing to wash out my mouth.

We wander for a few minutes, and somehow the planets align. Antonio and Fabio return with our orders, and the four of us stand together with small glasses of prosecco. I probably insult Fabio when I ask how much our drinks cost, although even as I do, I suspect I know the answer. It is complimentary, and he seems surprised I would think otherwise. Okay, I just want to make sure I wasn't assuming something. To their credit, the two of them chat a bit and stand with us. Before taking some serious drinks (or sips in my case), I take the plunge and propose a simple toast in Italian: *"To the Goose!"* They agree, probably a bit amused, and we all take a drink. They really don't think that Guess stands a chance, but they appreciate the gesture.

I am still standing there with a nearly untouched glass of prosecco. Noticing my nonverbal cues, Linda comes to the rescue. After downing her portion almost immediately, she quickly swaps glasses with me while the others are not looking. Now she has more, and I don't need to stumble around for the rest of the afternoon. *Clever girl!* (To quote another favorite film, *Contact.*)

At this point I fear that the moment will rapidly descend into awkwardness, which I know can happen depressingly fast. I sense that Antonio and Fabio don't really know what else to say, and I don't want to push my luck. I make reference to the adjoining hall through which we entered and ask if we are allowed to walk around and look. They nod and say, *"Certo!"*

FIRST CONTACT

("Sure!") in approval, and we start moving off with the intent to look around, the way we would in a museum. In a way, the hall is just that. It is a living museum where the energy of today's community is literally on display, surrounded by past heritage and symbols representing deep community pride. This is the extended family of the contrada, and this is one brief window into their family. All age groups are represented, and they all seem to feel a belonging and sense of being a part of something larger than themselves.

We extend our thanks to Antonio and Fabio, and they go their own separate ways, back to the tasks of the contrada, to their local world. I am thankful for having behaved gracefully, and I am feeling more comfortable in their space. Nobody is really paying attention to us, which is a good sign. With the social component successfully concluded, I breathe out and relax a bit as we wander the hall and enjoy the giant, wall-sized photos of recent and past Palio wins. The photos generally consist of posed, all-male group shots, sometime during the colder months. After soaking up a brief sense of place and community here, we silently say good-bye and slip out quietly into the realm of Via di Santa Caterina. This will be a treat that we will no doubt cherish for numerous Goose victories into the future—which may take quite a while if the odds are not "ever in their favor." Overall there are sixteen other contrade that also hope to run and win the Palio in any given year. The Goose, with an apparently mediocre but beloved horse named Guess, will face nine of them in a matter of days.

CHAPTER 9

Building Confidence

I HAVE BEEN WAKING UP AROUND EIGHT IN THE MORNING IF I SLEEP WELL enough, enduring the ceaseless, if entertaining, noise of Goose dinners and concerts, scooters, and other distractions outside our second-floor window. My normal bedtime back home hovers around ten thirty. In Siena, getting into bed, let alone thinking about falling asleep, is rarely accomplished before midnight. Needless to say, rising with the sun for a brisk morning jog at six o'clock is not in the cards here. I gave in to this night-owl schedule after our first week, when I noticed that we were not entirely adjusting to the time zone. Instead, on average, we stayed consistent with a midnight bedtime. Add to this mix an occasional three-hour dinner—sometimes with students—and evening festivals or class events, and I found it was not a simple task to improve on this sleep cycle.

Of course, much of Siena is already up and kicking before we are—and the Senesi do everything possible, it seems, to make this fact quite apparent. One of us usually wakes up briefly around six o'clock, most often with the advent of the morning scooter commute and city bus traffic charging up Via di Fontebranda. Of course, the Senesi are simply behaving normally on a typical workday.

Most noticeable, however, is our massive neighbor perched on a ridge across the valley, the Basilica of San Domenico. Naturally, the bigger the church, the louder the bells—and louder still when someone is trying to sleep. The otherwise impressive gongs of San Domenico penetrate deeply into our little studio apartment as if the thick shutters, glass panes, and inside window panels were all missing. "Cock-a-doodle-doooo!" I quipped to Linda numerous times until we tired of the joke, the basilica serving well as a substitute for a more traditional rooster. More often than not, we are tired enough to sleep right through it. We haven't ascertained a standard schedule of the bell concert throughout the day, but the ringing is often and furious. "What are those bell ringers doing—running around in circles up there?" Linda asked once in mild frustration (to my great amusement).

The silver lining? They are real bells. It was a sad day when Linda and I doubted our ears, wondering how powerful an electronic speaker system would be necessary to reach across the valley. More often than not, bells for colleges or churches in the United States are set on an electronic schedule and system, sometimes not even requiring real bells at all. No doubt, these are the real thing and mighty impressive—if a bit less so at six in the morning.

The Medici Fort

Today the bells toll, reminding me that it's the first morning *prova* (trial). With yesterday's *tratta* and first evening trial behind me, I plan to stick with my jogging routine. I am determined to stay on my workout schedule of every other day now that I've discovered a rather pleasant and scenic arena of my own. The Medici Fort, or Fortezza Medicea, was completed in 1563 after Siena's last military stand against Spain and its ally Florence. After Spain and France (Siena's previous ally) signed a peace treaty in 1559, Siena's fate was sealed. Spain handed control of the defeated city over to Duke Cosimo of Florence, one of a long line of Medici overlords. Cosimo purposely ordered the construction of this new fort atop the old Spanish citadel that stood there previously. The fort and its Florentine military did not exist so much to repel future invaders but to quickly subdue any uprising from the Senesi themselves. With the construction of the fort, Siena's chances of an independence movement all but vanished. To this day, the six balls that make up the Medici family coat of arms can be found placed prominently above Siena's city gates, on the walls of the fort, and even slapped onto the Palazzo Pubblico itself—in case anyone had any doubt about which family was in control in Siena. Today, the fort is home to more-civic uses, including an open-air theater for movies and an elevated public park that can double as a jogging track.

I've reflected often on the fort's past military activities while hiking there every other day to begin my official workout. For probably three weeks I've kept this schedule with minor exceptions, and today, June 30, I plan to do the same. With Linda still asleep, I quietly dress and bolt into the street below, greeting the rising sun before it gets too high for fair-skinned people like me. Intent on turning left to conquer the mountainous set of stairs beside San Domenico, I stall, noticing the atypical density of determined Palio fans trudging up our hill. The occasional scooter and bus whizzes upward, intent on getting riders up the hill a bit faster.

Scanning the traffic passing me, I think, *Do I really want to jog at the fort to commune with the Medici regime? Or do I actually want to see the action up at the Campo to possibly repeat yesterday's excitement?* The answer to this question comes easily. Following a quick return to our apartment to scoop up my camera and phone, I find myself blending into the commute up the hill, wearing jogging shorts, an unsightly T-shirt, and my baseball cap. Because I had intended to jog, not spend three hours or so locked inside the Campo, I'm not quite prepared for the sun, but it's a gorgeous Sunday morning. I find myself hiking up the hill, only somewhat berating myself for missing the jog. How often can people see bareback jockeys riding horses around the city's main square? Yesterday's trials had impressed me to the point of wanting to see more.

I do need some water, however, before getting locked into the Campo. Linda and I have learned how to find it cheaply, and this has made us feel even more like locals. First, we always carry a few of those fun one- or two-euro coins in case we need a snack or another bottle of water or, in Linda's case, another diet coke. With coin in hand, I decide to play it safe and dart through the incoming crowd to the nearest *tabaccheria* (tobacco shop), a funny type of store that is almost more numerous than fruit stands in Italian cities like this one. It seems to me to be a blend of a small soda fountain and newsstand that might have appeared in the United States prior to the 1960s.

These *tabaccherie* (plural) are much more exciting than their name implies. In addition to cigarettes and cigars, one can also buy bus and lottery tickets or perhaps add more minutes to a pay-as-you-go cell phone. Adding phone minutes here is an intriguing process for Americans because it takes place in the least likely of places. But the process is easy enough: give the phone number to the fellow behind the counter, who enters it into his computer, and tell him (not often a her) how many euros to add. Just like that, your phone is back in business.

BUILDING CONFIDENCE

Oh, and the tabaccherie happen to sell bottles of water for one euro. The same water will cost two or three euros where the tourists roam. Even in the historic core, most tourists are understandably hesitant to dive into these typically dark, cluttered places. This is where I can pretend to be an Italian local—darting in, finding the water, making my greetings, and getting out. That's confidence—the type that we hope to instill in our students. At this point in our stay, I am no longer flustered by the sight of an actual Senese local standing in front of the shop's short refrigerator, chatting it up with the storekeeper as one is doing this morning. In this case, they each turn one friendly eye on me and notice that I'm in a hurry as I visually scope out the fridge. With nary an interruption in their conversation, the man calmly bends down, opens the fridge, and acknowledges my words of appreciation. I confirm the one-euro price, and out I go.

A Morning Trial

With water in hand, I squeeze under the double balcony and scope out the situation in the Campo. *Am I too late for a prime spot this morning? It would be relatively easy to find my hangout at the Casato again. I've got plenty of photos from there, however, so why not get creative and find someplace else on the route? Do I see what I think I see?* Now on a personal mission, my feet and brain shift into higher gear. I scurry along the track past other arrivals who lumber around as if they are window shopping. Through the gate near Fonte Gaia I go into the center. I turn right and move quickly to a yawning open space right along the barrier, within sight of the *mossa*! When that rope drops, the whole mass of horses and jockeys will thunder past my spot here. And it's a bright, sunny morning with the sun behind me. It doesn't get better than this.

Then my overconfidence gets the better of me, a stark reminder of how little I know about the Italian language and Siena. There is a fine line sometimes between feeling confident and feeling too confident. An Italian mother and her child are lingering nearby, and the three-year-old is wearing a *fazzoletto* that I recognize: it's from our beloved Bruco (Caterpillar). Since I've been to the Caterpillar museum and conversed with Dario Castagno, I am feeling confident. In Italian I say, "Ah, you are a Caterpillar today." The kid ignores me, something I had expected, while Mom just gives me a strange look and a polite smile. She slowly backs away—something I had not expected. Usually, they start chatting incomprehensively. *Okay, fine,* I think.

Then it dawns on me that there is another contrada with colors similar to the Caterpillar, that of the Drago (Dragon). Oh boy, I probably just insulted the pair and showed that I really haven't learned my contrada designs well enough. Though not formal enemies, the Dragon and Caterpillar don't care too much for one another. One of our students discovered this fact the hard way when, having been invited to a Dragon event with some friends, he mentioned the word *Bruco* at the table where he was eating. He thus recalled, "The Dragon members around me just stopped and stared as if I had said something insensitive." In this case, I swallow and tell myself that it's a learning opportunity. This is the chance one must take sometimes if one hopes to converse with the natives. *And are they really from Siena, or had the child randomly asked for the lowest-hanging scarf at a nearby kiosk?* Perhaps he was a Caterpillar anyhow. *Let it go,* I tell myself, but sometimes this is easier said than done (and I am apparently now counseling myself with music from the smash Disney film *Frozen*).

It's showtime. The *mortaretto* does its booming thing, and the track is swept of humans and, soon thereafter, trash. Then our four-legged heroes emerge from the Palazzo Pubblico to the mild roar of the crowd. This may not be the actual Palio race, but this front-row seat to the action is unbeatable—and the right price. The lineup at the *mossa* (starting line) is different today. The Senesi have specific rules, even during the Palio trials. The horses and jockeys do not all start in the same position each time. This is my third time as a spectator at the days of the Palio, and the educator in me now thinks about our current and possibly future students. To learn the intricacies of the Palio race and how it all goes down, it's important to be at the trials. By the time the real Palio comes around, you'll then be an expert and will probably teach a thing or two to those around you. *Give it a week, and you'll be teaching at Caltech!* (from *The Hunt for Red October,* likely the favorite film of all time for both Linda and me).

I spot Guess and his jockey, Giovanni Atzeni (nicknamed Tittia), making their way to the *mossa,* and I realize that on some minimal level I have become a Goose fan. Tittia is a veteran of the Palio, having raced here eighteen times since 2003. Both of his wins to date have been for the Goose. I manage to snap close-up photos of all the horses as they make their way around the track, for the later creation of a who's who of Palio competitors. Amazingly, sometimes the riders are actually too close for decent photos because there is only the barricade separating us.

The little voice on my shoulder pipes up again, asking if I should be thinking like a social scientist and remain unbiased or if it's okay to display some emotional favoritism for the Goose. The Caterpillar isn't running in this Palio, so that's not an issue here (although our students are mildly disappointed). *I am here to remain objective*, I remind myself, observing all seventeen contrade as impartially as possible, in true social-science tradition. Although there is no hope of integrating into a contrada much beyond the repeat-visitor status for a few weeks, I am personally comfortable with that. Eventually these reflective thoughts pass, and I obtain as many quality photos of Guess and Tittia as possible. So much for social science! It's a strong attachment to place that drives my motives now, particularly to one hilly neighborhood near Fontebranda.

I keep wondering if Guess is the infamous white horse that threw its jockey at San Martino. Only one other white horse (named Indianos) is racing, that of the She-Wolf. Despite my efforts, I cannot tell the two horses apart, and I would have to conduct a rigorous photo analysis later. It's a good thing the animals are wearing different colors, as I am not visually aware enough to notice subtle differences between them. White horse versus brown horse is about as good as I can do. There is one sleek, tall, shiny brown animal that has stood out since the trials, however, and I believe that was the other free spirit who threw his jockey. This one is the favorite hope of this Palio, and it is the race contender for the Ram. Its jockey is hard to miss; he is wearing a solid, dull-pink outfit, which I seriously hope has some deep-seated meaning for the Ram faithful. Oh, well, it's not for me to judge from my American cultural perspective and associated color biases. Pink, fluffy jacket or not, the Ram will be the contrada to beat on July 2.

I would ideally like to be the only spectator with a camera held in the sky this morning, but alas it is not to be. All in the Campo have brought their own versions of digital wizardry, and so my arms are not the only ones lifting a camera above the crowd. With all those electronics in the air, I need to get my own devices around the raised arms, not just the actual human bodies in front of me. Finally confident with my current camera strategies, it's time for the hooves to hit the pavement, so to speak. The *canape* (rope) drops with little warning. Note: It's important to watch the *mossa* like a hawk, lest you miss the first half lap!

The thundering herd rushes toward and past me within seconds, and I manage about six photos by simply panning and holding the shutter down. I learned yesterday that I just get what I can and check out my digital prizes later. The horses make good time, albeit not at full throttle—with the possible exception of the Panther jockey, Silvano Mulas (nicknamed Voglia), atop a horse named Pestifero. *What's up with this guy?* I think. *He's been hauling the mail* (Rodi might say, "balls to the wall") *and shooting past his competition each time now.* I wonder if he's thinking, *I don't have a chance with this Old Paint, so let's open 'im up now and enjoy the ride.* In that case, he may be underestimating his muscular horse from what I see. I suspect that Pestifero has a fighting chance. Actually, Pestifero is no *debuttante* (novice) but is a veteran of the Palio. Sometimes horses want to run, and it's not the easiest of tasks to hold them back. In any case, no one succumbs to San Martino today, so we may get these competitors to the final games in one piece after all.

CHAPTER 10

Prova Generale

LINDA AND I SLITHER OUR WAY INTO THE PIAZZA DEL CAMPO JUST AFTER SIX IN the evening, hopeful that we might be able to land some bleacher seats for this evening trial finale. I had found my way behind the bleachers near the Casato earlier today and asked a gelato shop clerk how the process works to get bleacher seats for tonight. After struggling with my Italian to explain what I wanted to do, she smiled and said, "In English?" I sighed and resigned myself to another embarrassing attempt to communicate. Siena's shop owners are likely to know at least some English, given their location at the hub of visitor activity. "Plan on being here by 6:15 p.m. at the latest, and someone will sell you tickets and let you in." These pretty solid instructions had elevated my hope that if I did as she said, Linda might get a view of the action from above. The seats would only cost around ten euros each, quite reasonable for Linda's viewing pleasure as well as my own. Now we approach an opening in the bleacher gates from trackside, right around six o'clock, satisfied that I had followed the gelato lady's instructions and arrived about when she recommended.

Things always seem more difficult than they should be in Italy, an observation that comes home yet again. I am hoping to see a well-recognized bleacher attendant of some kind, someone I can pick out immediately who is selling tickets and who can perhaps even usher us to our seats. Nobody stands out with these qualities, however. Already I feel a letdown coming on, as I see few seats remaining in the bleachers that were, according to my gelato informant, supposed to be open to eager spectators at this time. Clearly, they have already been filled. My last hope involves two portly city employees wearing orange vests. I imagine that their proximity makes them experts, an assumption I hope will pan out. It does. They tell me and another gentleman that there is absolutely no chance of getting into the bleachers. *For how long have all of those people been sitting up there?* I wonder. No matter, we're late.

My level of alertness has shot up, however, as I realize there is no more time to waste. I report the bad news to Linda, and we make our way for the interior of the Campo. No good view for her tonight, I reflect, with some disappointment. She's a bit "vertically challenged" as she likes to say. In any case, back to the center, and quickly. My first instinct is to go to my comfortable spot at the Casato barrier, directly across from the bleachers that had just denied us access. *Note to self: Arrive at 5:00 p.m. and bring food to sit in the bleachers next year.* With mixed emotions I find that middle-aged couples have already claimed the coveted trackside spots, with one couple sitting on the ground. Still, I notice another destination instantly, the four-foot-tall hexagonal cement pedestal that serves as one of the few permanent features in the Campo throughout the year. Our chance is now. I quickly share the plan with Linda, and we make our way to claim the post. As long as nobody sits on it, we will both have an unobstructed view of the track in front of us. Linda hugs the pedestal to peer over the top, while I stand behind her and enjoy the view over her head.

While negotiating space around us, we watch the intensity of this final evening trial unfold. Even though we consider ourselves early, large clusters of contrada loyalists, who are wearing their home colors, are already perched in reserved blocks of bleacher seats. This wouldn't be so intriguing but for the fact that some of the most prized seats directly in front of the Palazzo Pubblico are occupied exclusively by children of grade-school to middle-school age. Lots of them—hundreds in fact. Gradually, parades of them, representing each individual contrada, make their way through the gathering throngs and climb into the precarious bleachers overlooking the Palazzo stretch. *This is really saying something*, I think to myself, *to place their kids in such prime real estate.* Then the youngsters start to chant something in unison, singing some kind of fight song in their high-pitched voices. They get busier still with various arm-waving routines, swinging back and forth in unison.

How ... My thought trails off in confusion. I try again: *How ... did they entice the kids to do this and in such a disciplined manner?* They all generally wear color-coordinated outfits. From right to left, it is difficult to mistake their identities, as long as one has done a little homework on contrada colors beforehand. Wave, Ram, Goose ... It's hard to miss the Goose, third from the right: their green shirts stand out. As contrada horses and their followers make their way into the Palazzo entrance for staging, groups of young people are doing likewise, finding their designated places in the bleachers.

The Secret to Adolescent Engagement

I think I have found one answer to the mystery surrounding the eerily conforming teenagers in Siena. As children, they are included front and center as an important part of the Palio tradition and spectacle. They are brought up with it and taught to enjoy it. They have a place and must feel as if they have a stake and role in their community. By the time they are teenagers, it is in their DNA, so to speak. Where they live is who they are.

This place-based loyalty, something geographers and others refer to as *place attachment*, is not just a coincidence, and it doesn't just occur naturally. Instead, the youths' affinity toward the home contrada is consciously and strategically taught and nurtured through social interactions. Children are learning how to view their own contrada—and that of their enemy—before they learn to talk. Little boys practice with toy flags and drums in the hope—or their parents' hope, more accurately—of one day qualifying for the highly selective *alfieri* (flag throwers). Little girls play Palio as well, until they are gradually encouraged to transfer to more "girl-appropriate" toys that may include ceramic bells or dolls dressed in medieval garb.[54] Children are taught at a very young age why their own contrada is superior to others, to the point of encouraging them to make nasty faces when their enemy contrada is mentioned. As Alice Logan explains, "Children learn immediately who their enemies are, how to regard them, and how to behave toward them."[55]

They further learn to recite the contrada cheer and may be expected to demonstrate their competence in front of proud relatives. The contrada is also involved at every important point in children's lives, including the traditional baptism in the chapel, followed by a secular baptism ritual at the contrada fountain. The contrada doesn't disappear after that; it is present in various ritualistic and physical ways at communions, graduation ceremonies, weddings, and even at funerals. Is it any wonder, then, that kids are yelling their cheers tonight in unison, taunting their playmates from nearby contrade, and generally supporting their miniature city-state?

PROVA GENERALE

In terms of social structure, contrada young people typically transition through three successive age groups. The youngest become a part of the Gruppo Piccoli (Little Ones' Group) until age twelve. As adolescents, they transition into the Gruppo Giovani (Young People's Group). This group is actually managed and led by teenagers themselves, including officers who provide an organizational structure. As adults, women will often join their own group. There is no men's group, however, given that "the men *are* the *contrada*, in the sense of being the locus of its power and authority."[56]

Of course, the social scientist in me can't help but also wonder how many young people are not here tonight. *Are these attendees volunteering?* I did discover that the Goose and Panther solicit interest by announcing on their websites how to purchase tickets for the bleachers. Still, tonight the answer is crystal clear: these young people are integrated into Palio festivities and strategically placed front and center. They are unmistakably perceived as a vital part of society, and they will be seen and heard. We further note that parents behave similarly regardless of their Italian or American roots; we chuckle as parents across the track from the bleachers yell and wave at their little contrada devotees perched in what otherwise would have been hundred-euro bleacher seats.

If my brief observations are any measure, Siena's contrada system is also nurturing some future museum curators and tour guides. Several weeks earlier I accidentally ran across a flier taped to the Goose contrada office that promoted a rare event. *Wow, am I interpreting this correctly?* I wondered. During an unexpected national holiday, all seventeen contrada museums would be open to the public during the afternoon and evening. This was enough for me to excitedly run back to inform everyone, starting with Linda.

Beyond this rare opportunity to go inside additional contrada museums, however, was a small statement on the flier and associated websites that truly caused my jaw to drop: *"a cura dei giovani contradaioli"* ("led by the young contrada members"). *Are they serious?* I mused. *What an awesome example of youth involvement!* As indicated earlier, it is challenging enough to encourage college-age people to appreciate such places—although Dario Castagno had succeeded wonderfully with our Caterpillar visit. Now the fliers were suggesting that combinations of teens and tweens would actually be leading tours? *I have to see this!* I thought.

LIVING THE PALIO

After a brief strategy session, I decided to focus my afternoon on two contrada museums—perhaps not surprisingly, those of the Goose and the Panther. These two museums ultimately organized their tours very differently. The approach of our home contrada revolved around a young rock star—a well-spoken and confident boy who could not have been more than fourteen years old. With no notes or older mentors nearby, the museum leadership had let him loose on his own with a large group of visitors. He methodically led our group through the cavernous rooms of contrada memorabilia and Palio relics like those we had enjoyed with Castagno. Though his Italian explanations were well beyond my comprehension, this young person impressed all of us with his poise, knowledge, and confidence, outshining even veteran tour guides. He earned a rousing applause at the conclusion of his hour-long tour. "There's no doubt," I shared with Linda afterward, "that kid is going to be running the contrada in the future!"

I was further pleased that I was able to introduce myself to the contrada's museum curator, Roberto, telling him an early version of why we were living along Via di Fontebranda. This earned us an opportunity to return a week later to enjoy the museum on our own time. One day Roberto made heads turn on Via di Santa Caterina when I walked past the società and museum. I was heading back to our apartment after watching the Goose host a contingent from the Turtle contrada, marching around the city on their patron saint day. I was admittedly amused when Roberto actually recognized me and yelled, "Ciao, Thomas!" At this point, everyone nearby stopped and looked at me, clearly puzzled when I returned the greeting.

Still reflecting on our young guide at the Goose, it was time for me to venture up to Panther territory. It turns out that my experience here would be equally captivating but in an entirely unexpected way. When I arrived at the museum entrance along the contrada's main street, Via San Quirico, numerous teenage Panthers were outside mingling with some middle-aged women clearly involved with the museum. Before I could mentally prepare to greet strangers in Italian as I was accustomed to doing, I was discovered by a friendly young woman who approached out of nowhere and asked, "Do you speak English?" Trying to internalize my instant surprise, I replied, "Yes, I'm American." With lightning speed she ushered me inside to the first main room, filled with all things Panther. Here she introduced me to her older, twentysomething friend, Carmina, who also spoke some English. I gathered that Carmina was there to help supervise her younger counterparts.

For the next hour I found myself being shuttled efficiently from room to room on my own personalized tour. Certain young people were assigned specific rooms to describe in English for visitors like me. One of the older teen boys, named Angelo, was particularly impressive with his language competency, and I complimented him after the tour was concluded. After accepting the praise with a chuckle, he humbly explained that he had only practiced for that particular room. His big dream, however, was to learn more English in either Britain or America. *Wow, big plans. He is well on his way*, I thought, and told him so.

I was also wondering how so many young Panterini became involved with the museum, and—more intriguing—how they learned this much English. *They seem friendly*, I further thought. *I wonder if they're interested in meeting our students.* Once back outside with Carmina and friends, I somehow mustered the courage to ask several of them, "Would it be possible to get together for lunch or dinner so that we could learn more about the involvement of young people in the contrada?" I fumbled through this a bit because nobody here was actually fluent in English. At one point Carmina and three other women were trying to determine a day for a special museum tour, having misunderstood my request. Finally I clarified that we would enjoy a meal with a few of them on their own, together with our students.

To my surprise, Carmina responded, "Sure, here's my phone number; feel free to contact me." By now my jaw was getting quite tired of dropping to the floor. "How do you like *them* apples?" I joked with Linda later, quoting from an early Matt Damon film, *Good Will Hunting*. "I got her number!" This ultimately led to a wonderful evening with about fifteen Panthers and Americans at a favorite local establishment. Some of their stories and anecdotes about contrada life are peppered throughout this book. As one of our students had suggested, "Sometimes it pays to put yourself out there" and interact with people. You never know where it will lead. Right now, I need to lead us back to the Campo and the trial.

The Song of Verbena

Back in the Campo, cutting through the background noise of socializing comes an impressive and recognizable melody. I have enjoyed this ritual throughout the past three trials, and now Linda has her chance to hear it. A large chorus of men down near San Martino are bellowing out a song in unison. *Do I hear harmony? Have they practiced?* The music is muffled a bit due to the distance of the chorus across the Campo, but it is captivating all the same. My first thought at hearing this at the first trial was a distant memory of a favorite motion picture, none other than *Close Encounters of the Third Kind*. In the movie stunned community members are chanting in unison out in the desert, essentially paying homage to the new "gods" that descended upon them the previous night. Creepy stuff. Although there are no UFOs here, I experience a similar sensation hearing the adults singing and chanting from across the open expanse.

In response, directly behind us the young men of the Wave contrada open up their voice boxes and send it back to the other side. Then, almost as if to outdo their neighbors from the Wave, a lively group of women wearing orange and white, belt it out themselves. They are of the Unicorn.

The song they sing now is one of Siena's strongest cultural indicators of city and contrada pride. Local pride is expressed throughout the year in various mottos, chants, and songs specifically designed to promote the solidarity and cohesion of each contrada and the community at large. The song we are hearing now is one of Siena's most cherished melodies, known as "Il Canto della Verbena" ("The Song of Verbena"). The *verbena* to which it owes its name is an herb or grass that is—or was—found growing between the bricks of the Campo.[57] Representing a sort of national anthem, the proud Senesi sing their song in unison at sporting events and other relevant citywide festivities. The words to the song speak directly to a strong Senese sense of place, focused intently on the Piazza del Campo itself:

> *Nella Piazza del Campo*
> *ci nasce la Verbena,*
> *viva la nostra Siena*
> *viva la nostra Siena.*
> *nella Piazza del Campo*

ci nasce la Verbena,
viva la nostra Siena
la più bella delle città.

In the Piazza del Campo
there grows the Verbena,
long live our Siena
long live our Siena.
in the Piazza del Campo
there grows the Verbena,
long live our Siena
the most beautiful of cities.

There are plenty of examples of the song on YouTube, for those who wish to hear it. Curiously, each contrada has adopted the same melody for use with its own unique lyrics. Apparently, there are several hundred versions of this very song, if all the unique verses of the collective contrade are added up.[58] The contrada-specific lyrics are decidedly more colorful and provocative than the actual "Canto della Verbena," which may not strike one as surprising. Each contrada rendition provides both a public expression of its own self-identity along with its image of others.[59] A bit less romantic than the Siena version, each contrada's rendition is sometimes used to verbally rip apart one's rivals while asserting one's own preeminence. This explains the singing back and forth across the Campo, with some groups focused on taunting their adversaries.

In song, the contrade are engaging in a sort of back-and-forth conversation through music, sometimes an insulting one. The Goose and Tower provide an example of this.[60] As translated into English, the members of the Goose sing these verses:

We have always commanded
And we always [will] command;
We are of Fontebranda
We are of Fontebranda;
We have always commanded
And we always [will] command;

We are of Fontebranda
And we don't have [know] fear.

The Tower contradaioli respond:

You said that you command
Instead [we are] commanding;
Down with Fontebranda
Down with Fontebranda;
You said that you command
Instead [we are] commanding;
Down with Fontebranda
And up your ass we will go!

Amusing taunts aside, I interpret "Il Canto della Verbena" as an expression of overlapping place identities for both city and contrada. With alternative lyrics built into the same melody, the Senesi are expressing their local attachment to city and contrada simultaneously. Note that there is absolutely no hint of attachment to Italy in the song. The Senesi identify with city first and contrada second. One young woman from the Onda (Wave) explained to Figliola that, "one is first of all Senese and then *contradaiolo* ... In this way, I'm a *contradaiola*, and I can also have adversaries from another *contrada*. But the thing that unites all of the *contrade* is the fact that we are all from Siena; therefore, we all feel the same sentiments and have the same cultural formation."[61]

From what I have been able to gather, the Senesi only identify as Italians when necessary or convenient. Here at the final trial, it is likely safe to presume that nobody is thinking now about Italy as a nation-state. Our time machine has taken us all back tonight to the days of the Republic of Siena—if we can ignore the mountains of digital cameras and smartphones all around us.

Defending Our Turf

As the melodic conversation continues, I am unpleasantly reminded of what one Siena School staffer told me days ago about the crowds here. "During the

Palio, people wait for hours and can get pretty nasty defending their space. It can become vicious and quite competitive in the piazza." We soon find that she is quite accurate, even though this isn't the real Palio race. At this final evening trial, the horses trot around with their jockey test pilots, getting a feel for the track while probably twenty thousand spectators take the event much more seriously than they had the night before.

This is why people seemingly line up to challenge us for our coveted spot at the pylon. First, a middle-aged, short Italian woman starts making a fuss about Linda's coat draped on the pylon. She seems to be suggesting that someone should be sitting up there to not waste the space, though I'm not entirely sure this is what her annoyed Italian comments are actually saying. Her friends or family are not far away, it seems, and she is clearly serving as the courageous point person. I sense that her whole entourage is just waiting to pounce if we show any weakness. Linda hugs the pylon even tighter, with both of her feet strategically spaced on the ground. She knows this will be a territorial ground war now. The aggressive Italian woman literally pushes her way into the couple standing to our left. We soon find out that the Italian woman has been bothering this English-speaking couple for some time, and the couple is now quite annoyed. The wife explains to us that they have been waiting for hours and are not about to give up their spots to a rude person trying to press in. *What if they are Senese, trying to see their own event?* I wonder to myself. *Should they receive some special treatment?* Part of me thinks they should. The problem is identifying them. Many "foreign" Italians are here tonight as well, muddying the local-outsider dichotomy even further.

At this point I'm starting to become uneasy and a bit uncomfortable with this display of human nature: too many humans, too little space; humans wanting space, humans not willing to give up space. Bad things can happen. We are enduring a preview of what Amy, from the Siena School, had forewarned us about the actual Palio race. Then, the *mortaretto* fires, surprising all of us once again. I still have not unlocked the mystery of the cannon and why there is no audible warning before its first firing. Pavlov and his famous dogs kick in later when they provide a drumroll in advance, leading many of us to hold our ears. Never mind, the crowd is thickening and pressing in. A group of Italian teenagers, it seems, is likewise eyeballing our precious pylon, with the hope that one of them will soon be atop of it, blocking the view of those of us behind. I learned that lesson two mornings ago, when a teenager sitting atop a similar pylon blocked about 40 percent of my view down the track. Linda warns me that the teens are gradually pushing in, presumably getting ready to make a run for the pylon. One of them actually points and provides a sheepish request to get in. Linda stands her ground and denies the request.

In the meantime, we have befriended a determined Dutch couple sitting to our right. I am relieved when they finally decide to stand. I was secretly worried that someone would use them as a stepping-stone if they didn't get up soon; by sitting, they were relinquishing their air rights, which seem to matter here. Following some conversation that unites us against the intruders, the four of us form an unwritten, united front at our barrier, and by the time the Carabinieri (Italian military police) make their appearance on the track, the threats from behind us have subsided. The mad Italian woman has taken her fight elsewhere. Linda has made friends with the Dutch woman, just short of trading contact information. The woman reminds me, lovingly, of my great aunt—friendly when you get to know her, with a decent sense of humor, but don't ever mess with her or she will flatten you without much regret. She and her husband are great allies to have standing beside us.

I realize another challenge now that we have secured the pylon. People will crowd in—and upward—as the cameras rise in one unified mass into the air. I am mentally prepared for this, given yesterday morning's lesson. But even my six-foot stature doesn't provide me with a clear view down the track toward the Palazzo Pubblico as the mounted Carabinieri make their way toward us. They are impressive and gallant with their polished uniforms, graceful mounts, and layers of medals and regalia clanging along. This is the bonus for attending the final, most festive evening trial, known as the *Prova Generale*. Not that we can see much. I mention to our Dutch friends that their second trip around the track should be at breakneck speed, swords extended in front of them as they ride courageously into an imagined battle. *Actually, what are they really supposed to do on these horses when called into action? They will certainly go to war in style*, I think.

After another half lap around the track, I wonder if the promise of a full-on charge is not to be. Then past the starting line we see bobbing heads increase in speed, and the crowd roars with delight. Bread and circuses, indeed. I manage a few acceptable photos of the mounted police as they blow past, albeit with the intrusion of some arms and heads. As they finally complete one full circuit, we soak in the scene and ambience of this thrilling tradition once more: the unified singing, the contrada pride, the electric crowd, the sea of spectators across the Campo. Everything tonight is more intense, more elevated, with seemingly greater stakes for everyone involved. Tomorrow night at this time, it's game on. Whether we are present or not for the grand finale, I am more satisfied that, for all intents and purposes, we have just experienced the Palio.

PART III
PALIO DAY

❋ CHAPTER 11 ❋

A Tough Decision

FOR SEVEN WEEKS WE HAVE WAITED FOR THIS DAY: THE MAGICAL DATE OF JULY 2. Now what to do with it? There is a dizzying array of activities associated with the Palio all day long, and it takes an expert in time management to keep track of them all. As a novice, I'm relying on online calendar supplements and a detailed preview from the Siena School staff just to get my head around it. The *fantini* (jockeys) need to be awake quite early, as their first obligation is to be blessed at a special mass at 7:45 a.m., presided over by the archbishop of Siena. Following the mass, they gear up for the sixth and final trial known as the *Provaccia* (bad trial), so called because "there is a general indifference" among the contrade for this particular trial.[62] Jockeys are expected to hold back their horses to avoid injuries and especially to keep them fresh for the final race tonight.

Now I understand better why so many jockeys get thrown off their horses in the race. They're simply exhausted, having endured blessings, trials, parades, final negotiations, the seemingly endless procession in the Campo, and probably an hour just trying to line up at the *mossa* without too many false starts. According to Sydel Silverman, "In the Palio, it's not the best man who wins; the man who wins is the one who comes in first."[63] I am increasingly of the opinion, however, that the winner is simply the one who hasn't fallen asleep prior to reaching the finish line.

For my part, I manage to wake early enough to saunter over to the Church of Santa Maria di Provenzano for one of the more peaceful events of the day. I understand that the *palio* banner (*drappellone*), which will be awarded to the victorious contrada, will be on display prior to a separate mass. It is still well before the mass begins, and only a few individuals and families are making their way inside. Because it is my first visit inside this magnificent Renaissance structure, I sneak in respectfully to not arouse much notice from anyone who may be religiously inclined to be here. Sitting silently in a wooden pew near the back, I soak in the centuries of Baroque-style decorations and religious iconography. Most striking are the banners, representing the colors of the ten contrade running in the Palio later this evening.

Dwarfed by the sheer scale of the interior, the *drappellone* is perched high on a pole (known as the *asta*) above the floor. A short queue of Senesi from various contrade has formed near its base, some simply sitting in nearby pews to enjoy its artistic design. As time marches on, the small crowd thickens, and individuals of all ages make their way to its base. Most are sporting their respective contrada's *fazzoletti*, waiting serenely for a chance to commune up close with the *drappellone*. Of course, this wouldn't be Siena without some kind of wrinkle.

I am surprised and puzzled to see people throwing something at the *drappellone*. Some youngster takes his own *fazzoletto* and tosses it toward the prized banner. The *drappellone* is high enough up on the wall that it takes some effort to actually hit the target (whoever placed the banner that high knew what he or she was doing). A few more people try their own luck with target practice, enjoying some success. *Okay, there's some sort of ritual going on here*, I conclude, *rather than simply the antics of a misbehaving young contradaiolo*. Family members clearly approve of the activity. Now sitting with a Siena School staff member, I learn that tossing a *fazzoletto* at the banner is believed to bring good luck to the contrada during the upcoming race. Since the mass is expected to begin soon and the pews are filling up with well-dressed Senesi, I make a graceful exit and return to my own home base to discuss our plans for the rest of the day. If my observations are accurate and the superstition holds water, the Panther should have a fair shot later this evening.

How to View the Palio

At the risk of being judged fools by our students or colleagues, Linda and I contemplate the pros and cons of viewing the actual Palio race somewhere other than in the Campo. We clarify our decision only this morning, the day when ten contrade will send their horses and jockeys into the arena to decide the next chapter of Senese history. Here's the deal for those who want to witness this history firsthand. There are two basic options for in-person viewing, each with a serious downside in my estimation. The most inexpensive approach is to arrive hours early and stand somewhere in the central public space of the Campo until the race is well over. This option costs nothing financially, if you're still standing in one piece at the end.

The second option is to purchase elusive tickets well in advance to enjoy the comfort of a simple wooden bleacher perched between the buildings and the race course. The catch is that this latter option can cost a few hundred euros or more per seat. A few weeks earlier I had thought about investigating bleacher seats, emboldened by simple signs that read "Palio Tickets" in a few café windows. No prices and no instructions—Italian or otherwise—on how to acquire them. Not so surprising, perhaps. This is understated Siena, after all. I would need two tickets if I wanted to stay married. We thus decided to scratch the bleacher idea this year. *It's still only a ninety-second horse race*, I comfort myself. It turns out that the bleachers, known as *palchi* in plural (*palco* in the singular), are essentially owned and controlled by the shop owners located behind them. Thus, there is no centralized office where one can inquire about tickets.

For those determined to tough it out in the Campo, the encouraging news is that you are essentially guaranteed some spot on the inside of the racetrack if you simply show up on time. According to numerous acquaintances in town, we would need to arrive in the Campo around 5:00 p.m. for the scheduled 7:45 p.m. race. The preferred arrival time differs by several hours, depending upon who provides the wisdom. It's fine to arrive at Piazza Mercato behind the Palazzo Pubblico before six o'clock, after which time you swarm in like cattle, according to one informant. This is the staging area, as I call it, for the final hours of Palio attendees who decide to not stake out a claim within the Campo before four o'clock. At some time after then—the exact timing is not clear—the other entrances are closed off.

Surviving the Campo

In this case, my week-long poll of asking about this process yielded consistent answers. "Enter through Wave—Onda," Viola tried to explain in her English-Italian combination. During one of my recent visits to their shop, she and Riccardo dug out a book about the Palio and reviewed an aerial photo with me. I pieced it together, but it took more cognitive effort than I expected. After a certain time of day, the only available entrance would be along Via Giovanni Duprè, a narrow street entrance from the Onda (Wave) contrada. Upon later inspection, this strategy for controlling the entrance made geographic sense; after all, the Senesi have had more than a few centuries to figure this thing out. The two imposing buildings sandwiching the narrow Via Giovanni Duprè provide convenient, effective crowd control.

Those who actually arrive earlier in the day to valiantly stake out their space along the barriers must still protect their prized territory from the inevitable press of the gathering crowd. As the density of people increases, it is not hard to imagine these latecomers becoming pushy and rude. As explained earlier, Linda and I experienced this type of behavior ourselves during the *Prova Generale*. Our own preview was compounded by stories of medics stationed in the center to assist those with heat exhaustion and lack of food and water (although I understand that three kiosks sell water during the event). I seriously cannot envision how the benefits of personally viewing the Palio would outweigh the potential costs.

Thanks to the trials of the past few days, I had already accumulated dramatic photographs of the action from various close-up vantage points. I could imagine littering our house with framed images. I had experienced the electric crowds, the singing in unison, and the festive nature of the Palio events, and I had endured three hours of lockdown during the *tratta* Friday morning. I had essentially experienced all these Palio rituals without actually attending the final event. How convenient! For me, this was satisfying enough. Though Linda had contemplated toughing it out, she eventually became even more convinced than I was to avoid the mess in the Campo. No, she would not commune with the verbena. She happily assured me that I could do what I wanted, if standing in the center with the students was really my thing. I could even arrive at ten in the morning to secure a precious spot, but she would not be a part of it. There are two words to describe her point of view: rational thinking.

Remote Viewing

Days earlier Linda speculated aloud whether our feel-good restaurant deep in Panther territory, Due Porte, would host its own viewing on their flat screens.

LIVING THE PALIO

Linda and I consulted on options, which included a Robert Rodi–esque hope on my part that we could join the Goose or Panther loyalists at their società. It would be similar, I supposed, to watching an NFL or college ball game at a sports bar within sight of the stadium. Many Senesi do just that, according to multiple sources. They may have endured the Campo once or twice to soak in the experience, but then wisdom kicked in as the Palio races added up and blurred into the past. These folks now happily watch the event at a local bar or some other place with a comfortable seat and television. Some contradaioli, we found, get so nervous and anxious during the lead-up to the race that they simply prefer the solitude of being alone.

One of our Panther friends, Silvia, was even more specific. Having joined us for the mixer dinner with her friends, she explained, "We [Panterini] typically watch the Palio in one of two places: at the società or in the Campo. During this time the city is dead; a strange calm exists because nobody is on the streets." I asked our friend's sister if they allowed visitors to watch with them at the società, and the concern was one of possible embarrassment on their part: "We go nuts during the Palio, so you will think we are crazy. We will not be in a good mood if the Eagle has a good horse or if we lose." Another friend chimed in again, adding, "Yes, you can watch it at the società, but you would need to stay in the back and remain quiet." These comments were enough for me to conclude that it would be best for everyone if we watched the Palio from elsewhere. Their società is their veritable living room, and we certainly don't want to disturb the extended family during this emotional event.

Thus, on this fine Palio morning we confirm our decision to watch the race at Due Porte, in the comfort of a familiar family restaurant with decent televisions and personal pizzas to boot. Of course, I imagine the students will most likely choose to view the Palio from within the Campo, given its once-in-a-lifetime status. They will undoubtedly fill us in on their adventures tomorrow when we plan to meet for our final debriefing.

Our decision to alight at Due Porte is leading to some unintended yet happy consequences. Not being stuck in the Campo for hours on end will free up much of our day for other events. One is the *corteo storico*, a medieval procession, which actually originates at the Duomo (Cathedral) before meandering downward to the Campo. We determine that an arrival at the Duomo around three thirty or four in the afternoon will be sufficient to see the action there and perhaps with better views than the Campo would afford. The day is heating up, but it is not oppressive. The rain and clouds are holding off for a change; the weather has been so unpredictable over the past month or more, but today it is nearly perfect. A little sunscreen, a couple of water bottles, and our distinctly American wide-brim hats should be all that's necessary to explore the *corteo* fun.

Prior to this event, however, I am eager to witness one of the most distinctly Senese rituals associated with the Palio—the blessing of the horse. It was the intrigue of this very event that encouraged Roy Moskovitz to learn more about the Caterpillar and ultimately become an active member. Although visitors can occasionally sneak in to "catch a blessing" as my colleague nonchalantly mentioned, this is certainly one of the more mysterious and peculiar events of the days of the Palio. Thanks to some encouragement from our Panther friends, there is a real chance that we can witness this event with our own eyes.

The Blessing of the Horse

The blessing, or benediction, of the horse tends to occur around three in the afternoon on Palio day, at each contrada's respective *oratorio* or chapel. Apparently, visitors are welcome to attend this bizarre event, although the chapels are typically small and crowded with their own contradaioli. Any visitors are, as tradition would have it, carefully scrutinized, given past accounts of enemies sneaking in undercover to sabotage a contrada's sacred animal.[64]

Following a brief ceremony led by the contrada priest, the horse will be blessed first, followed by a blessing of the jockey, once again indicating the relative importance of the four-legged animal over the two-legged one. At the end of the blessing, it is customary for the priest to diverge from his otherwise religious focus with a specific command to the horse: "Go! And return victorious!"[65]

As one might imagine, this is quite an abnormal event for a conservative religious organization; allowing any animal inside a church is generally considered an act of sacrilege. This would be true on any other day of the year but not on Palio day. In this case, not only is the horse required to enter the church, which is sometimes a maneuvering challenge in itself—directly related to the number of stairs it has to climb—but the contrada faithful will express satisfaction if the animal decides to relieve itself while enjoying the blessing. This letting go is viewed as a good omen. The contrada captain may carry this further with a carefully placed step into the offering.

"If you want to see the blessing, you should arrive around 2:00 p.m. at this back entrance," Silvia indicated as we walked past. She was referring to her contrada's church, the rather unpretentious Church and Convent of San Niccolò del Carmine. "I've walked past this church countless times," I responded, somewhat surprised, "and never realized that it served as the contrada chapel." Like the street it sits along, the church is found on the western side of Siena's Terzo di Città. I hadn't thought of this area as Panther territory, but indeed it is. In fact, the Panterini literally take over this entire wide, curving street for their pre-Palio dinner, the *Cena della Prova Generale*. Their church becomes the staging ground for cooking and setup, a process that serves more than a thousand people the night prior to the Palio.

Although we are clearly welcome to attend the blessing, Silvia had described one challenge with accommodating visitors. "Before the horse comes in, someone tells the visitors to turn off their camera flashes, because the flash can scare the horse," she explained. "This is announced in English and even Chinese." She laughed, somewhat frustrated. "But every year when the horse walks in, flashes go off anyway." Despite this understandable dilemma with respect to hosting visitors, we were being invited to this very event, an exciting proposition!

Again, Siena is full of surprises. Now at the back door to the church at 2:00 sharp, our small group is patiently waiting at the rear entrance as directed. In contrast, the Panther contradaioli are entering through a streetside doorway. As we wait, more guests arrive, somehow knowing to join us here. *There really is no front entrance to this church*, I muse. Its sideways orientation to the street is not typical of most churches, which tend to display fully ornamented facades dominating their front entries. Our back entrance, therefore, actually consists of a set of unadorned double wooden doors in a small courtyard with direct access to the street. While contemplating this urban anomaly, our initial small group of visitors is turning into quite a sizable crowd. *How many people can fit inside this church?* I wonder. More than sixty people are now waiting with us, spilling out into the street. Our own group gradually shuffles a bit closer to the double doors, expecting that we

A TOUGH DECISION

will likely be among the first to enter. "Not that we're competitive or anything!" Linda quips, one of her favorite phrases.

To pass the time we scan the growing crowd, paying more attention to what others are wearing and where they might be from. "Oh no," I chuckle to the students, discreetly indicating a couple of women with sun hats at the back of the crowd. "They're wearing yellow. I guess they haven't learned the contrada colors yet," I joke. Yellow is the prime color of the Panther's rival, the Eagle. As the students consider this, I downplay the cultural breach. "I'm sure the contrada is used to visitors who don't know much about the culture here, so they'll be okay with it." It would probably be worse if the guests purposely wore Eagle colors as an insult, knowing full well what they were doing. I return to my original conundrum: *How have all these people found this place?* Somehow the contrada has become quite competent with attracting visitors.

Eventually we hear a booming knock on the double doors from within, signifying that they are about to be opened. Probably a hundred of us instantly swarm inward and fill every empty space in the rear of the church. Our group leads the horde that is now spilling down the sides. Linda and I are in the very front of the swarm, so we keep moving forward until a Panther contradaiolo indicates where we should stop. Within a minute, the entire back half of the church has filled with us visitors. We lose the students in the crowd but remain confident that they will still find a reasonable vantage point. *This place is humungous!* I think while looking around to scope out my new environment. The church appears larger from inside.

As for the Panterini, they are well disciplined. The youngsters are placed strategically on the stairs behind the altar to watch the event. Soon a contingent of Panthers parades in to the beat of a drum cadence, wearing colorful costumes and carrying contrada banners. The contingent climbs up behind the altar as if there are bleachers, forming a striking top row of red and blue. Before I know it, the church has essentially become a theater in the round. One young woman then approaches the altar's microphone and instructs everyone to not use flash. As we anticipate the guests of honor, I wonder how many people will not comply today.

Before I know it, we all turn our attention to the back doors. Here comes their sacred animal, Pestifero, being guided to the altar where he awaits the priest's blessing. Predictably, somebody uses a flash, and the woman repeats her request more firmly now. She hurries to the back of the church as if to chase down the offender. With everyone in place, the priest opens with a prayer, and the Panterini recite it in unison. As expected—something that does not happen often in Siena—the priest concludes his remarks and commands in a raised voice, *"Va! E torna vincitore!"* ("Go! And come back a winner!"). Strangely, there is no applause and cheering after this display of emotion—only silence. I remind myself that we're inside a church and not at a political rally where the candidate's speech is followed by jubilant cheers.

Just after getting comfortable with the standard silence, however, the place erupts around us. We are instantly startled with a brief, unified cheer as the Panthers let out what amounts to a war cry. *Wow, that was awesome!* I think, still in shock as the echo reverberates around the interior. The priest then places his Panther *fazzoletto* back over his head (he removed it earlier to wave it at Pestifero), and the jockey and horse make their way to the rear exit from whence they came. Just like the Palio race itself, the lead-up ultimately requires much more time and energy than the actual event. Within minutes the ritual is concluded. I do not detect that Pestifero has left any offering this time. *Oh well. Can't win them all.*

The *Comparsa*

Given that we were among the first to enter the church, we are also among the last to leave. By the time we emerge into the crowded street, the students have scattered, and the Panther *alfieri* (flag throwers) are providing a brief display of their talents to the delight of the crowd. They are generally not performing for adoring masses of tourists, however, but instead are seeking to honor their own friends and extended contrada family. There is a compassionate reason for this initial performance, as tradition would have it. Those individuals too old or frail to join the historical procession and Palio race are treated to a small performance of their own.[66] This street performance is essentially the contrada's send-off, a kind of "Godspeed" from the hopeful contradaioli to their representatives.

With their well-rehearsed routine having run its course, the crowd closes in for a round of backslapping, hand shaking, and otherwise local hero worship as they send their chosen *alfieri* off to "war." It is a joyous occasion for the contrada, and the crowd finally pulls away to let them go. Then suddenly my young acquaintance, Angelo, recognizes me through the crowd and informs us, "They are going to march now up to the Duomo, so you can follow along if you like." I thank him for inviting us to participate before I lose him again in the crowd. We don't need to be asked twice. We fall in behind the women and families marching with their *comparsa*.

Like this one, each contrada fields a *comparsa* that symbolically represents a group of soldiers headed off to war during the Middle Ages.[67] In this case, the Palio serves as a ritual war, and the comparsa is comprised of specially chosen contrada men who dress in medieval-themed outfits, showcasing their flag-waving and percussion skills.

Perhaps the most visually stimulating and skilled position within the *comparsa* is that of the *alfieri*, who are deployed to demonstrate their superior flag-throwing skills to spectators and rival contrade alike. Although each comparsa attempts to demonstrate its distinctiveness over its counterparts, each includes a standard membership of role players. One drummer leads the group with his repetitious cadence, followed by two *alfieri*. They are followed by one *duce* (leader) and two grooms. One page carries another flag, with two additional pages carrying the contrada emblems.[68]

We soon find ourselves marching with the Panthers toward the Duomo, albeit amid the less organized rear of the pack. Traditionally the *comparsa* would have marched elsewhere around the city before concluding at the Duomo, including a strategic stop at Piazza Salimbeni to honor their benefactor, the Banca Monte dei Paschi. One local acquaintance had informed us that every *comparsa* still does precisely that prior to heading to the Duomo, which would make for quite a hike through part of the city. As we make our way past Due Porte, our favorite family restaurant, I wonder just where the Panther will lead us now. Curiously, however, we need not worry about a lengthy hike. The *comparsa* instead makes a beeline for the Duomo and prepares for its brief performances there before lining up for the historical procession. It is nearly four o'clock, and Linda and I quickly scope out the scene to find some shade.

CHAPTER 12

Myth of the Republic

OF COURSE, THE MOST OVERPOWERING FEATURE HERE IS THE DUOMO ITSELF, or more formally, the Metropolitan Cathedral of Saint Mary of the Assumption. The age of this magnificent structure is as breathtaking as its polychromatic facade. Again, the centuries of time that have transpired here are likely incomprehensible to Americans. Locals were already showing up for mass here by the 1220s, and the cathedral's unique black-and-white marble was being delivered for the bell tower and facade around the same time.

An alternating marble, zebra-striped design was applied throughout the interior and exterior, representing a strong sense of place for Siena. It is no coincidence that black and white became the colors of the city's coat of arms. Perhaps even more surprising, the Duomo is not the first house of worship to be located here. The previous church and bishop's palace were located on this spot, constructed sometime during the 800s. That's only about three hundred years following the decline of the Western Roman Empire. It's worth noting that the Etruscans had already founded a town here centuries earlier, but they were eventually overcome by the Romans. By the ninth century, some version of today's urban Siena was already up and running.

The construction and use of the cathedral represent the heady days of Siena's medieval era. The city was a relatively prosperous place as the Senesi moved into the fourteenth century. For all intents and purposes, the Duomo could be considered complete by 1348, constructed mostly in phases during the 1200s. The urban population had reached an impressive fifty thousand during this time, and the city-state controlled another fifty thousand people within its *contado*, or agricultural hinterland and smaller nearby towns, which were mostly to the south and west.[69]

Even though Florence could boast of a population double the size of Siena's by the 1330s, it was the proud Senese leaders who decided to undertake a little project of their own. It was a modest proposal: simply to erect the largest cathedral the Christian world had ever seen. And they nearly pulled it off. Then came the tragic consequences of the Black Death in 1348. The city and its glory days would never recover completely; its various forms of republican government limped along until the arrival of the Medici rulers in the 1550s.

It is tough not to think about the Black Death and its tragic impact here. About one out of every two people, or half the population at the time, was wiped out. This particular rendition of the plague also destroyed Siena's cultural leaders at the time, carrying away every one of the city's established artists except for the presumably fortunate Lippo Memmi.[70] Though absolutely devastating, this was more a European problem than a Senese one. A staggering seventy-five million to two hundred million people perished throughout Europe roughly between 1348 and 1350. This was one tragic consequence of increasing global trade at the time—essentially an early round of globalization. This particular plague is thought to have diffused into Eastern Europe from Central Asia along the famed Silk Road.

Back here in Siena, construction on the largest church in the known universe ground to a halt and was never revived. A striking monument to this ambitious project and its tragic ending is found with the unfinished construction that bridges the piazza on the cathedral's eastern end. What appears to be an open-air loggia, with part of it bricked in for use as a museum, is actually the early construction phase of the envisioned expansion. A full line of pillars and vaulted arches still exists from this colossal project, which would have downgraded the existing cathedral's central nave into merely another transept.[71] This is why the Black Death looms at the forefront of my mind every time I view this structure or pass underneath it to the streets below.

The Historical Procession

Today the mood is a tad more uplifting. The *corteo storico* (historical procession) can be loosely compared to an American pregame event. More than five hundred people dress in costumes representing the medieval and early Renaissance heyday of the Siena Republic, well prior to the 1550s when the Medici overlords put down the independent city-state for good. More precisely, the procession can be viewed as a flashback to the "golden age of Siena," defined as beginning in 1260 with the successful Battle of Montaperti and the dedication of the Madonna, and ending in 1555 with the fall of the republic.[72] The *corteo storico* is designed to represent this flashback. In one sense, the procession is a nostalgic event demonstrating everything that was good and wholesome about medieval life in this once-proud republic.

As Drechsler describes, the procession comes complete with a stately marching band, banners, and regalia that likely provide an impression of a "big show event, which the race itself is not."[73] Like many contrived medieval reenactments elsewhere in Tuscany, this one is only loosely based on the realities of its Gothic-era city. Although designed to celebrate the former republic, the costuming has changed over the centuries, with the current medieval-themed outfits designed only after the 1861 unification of Italy. Uniformity of costuming actually dates back to only 1813, with the theming coming much later in 1878. And so it was that the *corteo storico* came to represent the "Myth of the Republic," as termed by Alessandro Falassi.[74] The event therefore reaches back to the nostalgia of Siena's pre-Medici glory of the 1400s but with questionable accuracy.[75]

Regardless of its shifting historical representation through time, the *corteo* is slow-paced, regal, and rather subdued without much flash or razzmatazz. The easily excitable Palio visitors are almost more energetic and frantic, struggling to climb over one another for the prized money shots. In fact, the procession actually proceeds at a crawl through the city as its participants make their way from the Duomo to the Campo. The symbology of the banners, flags, and military hardware is complex and might require a few college-level lessons for the first-time spectator.

Appropriately, the banner of Siena leads the procession, the black-and-white insignia known as the *balzana*. A group of trumpeters and other musicians play a slow, regal march, which was composed specifically for the

Palio in 1875.[76] The early procession is essentially populated by a who's who of Siena's local government and imagery. The procession then displays the territories and cities once included within the Siena Republic. A military contingent provides another sizable segment of the procession, followed by the more familiar imagery representing the seventeen current-day contrade with their respective *comparse* (plural of *comparsa*).

Also included are the symbols of six former contrade that were dissolved in 1729 following local territorial disputes.[77] Their representatives are marching as well, reminding spectators of the Lion, Bear, Rooster, Oak, Strong Sword, and Viper contrade that once existed.[78] Given that about fifty-nine contrade occupied territory in Siena at one time, I am unsure how this number was winnowed down through time to the present seventeen. The Black Death caused one reduction as the population was decimated, bringing the total down to some forty-two contrade after 1348.[79] By the 1720s, the number had been reduced by another twenty or so. Most recently, the 1729 dissolution by Governess Violante of Bavaria accounted for a reduction of the six mentioned above, ghosts of which are now marching in the historical procession.

The end of the procession as it enters the Campo is marked by the traditional *carroccio* (ox-drawn cart), meant to represent the triumphal chariot of the republic.[80] Probably overshadowing the cart and its impressive beasts of burden, however, is the *palio* itself, or *drappellone*, which rides on top to remind the contradaioli of what they will win should their horse return victorious. As the cart trundles leisurely past the spectators already assembled in the Campo, those closest to the cart participate in yet another curious ritual—that of waving their own *fazzoletti* in the air to honor the *drappellone*. Thinking like a social scientist, I would later realize how this behavior can provide some useful demographic information about the crowd. The waving scarves not only indicate where the members of each contrada are clustered within the Campo, but they also roughly reveal the proportion of true contradaioli in attendance compared with visitors like us. I would further discover that the cart itself is actually stored during the other 363 non-Palio days of the year not far from the Campo, in a vaulted garage along Casato di Sotto. The garage is typically closed and off limits to visitors, which is why I found it a bit puzzling that a standard directional sign on a nearby building points precisely to its location.

Contrada Performances at the Duomo

Having now arrived with the Panther contingent, we push our way into the L-shaped public space around the Duomo, only to find a mass of people already claiming the cathedral's expansive front marble stairs. The time is approaching 4:00 p.m., the hottest part of this July day.

We both agree to a trade-off: a little bit of shade is worth the potential price for not being precisely located at the center of action—wherever that might be. Soon my eyes catch a dark swatch just hitting the marble steps along the cathedral's side. There are already a few people sitting there to take advantage of the shade, created by the Gothic-era building itself. Dredging up my basic knowledge of earth-sun geometry, I calculate that the swath of shade will only expand as the sun continues on its clockwise path around the front of the cathedral. Not only that, but the side stairs provide a "natural" amphitheater from which to view this elusive procession. "I've heard that they all congregate inside this building with the courtyard," I say to Linda, pointing across to Siena's provincial administration building, "and eventually they process out and around the Piazza del Duomo before setting off for their final destination."

Settling in, it becomes apparent that we are actually in the wrong part of the piazza to enjoy an up-close view of the various contrade marching in. They are arriving on their own accord, as did the Panther, following their requisite tours of the city. They seemingly arrive with little warning, and they take their place just like airliners that queue into an airport. So far, the incoming traffic here is manageable. The Owl appears, for instance, with little competition from others for space in the piazza. The *comparsa* stops in front of the Duomo entrance at the base of a well-behaved throng. Here, the *alfieri* provide a preview of their eventual routine for the Palio, known in its entirety as the *sbandierata*. Banners fly into the air, the crowd roars, cameras blink and beep, and the *alfieri* do a U-turn to reverse their way back from whence they came.

Little beknownst to visitors, the *comparsa* has just paid its respects to the archbishop of Siena, who might be peeking out from his palace to receive the compliment, as tradition would have it.[81] To this day, the archbishop's residence is located just to the left of the Duomo when facing its façade. After their U-turn, they stop once more to perform for those confined to the hospital, the Santa Maria della Scala, so named for its location across from the stairs of the cathedral. Now a museum, this was one of the first hospitals in Europe, its mission to care for the sick and infirm, as well as pilgrims heading to Rome on the Via Francigena, women, and abandoned children. The esteemed Santa Caterina served here. If that weren't enough, the hospital is credited with sparing the city from allied bombing campaigns during World War II, given its role in treating the injured. Still somewhat shocking to this writer, certain contradaioli friends still recall seeing patients in the hospital enjoying the *sbandierata* as late as the 1970s prior to construction of the new facility outside of town.

Although tourists may presume that these successive performances are designed with them in mind, it should be evident now that the opposite is true. Paying tribute to the archbishop and those once confined to the hospital was of utmost priority to the contrade—and this time-honored tradition continues uninterrupted to honor that purpose.

Following this performance, the Owl *comparsa* presses onward through waves of incoming tourists and ducks into one side of the Cortile della Prefeturra (Courtyard of the Prefecture), the internal staging ground for the historical procession. Other contrade arrive in their own time, eventually making their way to the front of the Duomo for a similar routine: Shell, Dragon, Unicorn, Eagle, and so forth, before ducking back into the enclosed courtyard themselves. Once inside, the staged procession awaits a special signal to commence, that of the *Campanone*. Known also by its nickname, the *Sunto*, this is the massive bell atop the Torre del Mangia which formally summons the marchers to the Campo. If there is a more distinctive, low-pitched bell in Europe, I don't know what it is. Where they will exit from this massive structure in response to the summons, however, is anyone's guess.

Luckily, events actually unfold in front of us as we had hoped. The procession makes its first appearance. Still, I am not prepared for the participants to spit out of the east side of Siena's provincial administration building, opposite from where they entered (although to my recollection the buses in Florence pulled that stunt too!). To our left, a slow procession emerges and hugs close to the building, led by a military-style band playing the slow-paced March of the Palio, composed specifically for this occasion. It is wonderful to hear orchestral music again, especially bouncing off the stone structures. They turn left and continue to hug the building, opposite from us across the piazza but still technically crossing our path. The learning curve required for the tourist mob requires only seconds; I nod in approval at their collective reasoning skills. A veritable receiving line forms out ahead of the procession, with people dutifully lining up in anticipation of the lumbering marchers.

I wonder aloud, "Why is the procession hugging the building?" Oh well, it's not our show. We enjoy the relative comfort and shade of our prime seats, even if we are a hundred feet distant. We can still see the impressive showing of banners, band members, medieval warfare equipment, and period costumes slowly making their way past us. As various scholars have pointed out, we are essentially watching the (reimagined) medieval history of Siena unfold before our eyes—the myth of the republic.

❋ CHAPTER 13 ❋

Underdog

THE SITE FOR OUR RELATIVELY TRANQUIL VIEWING OF THE PALIO IS DUE PORTE (now called Vivace Ristorante), a family pizzeria and restaurant deep in the Panther contrada not far from the Siena School. We knew about this place prior to our arrival in May, as we ate here once or twice last July during a reconnaissance to plan our future program. Compared with its counterparts around the city, the square footage of Due Porte is impressive, not unlike a lodge-type dining hall. Just when you think the sea of tables has finally quit toward the rear, a magical surprise awaits. The restaurant maintains nearly as much real estate for dining on its two-level back patio area, which is essentially the entire backyard of the property.

Overall, the Due Porte staff is friendly and willing to put up with visitors, and the place seems to attract its share of student groups, Americans, and Europeans. I can see why. The menu is as extensive as its floor space, with literally pages of *primi piatti* (first courses), *secondi*, pizzas, and wines. *So many pizzas! Mama mia!* The prices are reasonable as well, a compelling reason to become repeat customers, sometimes with a contingent of students in tow. We recommended the place for our first pizza night with the class. In typical Italian fashion, we took over a lengthy interior table, enjoying our own company for several hours.

We taught the students early in the program about Italian restaurant etiquette and expectations, as Americans can get pretty surprised (at best) or frustrated or even rude (at worst). After you arrive at a *trattoria* (family-owned restaurant), the table is yours for the night. There is no sense of rushing you out to move more people in, and one should certainly not be insulted when the waiter fails to bring the bill. There is no tipping—the *servizio* is built into the final price of the meal.

Marco was our server for our first group dinner and for future return visits as well. He speaks passable English, compared to most Senesi we've encountered. Although he warmed up to our group as we made repeat appearances, he has a temperamental edge, suggesting a touch of unhappiness. He clearly works his heart out in the restaurant, but he once expressed some disappointment about the lack of time he had to join his Shell contrada peers or participate in Shell activities as often as he would have liked. Remember how work and/or family can get in the way of contrada life? Marco is a case in point.

On that first night with the students, the atmosphere of the place revealed a true family-run Italian experience, with female family members and customers alike decked out in Roma soccer garb, cheering on their regional team while we ate. Unlike American sports bars where there is typically more TV square footage than wall space, the staff had designed the restaurant for maximum viewing of its two television sets—placed back to back on a central beam in the middle of the main dining room. An HDTV faced the back half, while a regular TV faced the front. You could watch from either side and, amusingly, watch the reactions of the other half of the room simultaneously. This would prove to be a rewarding setup during the Palio. Given our rather frequent patronage of Due Porte, it was only logical that Linda would think about alighting here for the grand finale of our stay in Siena. And that time has arrived.

The Italians, especially at Due Porte, don't really care where you sit. On this magical night of the Palio, a 7:00 p.m. arrival works perfectly, and we choose a small table near the open window to the street, with a straight-on view of the television. My adrenaline ramps up a notch. The staff are airing what I call the Palio Channel, which is already devoting full coverage to the race. The standard commentators are dutifully making play-by-play comments while a variety of camera angles catch the historical procession nearing its final destination. Thinking like a fifth grader, I reflect, *Wow, we just saw them at the Duomo a few hours ago, and now they are being broadcast to millions!* The mood is festive, if not jubilant, around us at this point, with a manageable, small audience—including two families or groups of Americans actually only there to eat dinner. What a serendipitous surprise for them to be coincidentally entertained by the show of the year.

Amazingly, one family of parents and their college-age children are taking a break from walking a good chunk of the Via Francigena, the original, thousand-year-old pilgrimage route from France to Rome that I discussed earlier. They are exemplifying the fact that the route has become its own tourist destination. Linda asks them why they chose this type of vacation, clearly suspicious of the necessary workload associated with such an outdoor adventure. One responds, "It would be cool to walk part of it!" But they apparently got more than they bargained for. Like their predecessors, they are here in Siena for rest and refueling.

The Palio Lineup

One thing I realized during the *prove* (trials) is that you cannot lose sight of the starting line if you want to see the whole race. There is really no way to predict when the Palio will start. Blink at the wrong time or pick up that fork for a bite, and the race is half over. My cue to pay attention is when the *fantini* (jockeys) and horses are mostly lined up, the horses are behaving reasonably well, and there are only two or three horses remaining to join the pack. Even then, there are inevitably problems because the track itself is rather narrow, and there are no gates or stalls to separate the horses. Jockeys and steeds alike are more than a little anxious. In fact, there's really nothing much at all to contain the lot of them except a hefty rope, known as the *canape*, at which they line up. If a horse decides it really doesn't want to be there with its buddies or complains because the horse next to him throws a fit, then the jockey can't do much other than pull back from the lineup. At this point, other horses and jockeys inevitably do the same in a chain reaction, and the crowd lets out another exasperated sigh of disappointment.

The lineup ritual is nearly as suspenseful and complex as the race itself. After the jockeys have changed out of their costumes from the historical procession, they prepare to face the crowds and emerge from the Palazzo Pubblico onto the track. Before this captivating moment, they apparently splash water on the insides of their pants in the hope of getting a tighter grasp on their horses. Then, perhaps somewhat amusingly, they are frisked by the police for weapons. After this, in yet another touch of Senese irony, they are provided with new weapons as they emerge onto the track.

In this case, all *fantini* are provided with the same implement—and an odd one at that. They each receive a *nerbo* (whip), something that was not allowed in the trials. Again, this is Siena, so one might imagine that it's not just an ordinary whip. A nerbo is made specifically from the dried, stretched phallus of a calf.[82] For those who enjoy the gory details, the preparation of said phallus involves its hanging in a slaughterhouse with a weight attached to stretch it out. It is then cut at both ends to form a whip that measures about two and one-half feet. The nerbo can be used on one's own horse, on someone else's horse, or on another jockey to hold him back from the lead.[83] Unlike in the trials, the jockeys are also provided with a bit of protection in the form of metal helmets called *zucchetti*. A blow from the nerbo in just the wrong place, however, can produce a scar for life.

Nobody knows the order in which the horses will line up at the *mossa* (starting line) until they arrive. As with the assignment of the horses three days earlier, the lineup for the race is decided by one final lottery. Positions one through five, the closest to the inside of the track, are generally considered the most promising, not unlike what race drivers would call the pole position. Of course, one is better than two and so-on, favored by their inside advantage. The positions six through ten are not so promising, so the theory goes. The jockeys in these positions may try to make last-minute deals to suppress their rivals in more favorable positions. Otherwise, they just make the best of it. The *rincorsa* (position ten) is not considered to be an opportune placement, but anything can happen with that one.

It turns out that these assumptions about the starting positions are only partially accurate, if the last century of races has anything to teach us. My favorite website for Palio race statistics includes a detailed table that shows every winning position between 1899 and 2012.[84] To test the assumption that the positions become less successful toward the outside of the track, it was a simple matter of counting up the total wins for each position. Like all statistics, it depends how one interprets the data. In one respect, the assumption holds some truth. The positions one through five (131 wins total) are indeed more favorable as a group than positions six through ten (99 wins total). This isn't the big advantage that one might expect, however.

The bigger surprises are hidden within the data. The most successful position as of 2013 is actually the fourth (thirty-five wins), barely nudging out the first (thirty-one wins). Position five has been the third most successful (twenty-eight wins). Most intriguing, the second position (fifteen wins) is the worst—not the tenth (twenty-two wins). This tells me that the middle of the track is, in the least, more advantageous than one might assume. And there are other factors that determine the outcome of these races beyond the sole variable of starting position. One factor was made clear from a retailer on our street, a proud, long-time member of the Snail contrada. When I stopped in one day, he was clearly bored and tried to explain the start of the race to me. To bridge the language divide, he supplemented his well-worn Italian-English dictionary with a quickly drawn diagram of the starting line. Not unlike the playbooks of American football teams, his scribbles indicated any number of scenarios where one jockey and horse might attempt to cut off another near the beginning. I wondered if the number one and two positions tend to get cut off by rivals more often than might be admitted.

Prior to 1952, the starting order was determined through a lottery in the Palazzo Pubblico, requiring a rather risky hand delivery to the *mossiere*, who controls the start of the race. There are stories of keen observers who could read the list from afar and other mystical ways in which the order of the lineup would leak out somehow in the short time span of its journey between the Palazzo Pubblico and the *mossiere*.[85] If it leaked out to one captain or contrada ahead of the other contenders, a tremendous advantage could be realized. For instance, it would greatly affect the last-minute *partiti* (negotiations) and possibly alter the outcome of the race.

Consequently, the Siena City Council voted in 1952 to employ a rather unique mechanical device, operated by three officials standing up on the *palco dei giudici* (judges' stand). Its cylindrical pipe holds ten *bàrberi* (wooden balls) piled atop one another. Each ball represents one of the competing contrade. *Now all those little toy balls for sale in the gift shops around town are making some sense*, I think. The *bàrberi* are then dropped into a container, after which the pipe is screwed onto it. Then the device is turned upside down, which allows the *bàrberi* to fall back into the pipe. If that weren't enough ritualistic camouflage, there are "windows" on the pipe, which remain closed until the jockeys actually reach the Casato turn on their way up to the starting line before the race. At this point, the order of the ten balls is finally written down and handed expeditiously to the *mossiere*, who is standing only a few feet away from the judges' stand.

UNDERDOG

As the horses arrive at the *mossa* (starting line) this evening, we watch intently as the *mossiere* begins to announce the positions of the contestants, from one to ten, using their contrada names. Similar to the extraction (assignment) of horses, this process occurs slowly and deliberately. After the first contrada is called to line up, a few more seconds transpire while the horse and jockey arrive at the *canape* (rope). Then the second is called to line up, and so on, until all ten are fidgeting together at the starting line. Tonight's lineup proceeds as follows, from one to ten: Ram, She-Wolf, Tower, Porcupine, Unicorn, Owl, Goose, Wave, Panther, and finally the Shell (the *rincorsa*). *How did that happen?* Somehow the two contrade with the favored horses—the Ram and She-Wolf—managed to acquire the first two positions, even if the second position is not all that it's hyped up to be. *So much for the Goose and Panther!* I throw up my hands. I am nonetheless pleased to see that the She-Wolf, with its status of *nonna* (grandmother), has a fighting chance. The intensity of this process has only begun. As it unfolds from our viewpoint at Due Porte, everyone seems to expect a lengthy, drawn-out wait, so conversations kick in, and many of the restaurant patrons lose some measure of interest. The real intensity at this time is inside the packed crowd of the Campo.

An internal contest of wills then begins between the *mossiere* and the *rincorsa*. Technically, the *mossiere* has control over when the race begins. But the *rincorsa* certainly has something to say about it, although never a direct word is uttered between them. To start the race, the *mossiere* drops the *canape*, and the horses leap forward. This is Siena, however, and things just aren't quite that simple. The *mossiere* typically takes his time to line up the horses, one by one. The individual chosen for this role is generally an outsider, like the jockeys, which means that he is likely to be more objective—and patient, which the crowd decidedly is not. So here's how the *mossiere* and *rincorsa* relate to one another: In a perfect world, it is the *mossiere* who calls in the *rincorsa* to start the race once the other nine horses seem to be lined up appropriately. However, the *rincorsa* can decide to force the starter's hand by starting his gallop early, or the *rincorsa* can simply ignore the invitation to start the race and hold back until he feels that his own adversaries are at the proper disadvantage.

In the case of an early start by the *rincorsa*, the *mossiere* can play his own game and declare a false start. He probably still drops the *canape*, however, as the rope has the potential to inflict severe injury to horse or rider should one of the contenders trip over it. Meanwhile, as this back-and-forth continues between these two important role players, the other jockeys are likely engaged in last-minute deal making—the *partiti*—with their counterparts, right there in front of the crowd. It is no wonder that the actual start of the race can sometimes take well over an hour. We settle in and enjoy watching our own small crowd.

Although Due Porte is located within the Panther contrada, we are apparently only blessed with the presence of one or two Panterini. As noted earlier, most of the Panthers have settled elsewhere to share their collective tensions. Still, one of them has donned the requisite red-blue-and-white fazzoletto of her home contrada. Marco is quietly pulling for the Shell, he mentions, but refrains from full-scale fandom while dressed in black and white for restaurant duty. He is milling around like a nervous animal, though, occasionally visiting our table and providing us with an opportunity to chat with him. As we dive into our pizza, he pays us such a visit after the lineup of the horses is announced. "Do you give the Shell a chance tonight?" I ask. In broken English he laments, "No, he is in a very bad position—the *rincorsa*, the tenth spot. The *rincorsa* has control over when the race starts, but it is very tough to win from there." Marco is not holding out hope, consequently, at least from what we can see. Still, he gives us a reason to hold a small place in our hearts for the Shell, as it would be enjoyable to see his reaction. Without a doubt, a Shell win would result in Marco abandoning his post and darting out of the place at lightning speed. Contrada first; job second.

Another *fazzoletto* in the room belongs to Linda; she entered earlier with the Goose wrapped proudly around her neck. She suddenly remembers this fact during pizza slice number two. She now expresses a rare bout of discomfort with her own Goose identity, as unknown people are passing in the street, and numerous other contrade are now represented in the restaurant. I don't see anyone from the Tower here, however—the Goose's rival. Linda makes an instant decision to quietly remove and store the *fazzoletto*, stating nonchalantly, "I should probably take this off for now." This rare display of caution takes me off guard, but I don't disagree. We certainly aren't expecting any hostility or problems, but I can't help recalling a Siena School staffer's words of caution a day earlier: "You should be okay wearing it on Palio day, but you might unwittingly pass by the contrada's enemy near the Campo. You could attract some jeers." In any case, we decide to go undercover for our first Palio, choosing to be more publicly ambivalent and refraining from shoving our own allegiance down their throats. Sorry, Goose!

Eventually, all nine jockeys eventually do line up, and the ever-anxious crowd starts to turn its anger on the *rincorsa*, most likely because he won't start the race. It is understandable that people are outwardly distraught and even verbally vocal during this tense process. However, I view this frustration as an important ritual in its own right, one of many within the full Palio spectacle. The tense arm-waving and fist-throwing behavior would certainly be missed should the spectators miraculously become patient. As we watch from our table at Due Porte, I announce more than once, "They're getting close!" Each time I say it, the jockeys prove me a liar and retreat once more to the circling routine.

Then all hell breaks loose. The shell rushes the line, the *mossiere* drops the *canape*, and the Ram takes off in the lead that most everyone expected. He has pole position, the number-one spot, along with the alleged strongest horse. But then the *mortaretto* is fired, and the horses ramp down before the first turn. The crowd lets out a chorus of frustration (or relief, if not fans of the Ram), and the contestants trot around the track to begin the lineup all over again. False start.

Marco paces behind us in the street not far from our table, muttering, "*Domani, domani,*" ("Tomorrow, tomorrow") in exasperation. "The sun is going down; they are very close to cancelling the Palio tonight and running it tomorrow," he explains. If the sun sets too low and the track loses too much light, the crowd that gathered for some four or more hours in the Campo today would see nothing. Not that most of them can see much from the center anyway. I could not imagine how one might feel having protected precious Campo space for hours, only to have the grand finale canceled due to darkness. How dare the sun go down!

Ninety Seconds

As the lineup attempts drag on, our restaurant crowd lets its guard down, and people naturally turn to conversation instead of watching the television screens. Still determined, however, I've got my camera phone ready to go when needed, and I sense that the lineup just might work this time. Numbers seven, eight, and nine are all there, and I exclaim once again my standard remark ("They're getting close!") for lack of anything more intelligent to say. I decide to start recording my video. Then while few people other than the staff are watching intently, the wait is over. The Shell rushes the lineup, the *canape* drops, and the ten horses thunder onward toward the hazardous turn at San Martino. Now people are paying attention.

Shooting out ahead is the Tower, which held the number-three position. The Goose contradaioli can't be pleased with their traditional enemy taking the lead. Numerous observers in town have gossiped in recent weeks that this could be a particularly contentious Palio, given that four rival pairs are running in this one. The Goose and Tower comprise one such pair. On a bright note for underdog fans, the *rincorsa* does manage to catch the Ram off guard at the starting line, and the Ram never recovers. I suppose the power of pink didn't pay off. The Tower keeps the lead at first, with the Porcupine, She-Wolf, and Goose just behind. The She-Wolf has a chance, I think, which due to its status as *nonna* (grandmother) is perhaps the most desperate for a win. It's a wide-open race, it now seems. The Tower keeps a thin lead as the horses blast into the San Martino curve for the first time. Amazingly, all ten survive the turn without incident.[86]

What is that I see now? Are my eyes playing games? I squint persistently at the TV screen and determine that there is suddenly a new, unlikely leader. Guess, our own Goose horse, has wisely cut inside at San Martino and has now inched past the Tower. Wow, rivals neck and neck. Then comes catastrophe for the Shell, this time on the straightaway in front of city hall. The rincorsa who began the race is now nearly falling off his horse and struggles to stay upright. He then succumbs to gravity and falls into the middle pack of horses. He hits the turf and is trampled by at least one of his counterparts. The Shell's horse is now racing *scosso*, without a jockey—who is left literally in the dust and has about twenty seconds to get the hell out of there. Meanwhile, the Goose, Tower, and She-Wolf have the advantage as they move through the next turn at the Casato. Two rivals, one of them representing our own contrada, and the *nonna*. Can't beat that threesome from where we sit!

But there's a scare for the Goose here. Guess and his jockey, Tittia, get stuck on the outside at the Casato turn and body-slam sideways into the wooden barricade. This location is particularly dangerous for spectators in the bleachers, as injuries from collisions here can and do occur. I think it's over for the home team. But Santa Caterina is looking down from somewhere tonight, and her hometown horse literally bounces off the barrier and back into the pack, thereby cutting off the Tower once again! All of a sudden Guess has a commanding lead around the second lap, with Tower and now the Panther coming up from behind. *The Panther is in it!*

The Panther jockey, Voglia, then discovers the laws of physics at San Martino. The wall of mattresses proves useful as he gets thrown violently from his horse, Pestifero, falling backward and bouncing off the track into the mattresses. He quickly gets up and scurries away from the thundering herd. He's okay. Pestifero is now also *scosso*, along with the horse of the Shell. Amazingly, as if inspired by the loss of its load, Pestifero hangs in there and behaves as if he really wants to win. He's now vying for second or third position without his master. Seeing this development, I start silently cheering for the horse, as I would not mind seeing a Palio win by a horse without a jockey. Our Panther friends would likewise be more than pleased to say the least, having not enjoyed a victory since 2006. And no contrada has won without a jockey since 2004. As I have mentioned earlier, jockeys are expendable in this event—it's the horse that matters. As it happens, we are in Panther territory here at the pizzeria. If Pestifero pulls off the win on his own, the Palio celebration will come to us when the time comes.

Through the second lap it's a three-way race: Goose, Panther, and now the She-Wolf. The Tower seems to have lost its foundation and has dropped back a bit. Guess is still in the lead but is desperate to hang on. I watch with disbelief as our home contrada holds out more hope than expected. Despite all the backroom deals, predictions based on best and worst horses, and the starting lineup, much of this race is ultimately left to chance. And it's not over yet. Two horses are now *scosso*, and neither is giving it up early for sugar cubes.

Then Tittia takes Guess into a too-comfortable arc around San Martino, giving an opening to the stubborn Pestifero, who now cuts to the inside just as Guess had done earlier. He and Guess are now neck and neck. This makes one ask seriously how much the jockey really matters (contrada leaders could save a lot of money without them!). Now heading for the final turn at the Casato, Guess maintains his lead by inches, it seems, followed closely by the She-Wolf and Panther. This is the final run to the finish, and it's uphill. The She-Wolf and Panther are both gradually pulling alongside Guess, and then one final scare reminds us spectators how dangerous the Palio can be. The white horse for the She-Wolf, Indianos, tumbles with its jockey head over heels onto the track as they struggle for the finish line. It's between the Goose and Panther now as they cross the finish. A few precious seconds pass, and then I fall into disbelief.

Victory

The commentators shout, *"Oca, Oca, Oca!* Guess has done it! The underdog horse with the poor starting position has just pulled off the unexpected! The people of Fontebranda have won!" I think, *"We"have won! How did that happen? What are the chances that, out of seventeen contrade that might have raced during our brief stay in Siena, our home team would emerge victorious?*

My own emotions transition rather quickly from disbelief to cautious optimism and then again to sheer enjoyment accompanied by a big, if modest, grin. I remember Linda's *fazzoletto* that I had stuffed in my pocket, and now it seems to reemerge on its own and starts waving in the restaurant. Nobody else is really paying attention, although a few people smile at the sight of it. Others are deep into their own instant analysis of the race, which will continue in this city into the next year or longer. For my part, I wonder what's next. I have only one thought that sticks with me: *Get to the Giraffe. Get to the Church of Provenzano.* I invite Linda to leave with me, expressing my desire to see the first stop on the Palio victory tour—well, the second stop if you count the euphoria currently taking over the Campo.

At this point, members of the Goose have rushed the track in a state of ecstasy and are reaching for their precious *drappellone* at the judges' stand. Linda gives me a resounding "Go" and explains, "I can live without the commotion. I will have the cold pizza wrapped up and saved [I never see the pizza again], and I will make my own way home." So I don our silk *fazzoletto* and rush out the door. I am race-walking down Via Stalloreggi toward the Campo, opposite the flow of traffic. You know those movies where the city is being destroyed by nuclear weapons or invading aliens (think *Independence Day*), and the protagonist is the only fool driving into the disaster? That's me.

Now with the silk *fazzoletto* around my neck, I head for Provenzano, where I will enjoy being a Goose contradaiolo for one night. Linda will join in later at the Goose chapel, having decided to forego the crowds on the non-

Goose side of town. I imagine this is how Robert Rodi felt when his beloved Caterpillar pulled off a similar unlikely win a few years earlier. He shared the experience in the cleverly titled "Dark Horse" chapter in his book *Seven Seasons in Siena*. Tonight the dark horse is a white horse named Guess, now the instant celebrity of Fontebranda.

Though never a big fan of superstitions, I must truly ponder whether this is all a coincidence, or alternatively the result of a divine setup. This happens to be the sixty-sixth victory for the Goose. We were sitting next to a family that had been hiking the Via Francigena (Italy's medieval equivalent to Route 66, as I like to teach), and our class has been meeting regularly at a family-run pizzeria across from the Campo, called none other than Cavallino Bianco—White Horse. Seriously, you can't make this stuff up.

❋ CHAPTER 14 ❋

Goose Chase

WALKING AT FULL SPEED TO PIAZZA DEL PROVENZANO TO CELEBRATE WITH the Goose, I encounter a preview of sights to come. Halfway to the Campo entrance is a lone, middle-aged woman in the street, wearing a Goose *fazzoletto* like mine. She is ecstatic and clearly in disbelief, almost in tears. We exchange some version of a high five, although I say little, hoping to avoid an Italian victory conversation before she finds out I'm an imposter. *What is she doing here in the middle of the street in the Panther contrada? Probably the same as me, having realized the win while finding herself somewhere else.* In any case, it's fun to see my first Goose loyalist after the win. I'm moving quickly, so I don't think to inform her that the rest of her contrada buddies are going to be congregating at Provenzano. Unlike me, she is basically standing in one place, seemingly confused about where to go next. Soon, I somehow avoid the Campo mess and skirt through Piazza Independenza and into my favorite bypass route. *Wise choice.* I've made use of this relatively quiet backstreet route along Via dei Termini for weeks, but mainly for lugging groceries or rushing up to Piazza Gramsci to catch a bus. Now I could not be more curious to see what happens at Provenzano as much of the Goose contrada descends on this otherwise serene public space.

Celebration at Provenzano

Usually quiet and void of people, the Piazza del Provenzano is already overflowing with a growing, ecstatic crowd. This is where every victorious contrada congregates following a July 2 Palio win, while the August 16 Palio victors assemble instead at the Duomo. A more complete understanding of this difference is found in the depths of Senese history. Siena actually identifies itself as the "City of the Virgin," having offered itself to the Virgin

Mary at times of local crises, especially when there is an impending war. The first time the people here collectively decided to put their faith in the Virgin was during the famed Battle of Montaperti in 1260, when they clobbered Florence despite being heavily outnumbered and under siege. The Senese victory understandably sealed the deal with the Virgin. So although both July and August Palio races are held in honor of the Madonna, each of the two races is dedicated to a somewhat-different Madonna.[87] On July 2, Siena celebrates the Madonna of Provenzano, while the August race is dedicated specifically to the Madonna of the Offering, held one day following the Feast of the Assumption.

As for why this Provenzano neighborhood represents the Madonna and the Palio in her honor, the answer is, once again, not what one might expect. This locale served notoriously as a center for prostitution during the sixteenth century.[88] This same neighborhood, which now doubles as the hub of the present-day Giraffe contrada, was also known for miraculous curing of the "occupational diseases" contracted by the prostitutes.[89] Consequently, it comes as no surprise that Siena was also tagged "Civitas Veneris," the City of Carnal Love. *I wonder what that slogan did for their tourism industry.*

Finally, by 1594, the city had had quite enough with these neighborhood issues, and the decision was made to once again petition the Madonna of Provenzano to assist with the most recent stint of famine and pestilence. Prior to this in 1552, according to tradition, a Spanish soldier made a dumb mistake with an outcome that was interpreted as a miracle in this very place. Santa Caterina (Saint Catherine) had previously dedicated a shrine here. A drunken Spanish soldier fired his weapon at the shrine. The bullet ricocheted off the shrine and promptly killed him. Today, we might nominate the soldier for the Darwin Awards, which recognize individuals who protect the human gene pool by eliminating themselves in an extraordinarily idiotic manner. The Senesi, however, considered the event a miracle, a kind of intervention by the city's saint.[90] In 1594, the Church of Santa Maria di Provenzano was built near the shrine in the Madonna's honor, discussed earlier. That same year the July 2 Palio was instituted permanently as well. With all these human activities and miracles, this neighborhood was clearly a happening place during Siena's Renaissance years.

As I try to secure a reasonable spot to view the action, I weave in and out of high fives, tearful families, hugging friends, and old men congratulating one another as if World War II had just ended again. I step to one side, using a police vehicle as a crutch while I fumble with my smartphone. *I have to get some video*, I think. From my elevated vantage point just off the piazza, the star of the show becomes evident. And it's not the jockey, though he is certainly to be found somewhere within this chaotic mix. The true hero is Guess, the Palio champion. He is mingling in the center of the piazza with little sense of what is transpiring around him. I can nearly imagine him giving postgame interviews to reporters with microphones. "Well, it was a strong field this year; they were impressive coming up on my tail and kicking up all that dirt," he might say. Aside from watching Guess give imaginary interviews, I can't help but wonder how he and his entourage arrived here so quickly after the win. *Were they beamed down? Guess is fast but not that fast.*

I recognize yet another benefit of a true walking city, where pedestrians take precedence over cars and where the density of urbanity allows one to traverse large swaths of the city in a matter of minutes. Crowds can easily materialize on foot, literally falling out of the woodwork (and stonework). Then the celebrants can shift to another part of the city without the ritual of finding their cars in an ocean of parking, getting stuck in traffic, and making their way across town. No need to do that here, as the Goose faithful are more or less instantly mobile. Similar to the earlier trials, Guess is led by his *barbaresco* (caretaker of the horse, or groom) in a tight circle as if the two of them are inside a small fenced area; the *barbaresco* is displaying the horse to the adoring crowd and, more important, keeping him calm amidst the chaos. Instead of pushing into the center, the polite spectators actually step back and make a hole as Guess makes his rounds.

A few Goose contradaioli wave green-and-white banners in the air, along with a puzzling mix of blue and white, the colors representing the Wave contrada. *Did that contrada help them emerge victorious? Perhaps they are happy enough that their mutual enemy, the Tower, did not win.* This interpretation of why the Wave contrada is celebrating here is likely accurate. The Wave does not have a traditional reciprocal enemy as do other contrade. As we have seen earlier, the Wave claims the Tower as its enemy, although the Tower supposedly doesn't pay much attention to its smaller, upstart contrada next door.[91] The Tower is more typically concerned with its reciprocal enemy, the Goose. Putting two and two together, we might logically deduce that both the Goose and Wave had it in for the Tower this time. Given the Tower's early lead, that contrada was likely humiliated by its loss. In this case, the Wave may not have won the Palio, but there is a strong "silver lining" when a contrada's enemy loses. It is not unreasonable to assume that there was some serious *partiti* taking place prior to the race, between the Wave and Goose in particular.

A Chaotic Crossing

An overwhelming feeling of happiness surrounds me. After milling about with its massive extended family, the crowd somehow senses that it is time to migrate. The celebrants are finished with Piazza del Provenzano and start to seek paths to the Goose homeland around Via di Santa Caterina. Guess and his *barbaresco* lead the way, as a quiet signal that it is time to move out. The crowd naturally transitions into a unified if ecstatic mob as we shuffle our way toward Goose territory. Reminding me that the celebration is still somewhat a family affair, various children are enjoying the best views from atop their fathers' shoulders.

It would take a struggle to extract myself from the cheery mob anyhow, so I just go with the flow. That is, until we hit the intersection with Banchi di Sopra, the northerly main street heading out of the Campo. The Goose faithful form a veritable passenger train attempting to cross, but nobody has bothered to put down the crossing gates. Instead, our Goose horde is met from the left by another, less pleasant crowd attempting to stumble home from, what was for them, an unfortunate race. It is wise to keep in mind that all the other competing contrade lost tonight, save for moral victories if their enemies lost as well.

Many of these arrivals represent the She-Wolf, heading back to their own territory to probably drink off this disastrous night. Thanks to their *fazzoletti*, I can at least tell where people are going. Despite how close Indianos took them to victory, the She-Wolf remains the *nonna*—the contrada that has endured the longest period of time without a Palio win. I can't begrudge them the fact that they are not giving the Goose any leeway here. I'm glad these contrade aren't official enemies, or I could end up in the middle of a serious brawl right now. This is not the most romantic of thoughts.

The intersection does turn into mayhem, even if fists aren't flying. It is all nonviolent and rather slow motion but still somewhat uncomfortable as

LIVING THE PALIO

Goose contradaioli try to move fifty feet east-west across Banchi di Sopra while She-Wolf contradaioli and friends move northbound. Amusingly, many of us are carried like a river downstream with the new horde vectoring in, temporarily taking us off course. Once across the river, the Goose faithful turn to a variety of convenient paths and recalculate routes to Via di Santa Caterina, including me. Aside from the discomforting mass of people, the whole episode is rather humorous. I can't help but chuckle at the whole thing as I'm shuffling across the street.

Almost like a small child suspicious of the scary forest, I spy the chapel area on Via di Santa Caterina, and I contemplate making my own gradual approach. As I do, I pause numerous times to observe the celebratory behaviors of young and old. Youngsters are still on shoulders enjoying a prime view. There is no rioting or shoving cars on their sides, as with various sports celebrations elsewhere. Actually, there are no cars here to overturn. In this respect, it is a wonderfully safe and comfortable space, save for the occasional spilled wine or low-speed collision with a reveler. Banners are waving but not in an organized fashion. Anyone—from teenagers to professional adult men—can acquire large banners and randomly wave them through the streets. A drum cadence ramps up somewhere but stops before kicking into a permanent parade; then another drum starts up on an adjacent street. The sound reminds me a bit of trying to turn over a car ignition. But this is a rather disciplined crowd, which is impressive. Even their collective jubilation is tempered; banner wavers carefully pull in their banners when the crowd thickens. I do end up with a Goose banner in my face at least once, but I easily accept this as part of the fun.

Mingling among the true Ocaioli are others capturing their share of photos and video footage; some are clearly not Italians and others are not wearing *fazzoletti*. I somehow feel comforted being with my fellow outsiders here soaking in the atmosphere. There is clearly enough room for everyone to enjoy the moment, and part of me is surprised that the mayhem is not off the charts. Perhaps the tempered mood would be different if this win was the first in decades. But the Goose has been flush with Palio wins of late, having pulled off wins in 2007 and 2011 as well. The odds have indeed been in their favor.

Guess Returns Home

I am ultimately rewarded for my patience at street side, as a series of events begins to occur. The crowds seem to know how to manage this type of win. There is a party forming somewhere as a small truck stops in front of Società Trieste to pick up trays of pastries destined for elsewhere. I notice a minor commotion farther up the street and see the crowd part, encouraging a bit of hero-worship of my own. Guess is about to clop right past me on his return home! It's not Harrison Ford, but Guess will do. All I see at first are the steed's humble eyes and cute white ears popping up above the crowd: This is certainly not anyone's idea of an intimidating or overpowering animal. But he seems to blend right into this dense district and mass of humanity. He is not fazed by the crowd and celebration around him, so he seems to be a natural people horse. As he did earlier, Guess trots by my spot. I obtain my precious video, and I see him led down to his stable where he unceremoniously disappears.

Once again, I am actually taken aback at the restraint of the spectators. There are some reserved cheers and clapping as he passes (one fan raises his wine glass and blurts out "Guessy!"). But it's almost as if Guess has already become an Ocaiolo and is simply showing up for the party. There is no bowing, feeding, blessing, foot stomping, singing, or crowning Guess into some kind of Horse-God. He's just here, passing by on his way home, likely unaware that all of us are actually celebrating because of him. He is the epitome of modesty. As a recent pop song goes, Guess might simply sing, "I just came to say hello."

The next few minutes are essentially a blur. At some point I make it nearly to the front of the Goose chapel on Via di Santa Caterina, with its bells tolling wildly. They are higher pitched and less intense than those of the monstrous Duomo or San Domenico up on the hill above us but just as joyous. The bells are adding greatly to the festive spirit of the neighborhood, though it is clear that this is a special occasion for this otherwise obscure church. Its humble Renaissance facade fits naturally into the multifloor streetscape of medieval-era buildings. There is little to indicate its role as a church other than a few projecting pediments and the entryway, which is surrounded more prominently with Goose statuary. I am dumbfounded to see that the chapel doors are open, unlike all other times I've walked past it. Some contrada chapels are only opened to the public a handful of times a year, if that. With dusk coming on quickly, the interior and wall-sized frescos are lit up and visible to those of us outside. This scene is nearly a metaphor for my own role as an outsider looking in. Some people—but not throngs—are calmly making their way in or out of the chapel entrance.

The People's *Drappellone*

What gains my immediate attention, however, is a slender, elegant banner I recognize immediately from my morning visit to the Church of Provenzano: It's the *drappellone* up close, in the flesh, so to speak. One chosen individual is rather simply holding the black-and-white *asta* (pole) to which the *drappellone* is attached, standing on the church steps to the right of the entrance. Again, there is no dancing in the street or other fanatic type of behavior at the sight of this magnificent piece of art. Instead, a small gathering blends into the larger street scene and patiently awaits a turn for a photo op, as if they were in front of a tourist landmark. Though unthinkable to this outsider, there is no doubt that I could easily make my way to the cloth prize and touch it myself. I really don't feel the need to do so, as I am enthralled with getting this close—even closer than this morning when it first went on display. This is the Goose's Palio, in both senses of the term, so I refuse to interfere.

Some individuals touch the banner and rub their fingers on its edge, and even the *drappellone's* caretaker holds up one corner of the bottom so that he can see through to the crowd. I am impressed that it has not been encased in glass yet or taken out of sight. I suspect that it won't be cleaned, either, before it is immortalized behind glass in the Goose museum. Other banners from more recent wins were clearly soiled with the grime of human hands, and that's the way they remain to this day. Of course, this fact was made all the more visible on those with light-colored backgrounds. The white ones didn't stand a chance.

Tonight, the banner is available for all to see, photograph, and even touch. It is the people's *drappellone*. Then, as if on some magical time schedule, the *drappellone* eases down the steps and back into the street. It is on the move once again, setting out on its own victory tour, all on foot. From what I gather, it is destined for a trip around the Campo. Eventually other Ocaioli realize this as well, and an impromptu parade forms, complete with waving banners, drums, and loyal fans now headed back up the hill. The proverbial ignition has finally turned over as the drum cadence ramps up and continues. I don't know if there is a planned itinerary for the *drappellone* or for other aspects of this celebration; it is all happening at a rather natural pace and free of elaborate promotion or fanfare. These fans are not getting all mad and rowdy; they are simply happy, enjoying spirited conversation in their hometown streets.

Having encouraged Linda to join the party, I give her a brief tour of "our" contrada headquarters, proudly showing off the house of Guess and the chapel across the street. I also gladly surrender the *fazzoletto* to Linda, while I clumsily install a cheap polyester version around my own neck, a feat more complicated than one might imagine. It can't possibly require this much effort and engineering, but it still turns into a jumbled mess. Nonetheless, we promptly notice that the chapel is still wide open to visitors and that it is enjoying surprisingly few takers. I suppose the Ocaioli locals have all been here before. I learn later from a guidebook, however, that it is a rare treat to find this church open at all. For now, I am genuinely flummoxed about the accessibility of the church to anyone who wants to enter, including us. Without any resistance from crowds, we march up the stairs and into its depths.

The Chapel of Saint Catherine

The Chapel of Saint Catherine is striking with its magnificent frescoes, vaulted ceiling, deep-blue background, and star-painted foreground. Some simple benches on the side provide a chance for us to sit and stare at the frescos and chancel area, which features a rather modest, if massive, marble altar piece, carved with inlaid goose figures. The contrada iconography is literally carved into this house of worship. Ostentatious contrada banners are proudly displayed on both sides of the altar. More-tasteful Goose medallions and related icons appear to blend seamlessly with the traditional religious symbols here. And apparently Santa Caterina herself was a proud contradaiola; her otherwise sullen statue has donned a silk *fazzoletto* for the occasion. I do like these people.

Then Linda discovers the chapel bells. Their incessant ringing seems to depend upon kids and adults alike who take turns pulling ropes in a side room. I quickly observe that should these volunteers abandon their posts, the neighborhood will fall silent. We can't have that! With few adults to hinder us, Linda encourages me to "come on," several times before I relent and join her. Nobody seems to care as Linda's non-Italian blonde hair starts bobbing up and down in sync with the rhythm of the ropes; she is intent on keeping the bell tower in business. *Wow, I contemplate, we are so close now to the cultural focus of this contrada, and no one seems to bat an eyelash or fazzoletto—even though this is not our place, not our church, and certainly not our community.*

Linda is having a blast joining in the celebration, volunteering to keep the party going outside. Her sense of adventure is admirable. Linda then shares the ropes and teaches others how to ring the bells—some of whom are clearly imposters like us. Then she encourages me to grab hold and let them ring. I tug the lines but can't tell if my efforts are having an impact, until I vaguely hear the high-pitched bells outside. Then I pull harder as Linda takes too many photos. After our turn with the bells, a larger crowd grows, and we gladly give up the reins to others. Linda even starts teaching some Italian kids how to pull harder to ring the bells.

I wander around, and my awe continues. There's another, smaller vaulted room immediately off of the main *oratorio*, with entrances connecting the two at either end. There are historic banners on the wall, one dating to the mid-1800s. A simple ceramic tile on the nearby wall announces Capella di Santa Caterina (the Chapel of Saint Catherine). *Isn't the chapel in the other room?* I obviously have a lot more to learn about this place.

Once again outside, I decide to call our students to give them our location, in the case they would like to experience an actual victory celebration. *Why aren't they here, anyway?* One student in particular has a higher percentage chance of answering his phone than anyone else. Since he is typically grouped with at least one or more students, I learned weeks ago to use him as my gateway to the rest of the class. Most students have actually abandoned their smartphones, which turned out to be rather dumb in Italy. Thanks to the helpful staff at the Siena School, three of us were provided with simple pay-as-you-go phones to assist with communication during our visit.

After a bit of phone tag, I finally make contact, desperately trying to hear over the surrounding crowd noise. No good. I call back as we retreat down the street a bit, and within only a few minutes we meet the students at the top of Via di Santa Caterina—no driving required. They were getting some pizza and relaxing a bit following their Campo ordeal. I am delighted to see their familiar faces appear, and we welcome them to our "home," commencing with my now-familiar tour—the società, house of Guess, and chapel with its tolling bells.

The night has transitioned into a buzzing, although disciplined, street celebration. With three students joining us, we once again discover that Guess's stable door is wide open, with adoring fans in green and white gathered around the wooden barricade. Directly opposite the stable entrance is a conveniently steep alley leading to a street above. From a few steps up the alley we can look over the people and straight down into the house of Guess.

We take our turns photographing the horse of the year and then simply hang around the chapel outside, sharing our respective stories of the remarkable evening. Plastic cups of wine and water are available on folding tables across the street, staffed by a few women. After a brief hesitancy on my part, my thirst overwhelms any worry of intrusion. I pour myself some water from the half-empty bottles that aren't getting much attention anyway. The wine is another story; it is quite hard to come by right now aside from what has spilled on the tables and street.

Linda and I soon learn about what life was like earlier in the Campo. All our students survived the experience together, albeit with stories of verbal conflict between nearby individuals defending their hard-earned turf. Otherwise they enjoyed the experience of a lifetime, now completely exhausted from four hours of late sun, continuous standing, and struggling to see the events.

Just above us on Via di Santa Caterina, we eventually focus on a group of younger teenage girls decked out in Goose colors. They are clustered together and sitting on the street, chatting excitedly and sharing their phone photos. I do a double take, as certain members of this young group have even spelled out *Guess* and *Tittia* on various limbs. Foregoing more typical tattoos and music icons, these teenagers have totally bought into the horse and jockey pair who led them to a victory. Once again the younger contrada members are displaying their strong sense of community pride. We debate, probably foolishly, among the five of us whether we should ask them for a photo. *Too touristy? Intrusive? Never mind, it's a festive atmosphere.* Linda once again takes charge. She easily makes friends with youngsters—Italian or otherwise. She calmly bends down and gestures something about a photo as we all stand in a circle and stare dumbly. Without hesitation several girls strike a pose together as Linda tries to click the shutter. Nothing. The flash on my camera has been acting up, and at this critical time the thing refuses to do its job. Linda doesn't notice at first, and neither do the girls. The moment has passed.

A Contrada Rebirth

At about this time I spot some young people fumbling with plastic pacifiers. Some kids are playing with theirs, enjoying the embedded, rotating, blinking lights. *Seriously?* Numerous, competing thoughts of amusement and recognition pop into my head at the sight of these gadgets. I suddenly recall learning that the winning contradaioli sometimes adorn themselves with pacifiers and baby bottles following their victory. This may all be too much to process for outsiders unaware of the symbolism here. After a Palio win, the contrada and its members view themselves as being reborn, with the members of the *comparsa* expected to display these items as they tour throughout the city. In more of an American corporate mode, the Goose may have distributed these modern pacifiers to the crowd at large, given that teens now sport them as temporary status symbols. I see no baby bottles as of yet.

As Alice Logan explains, a Palio win is interpreted as the birth of a baby, expressed with the phrase *È nato un cittino* (A little one is born).[92] In this case the contrada life cycle begins with its symbolic rebirth following a victory. This contrasts with the contrada that is unfortunate enough to earn the longest dry spell, without a win—the *nonna*. Logically, the longer the dry spell, the more meaningful the victory when the *nonna* finally pulls off a win. Consequently, "to win is to live; to lose brings the contrada closer to death."[93] As I've mentioned, the status of *nonna* currently goes to the She-Wolf, which nearly pulled off a win tonight but only managed a rather hair-raising third-place finish. The She-Wolf's dry spell continues, now at twenty-four years and counting. They have not secured a win since July 2, 1989.

Soon thereafter, a rather loud and giggly group of young women moves past our spot but not before one of them says something about tourists, pointing to us. It appears that they are trying to strike up a conversation with our students, who are clearly struggling with their novice Italian skills. I boldly step in and happily inform them of our eight-week stay along Via di Fontebranda. In this case, I quickly learn that the gregarious lady making contact speaks decent English, as her friend has just indicated. I get measurably excited at this and start explaining more about why we are there. It is rare to find someone who is comfortable speaking English, with the possible exception of the young Panthers I met. The young woman becomes very friendly and talkative—giddy, in fact. She is clearly still on a high from the win.

Going quickly into interview mode, I ask her if she expected Guess to win. She immediately confirms, "No, no, not at all. This is just amazing," she gestures around her. If somebody of stature in the contrada thought the Goose had a chance of winning, it was certainly not the everyday Ocaioli on the street. They had extracted a so-so horse and been dealt an unfavorable starting position for the race. Indeed, this contrada was taken off guard tonight. In the face of stunned surprise, however, I must say that the Ocaioli ramped up into celebration mode quite impressively.

The *Drappellone* Returns to the Goose

I eventually spy some incoming activity up the hill. I grin and nonchalantly announce to our small group, "The *palio's* back." After touring parts of Siena, its keepers are walking the vertical piece of art back toward the chapel, and we turn our attention to the minor commotion of viewers awaiting the *drappellone's* arrival home. After allowing for some photos in the street, the *drappellone's* keepers lower it horizontally and guide it sideways through the chapel doors: It has come home for the night. A small gathering follows the procession into the chapel, and we tastefully wait a little while to allow the Ocaioli to savor their prize. Soon, however, the crowd thins, and this time all five of us enter. I proudly point out the chapel's fantastic artwork and colorful ceiling to the students. I enjoy their gaping expressions of amazement. Linda and I take turns showing them the chapel's interior. The *drappellone* assumes its final resting place for the night, perched on a stand to one side of the altar. People are forming a rather orderly queue so that family members can take photos standing next to the icon.

There is more to the *drappellone* than just the actual cloth banner. Attached to its pole is quite the festive collection of artifacts, each with its own purpose and eventual fate. Somehow attached securely (we hope) to the pole above the banner is a silver platter that belongs to the city of Siena. Known as the *piatto* (plate)—no fancy name here—this one will eventually be deployed during a dinner organized by the winning contrada. Traditionally, a risotto dish is served on the plate at the January event, known as—you guessed it—the *Cena del Piatto* (Dinner of the Plate). The plate is later returned to the city. Tonight the plate is still on display with the *drappellone*, and black and white ribbons are suspended from the plate. They will eventually be removed and given as a token of appreciation to the *mangini*, the two lieutenants chosen to assist the contrada captain. Holding up this whole display is the pole itself, which is likewise honored by its own dinner. Known as the *asta*, the pole is presented to the contrada captain at this particular celebratory dinner, after which it likely becomes a permanent memento at the captain's home.[94]

One student is particularly eager to be photographed with the *drappellone* and its full contingent of icons. I am not sure about making such a brazen move, once again displaying my own reserved tendencies. I then comment, "You may have noticed that Linda and I have very different comfort levels in such situations," to which he replies, "Yeah, I have noticed that," grinning back. In the end these things are judgment calls. As long as one is respectful of the locals and aware of the culture, there is likely no right answer. Once again I am concerned about going too far. Sometimes my confidence does win out. I grab the student's smartphone and tell him, "Now's the time. Go, go!" He steps to the side of the precious piece of art, and I quickly snap the photo as probably twenty people linger patiently nearby. I take only one photo because I see that it is exposed enough to prove he was there. That's good enough.

The student then expresses his own wonder at being in the chapel tonight, in the midst of this victory. "This is just surreal," he muses. "I can't believe I'm actually here." Then he lists off all the contrada chapels he has seen during our time in Siena, in disbelief that this is number four. I am happy to see his enthusiasm, clearly having recognized the social magnitude of the centuries-old Palio-contrada system. Then he stuns me by saying, "I wonder if I can buy a *fazzoletto* tonight." I respond with a curious "Why?" I discover that he merely wants to wear one tonight as part of the celebration, to feel a greater part of the contrada. He seems deflated when he hears that the contrada office is likely closed and that a silk *fazzoletto* costs fifty euros.

However, I am still wearing the cheap knockoff around my neck. As he prepares for more photo ops with our group, I take mine off and shove it over his head. He acknowledges with a look of appreciation and then jumps up for a photo. We find him still wearing it for some additional group photos out on the street.

With the unprecedented events of the day behind us and the Ocaioli buzz subsiding, we collectively recognize our own exhaustion setting in, especially those who persevered in the Campo earlier today. It is now well past one in the morning, although one wouldn't know it on these streets. A contrada never sleeps after a victory. In between yawns, the wheels are already turning in my head. It is not too soon to start planning for next year. *More of our students and faculty have to see this extraordinary event and its aftermath if the fates allow*, I think. Tonight, capping a two-month journey, we have played witness to a veritable outdoor clinic in community spirit, deep attachment to place, and engaged street life that no classroom instruction could possibly convey.

Ceramic Shop Goodbyes

Our exit strategy from Siena would not be complete without one last stop to see some of our favored local entrepreneurs. With a Goose *fazzoletto* draped appropriately outside the doorway, we find Viola and Riccardo's shop wide open on the day after the Palio. As predicted, Linda bolts into the place, all inhibitions gone to the wind. My own inhibitions have admittedly taken a measurable dive as well. If there had been any other shoppers prior to our entrance, they have quietly slinked away. Fresh off the Palio win, Linda exclaims, "Go Goose, go Goose!" with fists raised, punching the air. She is having fun, which I now admire more than ever. As one might expect, Viola and Riccardo acknowledge her enthusiasm with smiles and expressions of reserved amusement. While they are certainly supportive of their home contrada, they are not what some might call superfans.

Following one of our last classes a day later, I can't resist one final, unplanned visit of my own. I give Viola a round of thank-yous and a hug. Even then, she continues to introduce me to one of her friends in the shop. I will miss even this level of community engagement, knowing I will not see Viola and Riccardo for at least another year, if not longer. Too bad the Senesi speak another language. The language barrier is, by far, the most significant and sometimes frustrating obstacle to communicating more deeply with community members. The students have expressed similar sentiments. Still, that does not seem to stop people, including us, from trying to communicate.

In my barely improved Italian I make a point to thank Viola for her continued patience with my limited language skills. Of course, she responds graciously by saying how she also enjoyed talking with me. Her sincerity convinces me that she is actually telling the truth. As a final token of kindness, she rummages around to find a couple of copies of *La Nazione* (*The Nation*), the most prominent of the local daily newspapers. On the day after a Palio win, the paper includes a color poster of the winner—the horse and jockey pair at some point on their race toward victory. Viola soon finds two color posters of Guess and Tittia battling it out with the She-Wolf, and she presents them to me. Although free of charge from the local newspaper, these are amazing gifts, and I can already imagine them framed at home and in my office.

Postscript

Following his July 2 victory for the Goose atop Guess, jockey Giovanni Atzeni (nicknamed Tittia in Siena) went on to race for the Wave in August 2013, riding Morosita Prima, and won, likely to the Tower's chagrin once again. This latest win marked the twentieth Palio race for Atzeni and his fourth victory (the first three for the Goose). Only one other jockey has won both the July and August Palio races in the same year since the start of the twenty-first century. That other jockey was none other than Trecciolino, winning for Rodi's Caterpillar in July 2005 and for the Tower that August—both times atop Berio.

After another diligent year of planning, our second cohort of students successfully completed a six-week program in Siena, culminating with the July 2014 edition of the Palio. Some of us made wonderful new friends in the Panther contrada and elsewhere, while our rock star pair of Rodi and Castagno performed their same educational magic. Linda and I visited Viola and Riccardo rather often, improving our Italian in the process. We even experienced the pre-Palio dinner, either with the Panther or Caterpillar contrada, depending on which the students chose. This was the very *Cena della Prova Generale* that we had shied away from the year before.

GOOSE CHASE

When it came to the Palio race, the Goose was not running this time, which explained the relatively peaceful Via di Fontebranda throughout our stay. The Panther extracted a strong horse (Indianos, coincidentally run by She-Wolf the year before) and held the number-two position for the race. Led by the veteran jockey Andrea Mari (Brio)—who had fallen off Indianos in sight of the finish line a year earlier—the race was the Panther's to lose. Alas, a victory for the Panther was not to be. The Dragon ultimately played the role of the underdog, just like the Goose had a year earlier, and pulled off an unexpected win—its first since 2001—riding a horse named Oppio. We were all happy for them, enjoying their joyful tears of celebration at Provenzano. As for Dario Castagno's Caterpillar, they never stood a chance with a novice horse in a poor starting position.

Though a dispiriting loss for those of us favoring either contrada, our academic program celebrated another type of victory—summed up in two words: group flight.

PART IV

CONVERSATIONS

❊ CHAPTER 15 ❊

Midnight Contrada Run

S OMEHOW MY PERSISTENT RECRUITING EFFORTS HAVE REWARDED US WITH A third cohort of students in as many years to experience the Gothic City. Let's just admit that I can't stay away from Siena for any great length of time. Nor have I heard any protest from globe-trotting Linda, also eager to set foot here once again. We now find ourselves in late June 2015 with the days of the Palio knocking on our door. Following two consecutive years of residence among the people of Fontebranda, the landlord gods have placed us this time on the main street of the She-Wolf, along the steep Via Vallerozzi. Our host contrada retains its designation as the *nonna*—a status that will remain unchanged for the race only days away; the Orange and Black is not running in this one. What has apparently changed, however, is my newfound confidence in initiating conversations with the locals, at least a notch or two above that of previous years. Aside from our unwavering dedication to our students, I also claim a rather personal goal for this summer—namely, to embrace further opportunities to engage with the Senesi. Of course, the real challenge comes with the elevated expectation that I can do so with minimal embarrassment and without memorable instances of awkwardness and humiliation.

With that goal in mind during one muggy afternoon between classes, I decide to take a stroll up into Panther territory with the secret hope of finding someone I know hanging around. Such a thought could easily be interpreted as self-flattering, given that I now know a grand total of probably ten Panterini out of some 1,200 or so. My chances of finding someone who recognizes me, consequently, are admittedly rather slim. Another, more pressing goal, however, is to determine when the società will be open to purchase our dinner tickets for the *cena della prova generale*, the dinner of the final evening trial. On the first goal, probabilities are playing out as I arrive, in that really nobody is hanging around at Società Due Porte. Worse yet, the place is all but deserted now in the blazing heat of late afternoon. The doors are wide open, however, an impressive sign of a true community hub. Just inside the foyer I discover a large bank of poster-sized sign-up sheets for various dinners, accompanied with a plethora of handwritten and typed announcements about upcoming events. *I still feel like an imposter*, I think, as nobody will know me from Adam (well, they might recognize Adam first). There aren't even any Panthers to say hello to and ask for information about the big dinner.

My nerves finally settle, and I zoom in to inspect the posters. I ultimately determine that the larger posters are serving as sign-up sheets for the bleachers, likely for the Panther kids and perhaps for adults as well. The cost, to my surprise, is ninety euros for the Panther bleachers, though I cannot ascertain whether this is for the Palio itself or for various trials. I then consciously remind myself, as I often neglect to do, that I am accompanied by my smartphone, and I capture the posters digitally for later scrutiny.

I then find two rather plain announcements about the *cena*, thereby piquing my curiosity. Actually, one of the posters is flopping over itself, having lost its top magnet. Being the problem solver that I am, I look around for any evidence of surveillance in a paranoid sort of way. I then find another magnet holding up a nearby poster and quickly shift it to hold up the failing sign. Success. Were I actor Ben Stiller, I may have inadvertently burned down the place or attracted the Carabinieri. But alas, this is reality, and simply nobody is around to care.

In any case, it turns out I have just taken my last phone photo, for no other reason than the battery has promptly died with no apparent warning. Why did I not receive the standard memo that the battery was running low, first at 20 percent, then 10 percent, then finally with a few desperate, last-minute warnings? Regardless, it appears that the *cena* tickets will be on sale starting Sunday night, June 28, for the next few nights, from 9:30–11:30 p.m. *Okay, I'll need to plan on returning here around ten*, I calculate, emitting a little chuckle at the times. I fondly recall a similar process last year when we finally discovered how these ticket purchases really work (cue the harp music and flashback ripples).

Elusive Contrada Dinner Tickets

Early in our second program last summer, I asked a Panther acquaintance how to acquire tickets for the *cena*. She originally suggested that she could get them for me, and so I was appreciative and waited patiently for some time. Eventually I called her a couple of times to see about progress on the tickets, but it was unclear how things would unfold. And, at any rate, how much would the tickets cost, and when and how was I supposed to pay her for them? I received no straight answer on either question. Finally she informed me that I could simply arrive at the società around eleven in the evening a few days in advance to purchase them, to which my jaw dropped once again. *Did I hear that correctly—eleven o'clock at night?* Wasn't there an office or something that I could visit? No, it turned out, not like the Goose. Don't expect standardization around here. I was just to show up around that time, and the tickets would magically be for sale. I had this rather startling approach confirmed by Dario, who told my colleague, John and I that the Caterpillar would be selling their own dinner tickets at around the same time. In fact, Dario assured us personally that he would be under the tent on the back patio of Società L'alba helping to sell tickets. Acting like it was no big deal, he instructed us to simply walk through the società and find him. Right.

Still unsure and a bit uncomfortable with the premise of waltzing into two contrada headquarters on one night without an escort, I asked John if he wanted to join me. We would need to visit both the Panther and Caterpillar to acquire *cena* tickets, as the class had decided to split up for the festive pre-Palio event. Given his persistent enthusiasm about the contrade, I presumed correctly that John would eat it up. After our initial discussion, I let out a sigh and probably a slight chuckle as I threw up my hands and thought, *Why not? Let's do this.* We consequently planned for what I quickly dubbed our *midnight contrada run* for the night of June 29, the first of the days of the Palio.

We met near John's apartment at ten thirty and quickly questioned one another, "Are you ready to do this?" Without hesitation, we set off first for the Caterpillar. It's not every lifetime when one undertakes such a quest. Our strategy was to visit Dario's home turf before doubling back past the Campo and up to the headquarters of the Panther. We were on a mission and enjoying yet another adventure. "Are you sure Dario is going to be around?" John asked as we hustled along, admittedly a bit suspicious of Dario's promise

MIDNIGHT CONTRADA RUN

to be instantly available. I reminded him, "Well, he said just to walk through to the back gardens and find him near the tent where they're selling tickets. We'll just give it a shot." We were about to crash not just one party, but two.

Arriving on Via del Comune near the società, we were met with a breathtaking view down the steep thoroughfare, with Caterpillar sconces lit at full wattage. Photo op. Their street was dressed for success, as they say, with an unwritten hopefulness that this could be the Caterpillar's year. Then inside we went, recalling our somewhat-recent museum visit. This time, however, we enjoyed no luxury of an escort as we made our way through the indoor maze, and at night the wall-sized contrada photos and trophies provided a living-room-type aura. Occasional contradaioli came and went, saying *ciao* to friends or moving quickly on a mission of their own. We found our way to the back patio and discovered a dinner already well under way. Our perch on the back stairs provided an award-winning view of the dinner sprawled out below on the lawn, awash with Brucaioli.

Moving off to the right, we searched for the mysterious tent where Dario should be perched. *Well, there he is!* Somewhat to our astonishment, Dario was precisely where he claimed he would be. Relaxing our collective nerves and shoulders, we made a beeline for him, taking comfort that our presence was legitimate because we actually knew someone here. To our delight, he even recognized us while mingling with his counterparts around the tent in a rather informal fashion. Relieving any lingering doubts, they were indeed selling tickets under the tent—outside with cash box and dinner floor plans, the whole works. After a few pleasantries he explained in Italian to his colleague that we were requesting tickets for the *cena*, and he confirmed how many we needed. I'd learned not to attempt a lot of small talk with Dario, as it would be too easy to become one of the annoying tourists that he writes about so humorously. And at this point we knew who he was and arguably should have moved past our original starstruck sentiments toward this prolific author of Tuscan culture. Well, maybe not entirely. Having completed our transaction, we recovered in the street again and congratulated ourselves on succeeding with phase 1 of our mission. "This is just a riot," one of us concluded as we exchanged laughs about how this all works. "Who else on the planet would ever know how to do this?" In any case, we kept an eye on the time, which was rapidly approaching midnight. How late did these people sell tickets? No matter; it was time to head up to Panther territory.

Talking up a storm as we hiked, we rapidly shared our own perspectives of the class cohort and their collective progress. How were the students doing, and how might we want to plan the next few days? Despite the time of night, the Campo was buzzing as we weaseled around clusters of people near Cavallino Bianco and past the judges' stand at the Campo entrance. The Panther contrada fountain was buzzing already, and we shared a grin as we watched contradaioli hanging around their favored community landmark—still with children and strollers at this time of night!

The Panther contrada's Via San Quirico is not only hidden but also uncharacteristically narrow for a contrada main street. On this night the street was packed and buzzing, with their designated steed, Indianos, perched in his stable at the top of the hill. The lower street entrance we entered was the only option, as the top of the street had been blocked off to protect access to the stable. We were, in fact, two of the few people here who were not sporting the requisite *fazzoletto* colors.

On final approach to Società Due Porte, we attracted a few curious stares, as one might expect, as we maneuvered carefully around Panthers of all ages simply enjoying each other's company under their own blue-and-red sconces and banners. Peoples' stares were more inquisitive rather than unwelcoming, however—a subtle difference that I was beginning to appreciate. They simply were conducting spot checks to see if they knew us or should say *ciao* before returning to their previous conversations—not unlike the familiar practice in any American neighborhood or small town where one enters a local restaurant to find nearly everyone screening the newcomer to see who is joining them.

"Should we just walk in?" I asked John sheepishly as we approached the società's open doors. "I don't see any table out here for tickets. Do you think they're inside?" To presume that two different contrade would employ the same approach to sell tickets was probably overreaching. Not being too sure, John and I just stood there while he insisted on continuing our personal review of our program to date. To his credit, John becomes fully engaged in conversations like this when the students are concerned, accompanied with arms excitedly waving up and down while pondering future planning strategies. "I wonder if" is a favorite beginning of his thoughts, in this case wondering if he could organize a student expedition next year along the Via

MIDNIGHT CONTRADA RUN

Francigena. In the meantime, my mind was distracted with my own burning question of what to do right now with the Panther.

Just as I was beginning to gain more comfort with this veritable stall tactic, my face instantly lit up as a magical sight materialized in front of us. My new Panther friend, Carmina, had somehow spied me through the lingering crowd and emerged through the società entry to greet us! The standard Italian greeting kiss followed—*Right cheek then left cheek*, I had memorized, from my own viewing perspective. Still puzzled at her sudden presence, the important thing was that she was actually here. Quickly she ushered us inside, with both of us thrilled to have a personal escort.

We didn't go far, and before we could fully comprehend what was happening, she pulled us into a small room crowded with Panterini. Immediately in front of us was a lengthy table with four older, distinguished gentlemen sitting behind it. Two of them were somewhat intimidating with their determined, businesslike expressions. Was this their idea of having fun? I gaped at what was draped over the table, a full-length seating chart—a veritable map—of the future *cena*, looking to me like a standard formation in a college marching band, complete with drumline in the center. Numerous parallel rows of tables led off to each side. The whole ensemble of tables was oriented at an angle to the stage, reminding me of jet plane wings. *Holy cow*, I thought, absorbing the massive scheme in front of me with the four men trying valiantly to manage it all. While I struggled to mentally assemble some Italian words for this inevitable encounter, Carmina quickly barged through and explained to them in Italian why in the world we were here and what we wanted. While eternally grateful, part of me felt that she was taking the challenge out of this, but I much preferred being relieved rather than being forced to repeat my standard awkwardness. With haste they mapped out some territory along one of the table wings, marked our seats, and handed her the tickets.

Then it was time to pay, so I needed to communicate on my own. I confirmed the cost of tickets and translated for John, who still knew virtually no Italian at this point. The cost per ticket was forty-five euros, slightly less for kids. He happened to have his entire family here in Siena for his debut teaching appearance, which of course meant that any per-person cost would usually be multiplied by four. Naturally, he balked slightly at this unplanned investment. "John, now is the time to decide. Are you going to do this?" I asked with firmness, as we probably had five more seconds to decide and close the deal. His indecision turned into resolve, and he confirmed, "I'm in," and presented his cash. Just like that, the tickets were sold. We would actually attend the coveted *cena della prova generale*, something we had bypassed our first year due to lack of knowledge and too much personal discomfort. We sang our praises to Carmina, who had just saved us, after which she quickly disappeared to elsewhere in Panther-land. We emerged back outside and slinked down Via San Quirico to take stock of our midnight contrada run. Two for two. We clearly would not forget this night anytime soon. This was life in Siena around midnight during the days of the Palio.

Return to Società Due Porte

I finish reflecting on last year's adventure; the time has finally arrived for me to seek those precious *cena* tickets once again. Although John has joined us for his second year, he is not available to share the adventure with me on this night. Still, I am more confident that I can undertake the ticket purchase on my own. The Caterpillar isn't running for the second time in three years—not their finest, nor most active, hours as of late. Our full cohort will therefore attend the *cena* with the Panther.

Now several hours after enjoying a home-cooked meal with Linda, I bid her farewell as if prepping for a commute to work. I still feel a bit silly as I venture out into the main street of the She-Wolf as the time approaches ten o'clock. At least I know the drill now, and it's not exactly rocket science: just show up on the first night of sales at the società with a reasonable arrival around ten. The intel I gained from the posters a few days earlier will further inform my plans. Following the proverbial cha-ching, I can then easily return to home base within an hour and enjoy a good night's sleep.

I arrive once again on Via San Quirico with sconces blazing. A few Panthers are lingering in the street outside Società Due Porte. There are no ticket lines in sight. My wimpy, American-style eleven-o'clock bedtime may be a reasonable goal after all. Someone is starting to set up tables in the street to sell red-and-blue "68" T-shirts for the kids. Each contrada has a special number, and this is the Panther's. Not feeling that I need to ask for permission to enter, I march into the società and aim for the infamous ticket room. The door is closed tonight, I notice, and only a few people are congregating here. I second-guess myself and think that maybe the tickets are for sale deeper within the società this time. *Never presume anything*—like a young Luke Skywalker, I have learned well. Just when you think you know how things work around here, they change it up to keep you on your toes.

Now with a bewildered look on my face, I start walking boldly up the stairs toward the bar area. Then a voice behind me says something muddled in Italian about the *cena*, perhaps directed at me. From what I quickly gather, a kindly looking, bald gentleman is asking me if I am here to purchase dinner tickets. Upon my reply, he gestures me back to the room I had pegged to start with. The door opens for a moment, and I peek inside to see the same four gentlemen (I think) that were there a year ago. Had they ever left that room? What had their lives been like during the past 364 days? Then suddenly a young couple exits, and the door closes again without anyone else being invited to enter. The bald gentleman is waiting and strikes up occasional conversations with passersby coming in and out of the società. I try not to look like an imposter, standing nonchalantly propped against the wall like I know what I'm doing.

Another younger couple beside me is clearly upbeat and energetic and also waiting for tickets. I figure, *What the heck, let's talk to these guys. I haven't made any new friends yet all month.* The jovial fellow next to me is now shaking hands like a politician as other men come and go—three, four, five greetings within two minutes or so. His girlfriend is smiling wildly as well, not unlike a dutiful politician's wife, taking in the scene as I am. This is, I imagine, simply a snapshot of typical behavior in the contrada. He is a Panther, and he clearly knows many of his counterparts, which should come as no monumental surprise. Still, it's fun to see people having a good time greeting each other. I can't help but conclude that he's no outsider like someone else standing here. Without thinking much, I decide to interrupt him and take the plunge, probably with bad timing, but what else is new? Just do it.

I interrupt in broken Italian, "Are you waiting for tickets to the dinner?"

"Yes, for the *cena della prova generale*." Someone else passes by on his way out of the società and shakes hands with the jovial fellow.

"Okay, great. I am in Siena with a group of students. Are you a Panther?"

He is smiling and remains jovial, not minding me interrupting him. "Yes, I am a Panther, and this is my girlfriend, Sofia. I am Carlo." At this point Sofia introduces herself with a wide smile, and I appreciate that they are even paying attention to me. In this regard I have also learned to have low expectations and hope for the best.

I continue with another basic question. "Are you from Siena?"

"Um ... yes, sort of." He responds in Italian and smiles a bit. "Yes, I am," he says more decisively, "from about two miles away. Sofia is from ... how do you say ... the countryside—a small town outside Siena. Where are you from?" Now we are in full conversation mode.

"The United States. I was here last year for the dinner," I say, trying to make it clear that this is not my first attempt to join a Panther event. Then I leave them alone for a bit as other people interrupt. Someone else exits the ticket room, and the door closes again.

Carlo then tries to relate to something familiar: "I like American football. The Patriots are my favorite." It takes a few tries for me to understand "Patriots," but eventually my internal lightbulb goes off, and it dawns on me what he is saying.

"Oh, the New England Patriots, that's great! I am actually from New England myself, from Connecticut." I'm just happy we've found something in common. Sometimes it's those small victories that matter most.

Then the bald gentleman gestures to the door as someone else exits. When had he entered? I hadn't seen him go in, and the line isn't any shorter. A good ten minutes have passed since my arrival. It's getting busier now and a bit more congested near the entry. We all are forced to talk more loudly over the increasing noise. The bar area inside is ramping up as well, and younger men are gathering and laughing.

The bald man gets my attention and points to the door, indicating a lined sheet of paper taped to it. Only half-consciously had I noticed that names were being crossed off the list as people left the ticket room. *Oh no.* "You need to sign up here for the waiting list," explains the bald man with his cheery disposition. I finally comprehend this after some effort, and I immediately feel deflated because of misunderstanding a key process once again. *There's a sign-up sheet, and I've been hanging out here for how long?* Then a mild crisis kicks in as I further come to realize that I don't have a pen. And, of course, there isn't one provided. In good nature I ask Carlo and Sofia if they have a pen. Determined, she rustles through one of the few purses in the Western world that does not include a writing implement. The bald

MIDNIGHT CONTRADA RUN

gentleman indicates that he does not have one either. We all seem to look around into thin air hoping one will materialize.

"You should go up to the bar; they have pens there," Carlo says, which I quickly suspect is not the best idea. I have never approached anyone at a società bar. None of these folks standing around me volunteer to go either. Why do *I* have to go? Aren't I the guest—the new guy? And why aren't they signing up? Whatever. I'm done being concerned. I have actually practiced the phrase "I need a pen" quite often at home, it being one of the first Italian sentences I put together on my own.

I take off confidently, gently weaving my way through a wall of young men forming a barrier near the bar. It would probably seem to anyone watching that I actually know where I'm going, and this is likely why no one is really paying attention to me. It's noisy with laughter, and someone's radio is playing. The inside flooring is not carpeted, so the noise echoes everywhere like a bar scene. Somehow I move to the left near the cash register and get the guy's attention quickly: "I need a pen please, for Carlo," I say in Italian, thinking that dropping an Italian name might confirm that I am just a delivery guy and that I'm not going to run off with his pen. "Sure," he replies and hands me one. That was easy! My short, anticlimactic quest complete, I proudly stomp off to find Carlo and produce the prize. Then I write my full name on the next line below two others that have since been added. The bald gentleman—his name is Paolo—needs the pen, so I hand it over. Soon thereafter I make my way back to the bar to return it.

Then the door opens again, and Paolo finally gestures to me that I should go in. *It's go time.* So in I march, ready to confront the front line. Someone else is still talking inside, however, and a larger gentleman gently nudges me to wait outside—just as a parent may have done to a ten-year-old child. Out I march as he guides me out the door. *Okay, whatever. I was too early, I guess, but I'm just being led around. Not my fault*, I think. In this way I am unceremoniously extracted from the room. And I got so close!

I turn to Carlo after the confusion. "This reminds me of a doctor's office," I state in Italian, to which he agrees and laughs. *Where is Carmina when I need her to show up?* I think, chuckling to myself. This doctor's-office waiting thing isn't going so well.

Then my turn finally comes. No more false starts, please. In I go, scooting around someone else, and I sit down in the third chair to the left for lack of a better idea. The dinner floor plan is sprawled out on the table like last year, so at least some of this is familiar. The door closes. Time to do business.

"Hello." I smile to man number three, and the others start paying attention. "I would like nine adult tickets please." They confirm the number and start muttering over the plan. I see that not many seats are taken; they have only started to fill in the center seats near the stage. I decide that I'm going to be confident and ask for what I really want. "If possible, could I have our seats closer to the center, near the stage?" After a quick consult, they agree, and one gestures with the lone pencil to the next available seats on the table that leads directly to the stage. *Wow, that's close*, I think, *and they don't seem to care if I'm a guest or a contrada member. They haven't asked.* The one with authority to deploy the pencil indicates nine seats on the map. Tickets are prepared and handed to me.

"Thanks greatly," I say while handing over the confirmed cash total. I say my good nights, and out I go. *Don't waste time*, I keep telling myself. *Be confident and move quickly. Don't try to small-talk with these guys, as they have business to do. And more importantly, I just landed front-row tickets to the granddaddy of all dinners!*

Paolo is next to see the "doctors," it seems. We all stand together for a short time, allowing me to say good-bye to all three of them and to somehow say hopefully that we will all see each other at this dinner. I want to recover a bit from my foibles with the language, so I open up a bit and indicate my frustration. "It's been a challenge for me to speak decent Italian," I say, shaking my head a bit in frustration. They all reply that I am doing a fine job, which I really appreciate. Rather than embarrass myself by hanging around too long and groveling further for more attention, I wish to exit gracefully. I'm done; time to go. Carlo is great, though; I've really enjoyed my time with him tonight and determine that I may have found a new friend if I can keep track of him somehow.

CHAPTER 16

Panthers

THE LONG-ANTICIPATED EVENING HAS FINALLY ARRIVED: PALIO EVE, ON JULY 1. As it turns out, the hearts and minds of this year's group have apparently been won over by the Panterini. It didn't take much convincing on my part to decide to attend the *cena* in Panther territory. If our students are any example, forging temporary loyalties can result from rather brief encounters. Their collective support for the Panther required little more than an impressionable, second-annual dinner with our twentysomething Panther acquaintances to sway our cohort toward the blue and red. Even our youngest student indicated that she was "switching loyalties" to the Panther from her original intent to follow the Shell. Following that dinner we enjoyed the added bonus of being treated at their favorite *gelateria* near the Campo.

Only during the past week have I learned the extent to which our students view that event as memorable. Some have already been asking about obtaining Panther *fazzoletti* and claiming to have become Panther fans for the impending Palio. One can never predict such things. I suppose that the natural inclination for humans is to support those we know best. My colleague Helen, joining the Siena program for the first time, said at one point, "I thought you'd all be supporting the Goose this year, after your prior adventures." Laughing, I replied only half-jokingly, "We're Americans, so our loyalties are fickle around here."

What of the Goose, our former victorious neighborhood? In fact, the Ocaioli have welcomed us into their territory as well. Within the last week alone, we have enjoyed two unprecedented dinners with the Green and Red of Fontebranda, both setting new records for our ongoing academic program—namely, our first meal inside a *società* and our first outdoor contrada meal prior to the *prova generale*. I had asked the Goose's museum curator, Roberto, to arrange a tour for us, and he pleasantly surprised me with a friendly e-mail more than a month ago: "After you see the museum, would you like to have dinner with the contrada at the società?" If that weren't enough, he continued, "You could join us for our dinner on June 29 at Fontebranda as well." For my part, there was no decision to be made. We had just been invited to two additional contrada events, and I couldn't wait to spill the news to our group. As we laughed it up outside Fontebranda a few nights ago, I inwardly smiled with some satisfaction at having moved beyond my initial forays into Goose territory two years earlier.

It is also wise to keep in mind that *more* is not necessarily *better*. How many Goose dinners would we attend before the novelty would wear off? As for our gracious stewards of Santa Caterina, it may be best to quit while we're ahead. "Let's see," I contemplated with the students one afternoon. "The Caterpillar is not running, we've spent time with the Goose, and there is no other contrada that we feel comfortable with at this point." So, with logical heads prevailing, to the Panther we would go for the *cena della prova generale*.

With some rather blunt prompting from us, our students have planned for this specific event since packing for the trip. "You need to pack some decent clothes," we instructed during our student orientation. "Guys, you don't need to wear ties or sport coats, but you should look respectable with button-down collared shirts, nice pants, and decent shoes." The women weren't getting off easily either. This pre-Palio feast is considered to be on par with a New Year's Eve celebration, and many contradaioli dress more formally to indicate the event's significance. I felt not a little satisfaction as two of our male students emerged surprisingly one evening to ask if their dress shirts and pants would be sufficient for the upcoming *cena*. They were not only anticipating this evening's arrival but also actively preparing for it and—gasp—asking for our advice. Who had replaced our student cohort, and what had been done with them?

Tonight we are scheduled to meet at Cavallino Bianco as our staging ground, as we have often done since our arrival. I believe that we have alighted here more often than in previous years, the pizzeria serving as a convenient meeting place to prepare for various outings. Given our location of apartments this year, Cavallino actually served as our first landmark upon arrival, as it was a rather conspicuous place that could easily be found. Some students even hang out here regularly, enjoying the place in the morning hours when most passersby presume the place is closed. Our coffee and tea drinkers have discovered precisely the opposite, with their morning beverages as proof. One student, having fallen ill for a week, was always here by eleven in the morning asking for tea while enjoying the quiet solitude of this normally buzzing pizzeria. He had thus discovered nirvana, otherwise described as the trifecta of hot tea, Internet access, and solitude for his sketching and drawing activities.

The *Prova Generale* ran a bit late tonight, due to three rare false starts caused by the new star jockey, Giovanni Atzeni, or Tittia. We had witnessed his rise to fame two years earlier with a horse named Guess. Earlier tonight he jumped with his horse three times from the *rincorsa* position but stopped short. Nonetheless, the other jockeys reacted, so the *canape* dropped, and off they went. Tittia just waited behind the *mossa* until they trotted around again. Now with the trial completed, we are meeting at nine o'clock at Cavallino to give everyone enough time to change into their best clothing. I arrive to find some of our women—including my colleague Helen and two students—sitting at a downstairs table awaiting the rest of us, impressively dressed for a night out. Our youngest student is beaming in her Sunday finest, so I snap a few photos of the group as our dapper fellows make their own entrance. There is a buzz among the class, focused on the impending *cena*. Some are still wondering if we are going to be late. Starting a meal at nine o'clock here is still a foreign concept to many Americans, let alone meeting here for a possible nine-thirty sit-down time.

For her part, my otherwise upbeat colleague Helen isn't thrilled with the upcoming walk across town to Panther territory, as Siena's challenging terrain and uneven pavement stones have been trying her nerves and tiring her feet for a full month. "Now, I expect that there's going to be much singing, flag waving, fanfare, and other festivities tonight to make this worth it!" she says, egging me on about what she expects in return for the sweltering hike in high humidity. Well, I can promise her the singing of the Panther *inno*, or anthem, but that's about it. "Oh yes," I reply with a smile. "They will be prepared to provide you with entertainment all night long." I say this with just enough sarcasm that I catch a mild grin from Brad, who keenly picks up that I'm not entirely thrilled with the comment. Of the numerous goals and interests of the contrada tonight, entertaining us is certainly not one of them.

It's time to set off. As a class, we depart Cavallino as if preparing for a road trip and bid the friendly pizzeria staff a good night.

Arriving at the Dinner

Upon making our last turn at the end of Via Stalloreggi, we pass under the first and only open arch of Due Porte. The two-arched entry was once part of the town's inner wall prior to expansion, and one of its arches has been bricked up in recent centuries. "Hey, everyone, I can't resist this," I call out to our group. "See these double round arches over the street? This is Due Porte, and it serves now as one of the Panther contrada's more symbolic landmarks here in their neighborhood. This is why they named their società *Due Porte* also." Feigning interest, the students soon eyeball the wall of plants and temporary floodlights further down the street, which is entirely blocked off as I had anticipated. *Friday-night lights*, I imagine. I almost expect an entryway into a lit-up football stadium. We walk up to the edge of human congestion, where hundreds of Panterini are already congregating somewhere near the entrance to the dinner area. We are certainly not late, if still rather hot and sweaty. The African heat, as it's called, has finally descended upon the Senesi, and there is no better time than ten o'clock at night to hold an outdoor event. Tomorrow, the day of the Palio, is expected to be even worse, probably the hottest I have yet experienced.

We linger by a nearby café with a few outdoor tables and umbrellas. On a normal evening the demand for tables likely matches the modest supply of outdoor furniture. Not tonight. Some two hundred people engulf the little café, and some lucky folks have secured seating—likely hours in advance. I joke with Brad, one of our more comical students, "I wonder what the chance would be of getting one of these seats right now," to which he wittingly responds, "Let's put our name in."

I may be the veteran here tonight, but the details of the past can escape me. I second-guess our "assigned" seats, given what transpired in the Goose a few nights ago. We had tickets to the dinner beside Fontebranda but no assigned seats. We actually hung out on the periphery of the dinner area due to our early arrival, eventually becoming more engrossed in personal conversations. Meanwhile the Goose contradaioli trickled in. "Maybe we should just go in and see about seats," Helen wisely suggested. We suddenly turned our attention to the nearly endless rows of tables, which were now filling up quickly. So much for our early arrival. People were swarming in, and we made a beeline for some of the tables. I fell into a mild panic as I figured out why there were lines and names marked across the paper table coverings. Groups had somehow already pre-reserved their blocks of seats, and it was clear that we were running out of possible tables the farther back we went. Now on a mission to avoid sitting on the cobbles, we collectively landed at a freshly set table. We ended up somewhat isolated from the rest of the crowd because we had sat starting from the street-side end of the table, with a large gap beyond us. Although a memorable dinner for everyone, students noted that we felt a bit isolated from the contrada membership.

Now at the Panther, I really hope to avoid the same mistake again. *I know we have assigned seats*, I assure myself, *as I saw those guys mark the tables and hand me the tickets*. What a let-down for the students it would be if my prized stage-side seats came up empty, should someone else grab them first. As we finally funnel into our places, I zip over to where we should be located per the seating chart I had briefly witnessed. Fussing between Panterini already at their places, I find specific numbers written on small red-and-white cards to indicate seats. *Wow, I forgot how organized these people are here*, I think, breathing a sigh of relief. We can simply match our ticket numbers with the individualized place cards. "Okay, I have 134, and Helen has 139. Who has the lowest and highest numbers?" I ask as students arrive in our area. "Who has the lowest-numbered ticket?" I ask, now realizing that I do not know our range of seats. "There are already four of us over here, so we'll need the other five opposite us," I explain. "Dillan, go around and sit over there." Our impromptu game of musical chairs finally allows us to take our places without competition from either end. I spot-check our numbers with those at the seats. We have arrived.

Making New Friends

We have barely sat down and begun to admire the table decor and Panther-themed wine labels when the prerecorded music begins. I privately smile at what's coming. "Time to get up, and you may want to get out your cameras," I instruct everyone. Our two youngest students display looks of surprise, not suspecting they would actually have to participate in a contrada-based activity. At the proper musical cue, the entire dinner population starts to belt out the Panther anthem, or *inno*, to my own delight. Sounding like a lighthearted military march, the melody is catchy and snappy. Although I don't remember all the Italian lyrics, I can still hum along with it. In fact, after recording it on my smartphone last year, I couldn't get the damn thing out of my head for months. Impressively, Panterini young and old can sing their song of solidarity without thinking twice, and they continue through both versuses reverently and respectfully. *As far as contrade go, this one is untypically reserved*, I ponder as I screen the crowd. I find the speaker system cute, with two giant speakers sitting on the ground at the base of the stage, providing somewhat-muffled but recognizable instrumental music to guide the singing. Siena is not a high-tech place, and something about this is rather refreshing.

I decide not to shy away from table conversation tonight but rather find ways to get involved without making a complete fool of myself. I can do that without trying anyway, so why not join in the fun without worrying about it? To that end, I quickly observe two contradaioli sitting next to and across from me. Given their own conversational banter, they are clearly old friends. Before I can introduce myself, I sit back and watch another conversation sparking up from the other side of them. The students are getting acquainted with their antipasti of melon and prosciutto that have just arrived, care of an energetic Panther youth. A middle-aged bald fellow catty-corner from me is beginning to talk with his neighbor, who is actually speaking pretty good English. I can't help but become intrigued. The bald fellow is clearly American and very well spoken and laid back but not afraid to ask some pointed questions. He is wearing a new, unfaded *fazzoletto*, which puzzles me a bit. *Where did he get that?* The bald fellow, Ryan, introduces himself to his neighbor across from me, and we quickly learn that he is from Chicago. I can't help but recall Robert Rodi's chagrin at being seated with other Americans like him during a Caterpillar dinner one night. Franco is our shared dinner companion, more refreshingly of Senese heritage. At some point I jump in and introduce myself to Franco and his friend sitting next to me.

I overhear Ryan say, "This is my family. We flew from Chicago into Zurich and Florence a few hours ago, so we're a bit tired."

LIVING THE PALIO

After waiting somewhat patiently at this news, I jump in and ask, "So, Ryan, I can't help but ask, how did you manage to attend this dinner after arriving into Siena this afternoon?"

"Well, my cousin," he says, pointing across the table, "lives here, and she told me that, since we were flying in today, we might as well attend this dinner tonight. But we are definitely dragging; it's been a long day."

I find it amazing that an American who knows very little about Siena and the contrade has landed here at the *cena della prova generale*! It took me two years just to figure out how to get into this event, let alone understand what it was all about. *Okay, the cousin explains it,* I think logically. *This could be fun tonight—we've got another novice, taking in all this stimuli for the first time.* He was already beside himself when they all rose up and sang the anthem in unison. A bit later, given his next inquiry to Franco and me, it must have dawned on him that this particular dinner event is not a normal occurrence. "So is it pretty easy to get into dinners like this?"

Franco gestures with his hand as if to say "sort of" but doesn't seem quite sure what to say. So it's up to me to carry on. "No," I say smiling, "it can be a challenge to figure out how to attend. It's certainly not intuitive." I chuckle. Then I tell him my story with some humor. "So for our class I had to know where the società, or contrada clubhouse, was located. Then I determined that they would be selling tickets only for a few days in advance, and I had to show up between nine thirty and eleven thirty at night!" We all chuckle. "It's safe to say that there aren't many Americans who can figure this out." I'm trying to convey that he has managed to attend quite a special and spectacular event.

Ryan then starts asking questions about the Palio race. Franco explains in broken English, "The contrade with the best horses tend to attract the better jockeys, and the horses were assigned in a lottery a few days ago."

"So there is no choice in the horse you get? That's curious," Ryan says.

Franco continues, "No, there is no choice, but the jockey is hired by the contrada and typically will make a deal with a contrada that has a better horse, as he wants a better chance to win."

I can see Ryan's wheels turning as he munches on a piece of plain Tuscan bread. Now I'm curious to see how an unwitting American thrown into the Palio-contrada system on this night will mentally absorb all of this. "Okay, so you don't have your own jockeys? Wow, not much loyalty there. Is there betting on the horses?" Ryan asks.

At this I silently cringe a bit and shake my head at him, quietly indicating no. *What is the fascination among Americans with horse betting? It must be a bigger thing than I imagine.* My colleague Helen asked this very question a week ago, suggesting that the very future survival of the Palio itself will in part depend upon allowing this activity. Naturally, I disagreed.

Franco responds thoughtfully after looking at the sky for an answer, "Well, no, not really, not betting in public as one might think of it." It's clear that this American has just asked a simplistic question that deserves a much more complicated answer. Franco gives it a shot. "The captains of the contrade make deals with each other, and there can be payoffs from allies to help them win or to help others win. If it works out and a contrada wins, they return the favor somehow."

Ryan tries to process this rather complex relationship, that of the *partiti*. "So you're saying that someone bribes you and then you pay him back."

I laugh at this elegantly simplistic interpretation. I would never think of it this way, though I can see his point. He's not yet judging but is certainly perplexed. Franco seems unsure of how to answer, and I sympathize. To explain the complexities of the *partiti* on a night like this in broken English is probably expecting a bit much. They will clearly need more wine. The cross-cultural conversation continues while I turn my attention to the students, who are feeling more comfortable with taking photos of the event and of each other. Brad then surprises me yet again with a modest invitation to view his phone's photo gallery, as he has occasionally done throughout the program. His eye for photography and use of the phone camera have been impressive, providing startling and creative images on an otherwise basic smartphone. This time he shows me a panorama of the dinner scene, which is stunning. Then I look beyond the actual scene and notice the moon.

We both look toward the south, above the other wing of dinner tables, to view a full orange moon surrounded by Panther banners and trees all grouped together. The composition of these elements is so perfect as to be ready for framing. Not as hesitant to walk among the Panterini as I once was, I inform Brad of my new plan: "I'm going to visit the end of the stage and see if I can get some decent moon photos." I've brought my new digital SLR camera tonight, so I'm itching to try it out. I bolt up and head for the stage. I'm nearly there when an older yet distinguished gentleman with combed-back gray hair practically grabs me from his seat at the end of the table. He is excitable about something, and I whirl around to see who is getting my attention.

His arms are waving excitedly, and he points to the moon. Aside from his hurried phrases I pick up *la luna* and *la bandiera* several times as he points to my camera. For a change I am quick on the uptake, and in Italian I tell him that's a great idea—without letting on that I already thought of it myself. I am pleased that he is paying attention to me as I mingle within this sea of *fazzoletto*-draped strangers. His friends are watching while this dialogue progresses. On the flip side, I end up making more haste than I had originally intended to get closer to the stage, flags, and moon. He has given me a mission. *Crud*, I think as I fumble with the new camera. *Should I use aperture priority or program mode, and either more or less exposure? What should I focus on?* Feeling some internal pressure to perform with a camera much more intelligent than its owner, I try my best on quick notice and scurry back to display my work.

I kneel down near his chair and show him one of the images with the moon next to the flag, indicating that it's only so-so, perhaps not great. "I have e-mail," he declares. "Can you e-mail the photo to me?"

Now I become more enthusiastic because he is offering to exchange e-mails and seems quite friendly. "Sure, no problem. Um, do you have a pen? I can write my e-mail address for you," I stumble through in broken Italian. I have no sense yet that he knows English, but we're doing okay.

None of his buddies have a pen, so I excuse myself and race back to Helen, whose purse, I imagine, is well supplied. She hands one over; yet another pen shortage solved. *What is it about pens around here?* I return and decide to take charge and use the little numbered place cards scattered around the table, now useless since everyone is more or less seated. They can be converted into veritable business cards. There is just enough room on the back to squeeze in an e-mail address. In later years, my continuing smartphone education would allow me to simply deploy the "Notes" and "Contacts" functions. For now, however, this is as good as it gets.

Upon receiving his e-mail address, I discover that it's a fairly simple account like mine. And this is the way I learn his name. "Matteo," he says, extending his hand.

"Nice to meet you. I'm Tom, a professor with a group of students from the United States," I add, pointing down the table. I make quick introductions with his friends as well. For what it's worth at this point, I have just made a new acquaintance, and we now have something in common to share.

The singing is ramping up again, and the first course is starting to arrive at our table. I bid my farewell and return to home base, somewhat flummoxed at what has just transpired. *That was so cool!* I relate the story like a schoolkid to Helen and Brad while returning her pen. "How do you like *them* apples? I got his number!" I deliver with a chuckle, recalling my original visit to the Panther museum. That visit is what ultimately led to our presence at this dinner.

The Dinner Progresses

As the *primi piatti* (first-course plates) gradually appear in front of us, the crowd is becoming visibly restless. This latent energy somehow magically materializes as the contradaioli start to sing as a unit, clapping to a highly energetic tune that is likely of local derivation and not related at all to "The Song of Verbena." It is highly participatory and seemingly requires dramatic shouting among the participants. Everyone is having a grand time. Occasionally one table of attendees stands up and sits down to the beat, all somehow in unison, and the next table does so in turn. Hands go up, hands go down. *Did they learn this stuff as kids?* Soon—and predictably—all types of dinner implements are being deployed as improvised drums, from glasses and bottles to entire chairs. My eyes gravitate to a giddy fellow who stands up, grabs his cheap wooden chair, and starts banging it open and closed to the beat while walking around the grounds. Our students are once again transfixed, and I can tell at least a few of them want to get involved. Even our group of visitors can at least clap on musical cue. Rather than ending quickly, the song repeats itself, and the contradaioli keep celebrating like Energizer bunnies. It's almost what I might consider to be good physical exercise for those most engaged.

All the while I reflect that these same Panterini weren't half as animated last year. Beyond singing their anthem it was a rather subdued affair, and they even had the Palio's new rock-star jockey Brio paired with a favored horse, Indianos. I wonder if they were too superstitious to carry on with abandon last year, thinking they would jinx their chances. Brio had most recently brought home a victory to the people of Stalloreggi in 2006. To suggest they were angling for a repeat performance is not out of line. This year, in marked contrast, these people are pulling out all the stops. And they appear to adore their jockey, Jonatan Bartoletti, nicknamed Scompiglio, who has won two *Palii* (Italian plural of Palio) and raced in fourteen of them. I am only speculating here, of course. I really have no clue why one year would prove to be so different from the next. Despite landing a mediocre horse in Quintiliano, the jockey is a minor success story with the Palio. The crowd occasionally cheers for him, and he is the subject of many a photo tonight from his admirers.

Likewise, I still covet some photos of the action around us, so I take an opportunity before the salad shows up. I once again grab the camera and excuse myself from headquarters. The students don't seem to miss me much anyway, for which I'm happy because they are conversing with each other and overall soaking in this lively evening. As for me, I am surprisingly more comfortable with moving away from the nest to explore the larger dinner scene. Last year I found myself behaving much more self-consciously, when I was certain that everyone was watching this blond-haired American take touristy photos of their neighborhood event. This year, no one seems to care, though in all probability they likely didn't last year either. Earlier tonight I even walked right up to the jockey and captain before dinner and snapped their photos, just as random Panterini were doing.

My meandering route through far-off dinner tables once again results in a nice surprise. I recognize Carlo and Sofia, whom I met while purchasing the tickets. This is actually my third encounter with them. One night our class was gathered at Cavallino to prepare for a walk to the Goose when they both entered and greeted the pizzeria's manager, Enzo, like they were friends. Then upon noticing each other, Carlo and I waved hello from afar. He and Sofia then joined us for a few minutes, thereby demonstrating to him that the students were not just a figment of my imagination.

Tonight is similar, as little visual effort is required to pick them out of the crowd, sitting as they are at the end of a lengthy table. I get down on one knee as I did with Matteo earlier so I can chat at eye level. Who cares about my pants at this point? This is too much fun, and the pants can be downgraded for airplane duty.

"How are you enjoying the dinner tonight?" Carlo asks in Italian.

"This is unbelievable, the energy and happiness here. People seem to like your jockey," I manage in broken Italian as fast as I can think. It's time for conversation mode, and my tired brain is in overdrive trying to keep up. Someday I'll hopefully run into Carlo when I'm not overtired for a change.

"Sofia is getting used to it also, not being from Siena."

She chimes in for the first time. "So you are interested in history? I enjoy studying medieval history as well. What do you think of Siena?"

I try to pick up important words to comprehend. In response I struggle to think of the last words of "The Song of Verbena," as I have used them a few times already: "The most beautiful of cities! The students are learning a lot about medieval architecture."

I open a new topic. "What was that song you were all singing earlier? It was great!"

Carlo thinks a bit. "I don't really remember, but I think it was an American song from the 1970s that the Panther adapted for ourselves." This is how I translate his response, at any rate.

Given my recent success with Matteo and his moon shots, I am on a natural high and simply ask if Carlo has an e-mail address so that I can keep in touch. He clearly thinks it's a good idea by his positive reaction, and I know the drill now. I find a numbered place card—or pseudo business card—but, of course, no pen. "Hang on, Carlo, I need to get a pen." (Again.) Helen is still back at base, and she knows in advance what I am about to request. I bug her for the pen a second time. I race back to Carlo, as if on a mission, before the next song erupts. We exchange e-mails and generally agree to stay in touch. *Cool!* Friends number two and three from tonight's dinner. I am now collecting Panther business cards in my wallet.

I return to base, and Helen bids us goodnight for what promises to be a sweaty walk home. She is the first casualty of this dinner, which is quickly pushing toward midnight. We Americans are lightweights, I have suggested somewhat facetiously with our students. While I would normally characterize them as night owls, our group has raised the surrender flag at two Goose dinners and other class events that push the limits of the evening. Tonight, I am impressed but not at all surprised that we are once again approaching midnight and that there is absolutely no indication of the Panterini giving in. And hey—this just dawns on me now—the stage party hasn't even summoned the first speakers of the evening. As if on cue, the crowd starts to quiet down. Our collective attention is now turning to their leaders. Thank goodness (yawn).

The first to speak is their *priore*, a heavyset man with a serious disposition the likes of which I would not want to mess with. He has a script and remains glued to it, word for word. Their elected contrada leader is clearly no showman or grandstander. He's not really trying to impress anyone. Meanwhile the jerry-rigged speaker system is trying to survive underneath him, and the distorted sound makes him barely audible. His words are nearly drowning in occasional whines of feedback. A determined assistant on the pavement fusses with the speakers and cables while the *priore* marches through his speech. Franco helps to translate for us, summarizing that the *priore* is proud of the contrada and is happy to have the jockey with us tonight. He expresses his full confidence that Scompiglio will perform his utmost best in tomorrow's big race. That is the hope, at any rate.

Then it's the captain's turn, the one who is elected to take the contrada to "war" during the days of the Palio. He is essentially in charge of the contrada business right now. He manages to make it through about half of his own speech before the speakers and amplifiers just simply fade and die away. Given that his mouth keeps moving, he fails to realize the fatal technological failure. Finally a few brave souls sitting near the stage start to distract him by yelling that they can't hear, to which he humbly stares at the microphone and stops talking while an agitated assistant on the ground vigorously shakes one of the speakers—for lack of any better idea at the moment. Not to be embarrassed by unplanned downtime, the younger contrada males start singing their own version of "The Song of Verbena," providing "intermission" music somewhat humorously until the speaker issue is resolved.

Following a good-to-go signal to the stage, the captain doesn't miss a beat. The singing dies down, and he calmly returns to his originally scheduled program. He then introduces Scompiglio to mild applause, and he rises to talk for a little while. In response to the intensifying roar of the crowd, he indeed promises to do his best tomorrow. No doubt. For some reason his humble antics strike me as something akin to a best man's speech at a wedding. Not long after he sits back down, his stage neighbors quietly relieve him of his duties in the hope that he can catch some sleep before tomorrow's marathon of events. Sometimes additional deal-making, or *partiti*, occurs at this point as well, while the rest of the contrada closes out the dinner. Regardless, Scompiglio will hopefully enjoy a few hours of precious quiet time.

With speeches concluded, the students are suitably impressed with the display of community energy, and the long-forgotten meal is revived once again. Dessert shows up, signaling the beginning of the end of an unforgettable evening. Even some Panterini start to rise and make their slow exit while greeting friends one last time. We are barely awake enough to thoroughly enjoy our scrumptious chocolate cream puffs, which I would easily continue eating if they would just keep appearing magically in front of me. But, alas, they don't.

Rather, I look around and am startled to see Carlo and Sofia walking toward our area. *Wow, a personal visit!* I sense that I can joke around with Carlo, so I open with some humor. "I saw you singing earlier, and I recorded it on my smartphone," I say, referencing the chair-banging song.

With mostly gestures and some Italian, he responds, "Oh, no, that wouldn't be good, very embarrassing." He laughs. "You can delete that."

Getting better with my nonverbal communication, I rub my fingers together to indicate that I will accept cash to keep the video off the Internet, and they laugh hard. I have finally succeeded with what is probably my first joke to Italians, and it wasn't with words. This is likely the last time I will enjoy much of a chance to speak with the Panthers while they are not only immediately available but also in a reasonably cheery mood (both of these variables will in all probability be reversed by tomorrow night). So I turn our attention to the impending race. "So what do you think of your chances tomorrow? Is Quintiliano a decent horse?"

To my surprise Carlo is more upbeat than I might expect. He says, "He is probably in the middle of the pack—not one of the best horses, but not the worst either. He is a novice, of course, so we'll see."

"So he is not a *brenna*?" I refer to the least likely horses to win a Palio.

"Oh, no, no," he laughs. "He's not a *brenna*. He has a chance."

"That's good to know! The contrada didn't seem too happy during the extraction."

"No, we didn't get one of the favored horses—those went to the Shell, Tower, and Goose. Brio is racing for the Tower, and Tittia is racing for the Shell. The good jockeys tend to follow the good horses," he confirms. As two of the most popular and successful jockeys as of late, both Tittia and Brio are competing to become the unofficial King of the Square. Carlo continues, "But we'll see what happens this time, as our adversary, the Eagle, is not running, so they won't be trying to disrupt us on the track."

I have been personally enthusiastic about this fact since the extraction; for once, the Panther will be free of its rival in the Campo. It was disheartening last year when the Panther lost despite having one of its best chances in perhaps decades to bring home the *drappellone*. During slow-motion replays of the start of that race, one can easily see the Panther's jockey, Brio, more determined to beat up the Eagle's jockey than focus on launching his horse. During our seemingly endless analysis of the race's start, my colleague John had reacted with disappointment as Brio lunged for the Eagle jockey. "Oh my, Brio, what are you doing?" John shook his head. "Just race. Don't mess with the Eagle. Just race." The Eagle didn't win, but then neither did the Panther. Sometimes it may be more advantageous to not worry so much about your competitors.

Either way, all bets are off for tomorrow. And betting in the traditional sense isn't condoned here anyway, so I will refrain from further speculation tonight. But I am learning that half the fun of this whole event is trying to untangle all the variables and to speculate about all the possible scenarios. As for Carlo, I promise that I will write and share something about American football. With speeches concluded and dessert consumed, it is time to say our good-byes and leave the Panterini to their own devices. Will my new acquaintances write back? Only time will tell.

CHAPTER 17

From the Bleachers

Sometime back in May, a thought flittered through my mind while I lay awake at two in the morning. *What if there are actually tickets available to see the Palio from the bleachers this time? If so, I wonder how much they might cost.* I ran through my mental contact list based on our previous summer here. Despite our numerous acquaintances, there was only one person I felt comfortable contacting about tickets, given his positive reputation and knowledge of the Palio scene: Dario Castagno. So I e-mailed him on a whim and asked if he happened to know anyone with tickets for the *palchi* (bleachers) and, if so, how much they might cost. I would need two of them, of course, for Linda and me. Not twenty-four hours later I received a startling reply from Dario: "I know someone who has four tickets to the bleachers, in very good seats near the *mossa*. A group canceled, and so he has them available. 400 euro each. Are you interested?" Like an eager child, I could barely wait to share this amazing news with Linda when she arrived home—and to make sure that she wanted in on the deal.

I was in the process of selling some of my model railroad equipment, so I immediately concluded that this would be a guilt-free way to justify such a purchase. As I expected, Linda agreed quite quickly to the scheme, so I replied to Dario that I would take two of the four tickets. Also, I said I would consult with my colleagues, who might appreciate a chance at purchasing tickets themselves. Soon I received word from Helen that she was in. Within twenty-four hours I had secured three tickets to the bleachers near Fonte Gaia, within direct sight of the *mossa*!

The deal went down at the end of our scheduled Caterpillar contrada tour with Dario in June, and we suddenly had three precious tickets that we needed to guard with our lives. Cash could get lost, and credit cards could be canceled if ever stolen—but don't mess with my Palio tickets!

Local Economic Challenges

While paying Dario for the tickets, he hinted somewhat grimly that the tourism scene in Siena has not lived up to expectations this year: "There are still tickets available for the Palio that would not have been available in the past. Usually they would not be available this close to the Palio." Something is still off with the local economy this year, which has been confirmed in bits and pieces throughout our third summer here. This issue was certainly on Dario's mind, as he asked me upon his arrival for our Caterpillar tour, "Have you noticed any changes in Siena this year?"

"Well," I said, "the traffic seems worse than in the past, but it could be my imagination."

He didn't agree that the traffic was worse. Instead, he reflected, "I think the city is dirtier now than it has been. There's trash in the street, and public areas are not cleaned up. There is vegetation growing on the city walls that wasn't there previously. Siena is feeling the real impacts of the bank's financial problems."

More curious, I then asked him about the status of the soccer (football) and basketball teams, and he explained, "The football team is no longer in the top division but is now in the lowest league. I mean, we Senesi were in some ways spoiled; we were used to hearing our name right up there with the larger cities and their football teams: Rome, Milan, Siena. It just didn't make sense that a small city like this would be competitive." I mention the gossip I had heard from other locals that there may be new sponsors on the way, even Coca-Cola or Nokia or something. He chuckled. "They dream about sponsors, but who is going to sponsor a team in Siena, a small town of which few people are aware? No, there are no sponsors on the horizon. And the bank isn't coming back. It's not locally owned anymore. They are not hiring. They are keeping people on until they retire or find other jobs, but they are not planning to hire replacements." With this discussion, reality was starting to sink in with me that certain conditions in Siena may be permanent. Welcome to the new normal.

At our first-ever class appearance for a dinner in Società Trieste with the Goose, I asked our host, Roberto, in between bites of penne pasta, "So does the società still provide assistance to less-fortunate members of the contrada? It seems this purpose of the società was reduced after World War II."

It turned out that Roberto knew better English than he had first let on. "Oh, yes, the contrada assists members who need some help, and it is becoming more important once again. The crisis with the bank in Siena has led to more people out of work, and so the contrada is assisting people who may need some help because of that." A couple of students at our end of the table listened to this conversation and were impressed that such a social safety net existed here.

Even some of our friends here in Siena have felt the economic pinch. One acquaintance had worked in the wine and agricultural industries for a number of years but was recently laid off when the company downscaled. He is currently looking for permanent work (soon after our return home he would find it). And even our ceramic shop friends from the Goose, Viola and Riccardo, told us that tourism is down for some reason, as Dario had indicated earlier.

On my first return visit to the ceramic shop a few weeks ago, I arrived to find Riccardo delighted and surprised to see me after a year away, though clearly a bit dejected. "How are things for you?" I asked enthusiastically. Although I struggled once again with understanding his soft voice, I picked up the essence of his disappointment. Sales were slow for this time of year, and he wasn't stooped over his workstation in the back as he had been doing tirelessly in the past. He gestured that they still had plenty of inventory for sale, so there was little need to create anything else right now. He was mildly pleased that the Goose was running, but he would be content to watch it on TV. Later when Linda found Viola during a walk, Viola indicated that she was perplexed with visitor behaviors as well. People still found their way into their shop, but this year they weren't buying for some reason. Travelers may not be as confident with their spending this year, though it isn't precisely clear as to why.

As Viola wrapped a few purchases of my own, an American family walked in, composed of a middle-aged husband, his wife, and three teenage kids. I paid some modest attention to them as they gravitated naturally to the colorful contrada plates and designs. Eventually I couldn't resist speaking up when Dad compared a Tower contrada plate to the University of Alabama. *Ouch.* I asked, "So where are you from?"

They seemed happy to hear another American's voice. "We're actually from the Chicago area, but she'll be starting at the University of Alabama," the dad said, gesturing to his daughter, "We've been traveling parts of Europe for the past year."

"How long have you been in Siena?"

"We just arrived last night, so we're wandering around and know next to nothing." He chuckled.

"Are you looking for specific types of ceramics?" Viola could hire me as a built-in salesman, perhaps.

"Not really. In fact this is the first shop we stopped in!"

"Cool. Are you aware of what these designs mean?"

"Well, not sure, are they symbols of the local universities?" This was a logical response since he had associated the crimson-colored design of the Tower with Alabama's own scheme, for which I decided to forgive him nearly immediately.

"You might be interested in knowing that each of those designs reflects a different neighborhood in Siena, known as contrade. That's the Tower contrada. There are seventeen of them in Siena that date back to the Middle Ages." I said a few more things about the local geography since he appeared to be fascinated, and he repeated some of it to his wife, who was browsing.

Viola commented quietly in Italian, "You are teaching," with a smile on her face, to which I replied with a smile, "Yes, I'm always teaching." For once I actually felt like the local translator who could serve as a communication bridge between the store owners and the visitors.

This didn't happen often, so I decided to take this newfound confidence for a test drive and introduce my local friends to the inquisitive Americans. "So everything is made right here in this shop," I said as I indicated the workstation in the back. "This is Viola, and her husband is Riccardo. They probably have the best shop here in Siena. The prices are a bit higher, but the designs are more intricate than anywhere." I explained to Viola that I just described this as the best ceramics shop, and she humbly waved away the compliment.

Then I suddenly recalled that it was a trial night—the first *prova* was on tap for this evening. The *tratta* and ensuing extraction had been held earlier today. I asked, "Are you planning to be in town tonight?"

"Oh, yes, we'll be here for a few days, but we're staying outside of town."

"You need to be in Piazza del Campo by seven o'clock tonight. It's one of the trials for the Palio, and you do not want to miss it! Your family will love it. Ten of the contrade are preparing their horses and jockeys for the Palio, and they will be galloping around the square. But you need to be in the Campo by seven, as they will close it off soon after that. You can't get in or out."

"Wow, that sounds fantastic. We'll do that!"

At this point, I explained the layout of the shop. The whole family turned their attention to the products on the shelves, not unlike the proverbial kids in a candy store—or game store, to update the analogy. At this point I made a graceful exit and said goodbye to Riccardo and Viola for a while. Perhaps I helped their sales margin today in a small way, or so I'd like to think.

Settling Into Our Seats

Tonight many Senesi are putting aside their economic concerns and turning attention to *la terra in piazza*. It's Palio night, and the city is buzzing with energy from visitors and locals alike. After assuring three times that I have the precious tickets on my person, Linda and I make the final trek down Banchi di Sopra around five in the afternoon to the Campo. "If we walk through that narrow alley, our seats should be just to the right of the entrance," I say hopefully to Linda. I scoped out the seats and location in advance, so I'm hoping I have enough accurate information this time. I am pleasantly surprised when someone in the alley across from Cavallino Bianco actually asks for our tickets, as they are already screening. With tickets in hand, the fellow quickly inspects them and lets us pass. *This is a good sign*, I think. I'm not even confident that they will believe our ticket numbers or that someone won't already be sitting in our seats. There isn't exactly a centralized box office for this event.

We brush past some other people standing behind the bleachers and emerge through a narrow opening onto the dirt track. From the alley we can already hear the steady hum of early discussions throughout the Campo. Some people are already sitting in their seats, while many seats still remain empty. It appears that we have arrived at a decent time. I look back behind the bleachers and see some decent access to cafés for later, if necessary. I point out this opportunity to Linda, still hoping that our two bottles of water, granola bars, and a few other goodies will hold us until around nine thirty. Now on the track, we start looking for guidance from anyone, anywhere. *Where do we go now, and how do we get to our seats?* I wonder.

As if on cue, one fellow sees us and asks for our tickets. Good. He takes them from us and confidently leads us to our seats. Things are going much too perfectly at this point, so I should know better. As we follow the usher who has our tickets, another fellow races toward Linda from behind. He asks in an elevated voice, "Your tickets, your tickets!" Linda is as confused as I am, and she simply turns to him and yells, "He has them!" For a brief moment I wonder if I need to chase down our host out ahead of us to calm down this guy chasing us from behind. Either we have to hold off this agitated fellow in order to retrieve our tickets, or fellows number one and two here need to have a conversation. Eventually fellow number one, our host, looks back and signals the okay, and fellow number two ends his pursuit. To paraphrase the words of actor Tom Hanks in *Apollo 13*, perhaps we just had our glitch for this mission.

Now at the base of our bleacher section, we turn our attention to our new home for the next few hours. There's Helen! She is already in the last seat of our row. She is always early to events, and this is no exception. I am also relieved to see that our seats are already in the shade, something I had retained just a smidge of uncertainty about despite calculating it days in advance. The past two days have been brutally hot here, and I didn't want to take any chances. At the last minute I had packed sunscreen and hats, just in the off chance that my sun-angle calculations didn't pan out. Sometimes I find that the laws of physics seem to take a unique twist here.

Our host confirms that our seats are in fact side by side, as I was curious from the ticket numbers if we would be sitting behind one another. We climb one by one up to our seats and find that they actually have round metal backs on them, rather than being simple bleacher seats as I had imagined. Luxury! *And there's Dario!* Perched a few seats to the left of us, he is assisting his client family from Australia as they become acclimated to the bleachers as well. The family includes Dad, who is sitting next to me; his wife sitting one row above; and two elementary-aged girls who are doing their best not to fuss around

LIVING THE PALIO

much. Dario says hi to us, but I don't plan to interrupt him, because he is actually gainfully employed right now. He is here until the other bleacher seats fill up, at which point he will make his exit. Apparently the Senese ticket holders tend to arrive just before the Palio, content to forego the *corteo storico*. As for us, we would not miss this, perhaps the greatest show on turf!

As a nice surprise, Dario indicates that either I or my companions can actually sit down a row or two until others arrive to fill them in. This would certainly provide my packed-in neighbors—Dad to the left and Linda to the right—with some breathing room for an hour or so. "Go, go, please," Linda encourages, hoping to gain some precious space for a while. She waves me away. I am also struggling within my cramped space to maneuver my waist pack beneath my feet along with two bottles of water, trying desperately to avoid shoving the whole collection off the bleachers into the abyss beneath us. To retrieve something from below will likely require a monumental feat of human effort, and I really don't want to test that suspicion.

Having found a new, temporary seat, I turn to the track and environs to finally pay some attention to the scene developing around me. Linda has settled into conversation with Helen. The *corteo storico* is due to show up soon, around 5:20 p.m. at the Casato, where they will enter the Campo. Looking across the Campo, we can see mobs of people filing in very slowly, like an amoeba covering the Campo near Palazzo Pubblico. It appears that plenty of time still remains for people to enter the center, though many die-hard fans are already camped on the edges to secure their favored spots.

I then hear Dario's voice from below me. "This is going to be a very interesting race," he says with no warning, directing his attention to me. Fortunately I can still hear his rather soft voice over the surrounding distractions. "I've never seen anything like this. There are seven adversaries in this one." The number of adversaries is curiously uneven tonight simply because both of the Tower's rivals are racing—the Goose and Wave. That's quite a threesome. The Owl and Unicorn are also racing, as are the pair of rivals from the Ram and Shell. Dario predicts, "The start of the race could take some time." As far as logic goes, the Tower doesn't have a prayer. It would be another interesting study to determine whether the contrade with modern-day rivalries are less likely to win than ones that do not. Perhaps there is no difference, but the assumption in town is that your chance of winning is considerably reduced should your rival be racing as well.

This logic bodes well for the Panther tonight, which has a mediocre horse and a pretty decent jockey with two wins to his name. This somewhat resembles the setup from two years earlier when Guess pulled off the win for the Goose. Most important, the Eagle isn't running, as Carlo and I discussed in Panther territory the previous night.

Dario's Wish

I am now apparently serving as a sounding board for Dario's speculations, for which I am grateful to be on the receiving end. Having him here with us is like having our own personal play caller up in the booth. "I really can't figure out the Goose," he continues, shaking his head. "They have Oppio, a horse that won last July, and they practically have their own loyal jockey, Tittia. But they sold Tittia to the Shell and instead hired a lesser-known jockey, Tremendo." (We are sticking with jockey nicknames here.) He continues with the who's who of tonight's Palio. "One to watch is the Unicorn," he continues in his calm, professorial tone. "Their jockey is a novice; he has never raced in a Palio, so it's really hard to tell how he will behave."

He is referring to one Elias Mannucci, who until this morning did not even have a nickname. A lightbulb blinks in my head, and I reply, "Now I understand why there was no nickname listed for him before the trial last night!" At least one small mystery is solved. His nickname—only hours old at this point—is Turbine.

Dario turns his attention to a few more people entering our area of the bleachers, but it appears that we don't yet need to return to our permanent seats. This race is clearly on Dario's mind, so he continues without any dissent from me, "I'm also not sure why the Ram hired the jockey they did. Their jockey, Massimo Columbu, is coming off of a ten-Palio suspension, so this is his first race after being suspended." Nicknamed Veleno II (Poison), Columbu was the jockey for the Eagle in 2006 and was apparently instructed to disrupt the Panther. He must have done quite more than that to warrant such a punishment.

"Then there's the Forest, which hired the veteran Trecciolino," Dario says, reminding me that the current King of the Square is returning once again for an encore performance. "He is trying to earn an all-time record for wins by a single jockey. If he wins tonight, he will tie the current record—it's still held by Andrea Degortes," explains a rather unenthusiastic Dario. What he is not saying due to his characteristic politeness is that he hopes the current record will stand. Trecciolino's real name is Luigi "Gigi" Bruschelli, and he can still boast of being the most successful Palio jockey in recent history. He has earned the *drappellone* thirteen times thus far, between 1996 and 2012, for a total of seven different contrade. *That explains why he's still competing*, I reflect. He is actually two years older than I am, having been born in 1968. This age in normal life is no great feat; achieving this age as a jockey, however, typically means approaching the end of a career. Aside from the seven rivals competing in tonight's race, the event is consequently representing a battle of generations, namely between the aging Trecciolino versus his younger adversaries such as Tittia. Along with Brio for the Tower, all three of these rock stars are looking to increase their victory counts tonight.

Dario adds, "Also, a few contrade will probably not even try. The Wave has won twice in the past three years and so is likely to focus on disrupting the Tower. And they have a novice horse with Osama Bin." This name sparks some negative emotion, not surprisingly, as no one in our American cohort can imagine why a horse's owner would provide such a provocative name to an unsuspecting animal. I saw his name emerge as a possible contender for the *tratta* in the past two years, but he never made the final cut. In those cases the horse's peculiar name was only worth a raised eyebrow or two. This time he has made it all the way to the big race.

I am not alone in my thinking, exemplified by a mocking photo posted on the website for *La Nazione* (*The Nation*). The altered image depicts the Wave's horse with Osama's face pasted in as the jockey. In other circumstances I may have found this rather humorous, but even my taste for creative antics has its limits here. I keep telling myself that it's not the horse's fault, but I have to admit that the horse's name has biased me against the Wave for purposes of tonight's race. Add to that the Wave's two recent wins, and they are just not one of my favorites in this one. Nonetheless, looking beyond the racetrack, I must say that there are few contrade as consistently enthusiastic, involved, and unified as the Wave, if their public presence has anything to say about it. They are an impressive bunch.

"The one to watch," Dario says, "is the Panther." My ears perk up like Scooby Doo. "They've got a pretty decent novice horse in Quintiliano, and their rival, the Eagle, isn't running." At this point I am totally focused on Dario's commentary. He is giving away personal perspectives free of charge, and I certainly wouldn't mind seeing the Panther take home a victory on our watch. "The Wave and Goose probably aren't going to try to win tonight, as they all have a good number of victories in this century. I think if the Panther makes a strong start and takes off in the lead early, nobody will try to stop him. The race will be his." Indeed, the Panterini seemed to be collectively enthusiastic about their jockey during the dinner last night, though I don't think any of them would say so personally for risk of jinxing their chances. In fact, their jockey, Scompiglio, has two Palio victories to his name, the most recent for the Ram in 2012—the aforementioned race that found six contestants piled up at San Martino. Incidentally, his horse in that race was none other than Guess, who tripped and caused the pileup. Of course, Guess would then carry the Goose to victory during our first Siena program in July 2013, thereby making up a bit for his earlier foible.

"As long as the Forest and Goose don't win this one," Dario says, "I'll be very happy." I don't feel the need to ask him why, but I silently think, *Add the Wave to that list*. I don't know much about the Forest, but they seem to be the sleeper, or upstart, who can come up from behind when least expected and yank the race away from others. And they have a revered veteran in Trecciolino. Tonight I can't help but silently agree with Dario. I have personally seen the Goose win, and I don't know much yet about the community of the Forest. I would be personally gratified if the Shell, Tower, Panther, or maybe the Unicorn pulled off a win tonight. Our male students have been living in Unicorn central, literally a few buildings away from their chapel and società.

If our collective logic holds water, there are only perhaps four or five contrade in tonight's race that are really itching to win, and some will be trying desperately to keep others from realizing success. I am the first to admit, however, that this personal logic reflects my own biases, perhaps blended with those of Dario. So be it. That's why this will be fun. I will at least enjoy having a few favorites to cheer for.

I am quickly reminded that Dario's priority here is the family that has wisely hired him to personally navigate them through Palio season. The girls are getting antsy, and one of them predictably needs to use the restroom. There's no mistaking his local status here, as he knows what barriers to jump over, what attendants to talk to, and what shortcuts to take through and around the bleachers to reach the ground and café restrooms nearby. He is technically employed right now, so he dutifully takes the daughter carefully along the bleachers and disappears onto the ground below us.

Future of the Palio

My own attention turns to the Casato, as the *corteo storico* is now preparing to enter the Campo. Although it is not uncommon to hear complaints from people who have "survived" the two-hour ritual displays of the historical procession, I am taking advantage of its lumbering progress to take copious digital photos and videos. After dizzying myself with unending photo shoots of the earlier participants, wisdom kicks in at some point and tells me to be more selective with my subjects. Simply, I need to slow it down with the camera. I have probably captured over a hundred images already, and the seventeen contrade haven't even shown up yet. But the lighting is still good, and this event tonight served as the primary reason for acquiring a new camera and zoom lens in the first place. The camera is certainly enjoying the workout I envisioned for it this evening, and the best is yet to come.

Eventually the Chariot of Triumph comes into view, and I yelp with enthusiasm at my first-ever site of this massive vehicle in motion. It comes complete with a bonus of trumpeters perched on both sides to play an occasional fanfare, sandwiching the *drappellone* that towers upward from the center. What gets better than that? Given Dario's absence, I temporarily play the role of Palio guide by asking the family's father what he knows about the cart being pulled by four gigantic oxen. "So this is the Chariot of Triumph, and it symbolizes Siena's victory over Florence in AD 1260 at Montaperti. That's the last time they clobbered Florence," I chuckle. "Typically the chariot of the opposing army in such battles was the ultimate prize. The prize for the winning contrada tonight is the cloth that you see at the center, the *drappellone*."

Speaking of the *drappellone*, this one is an absolute gem, if the enthusiastic applause at its first public presentation was any indication. Designed by Mr. Francesco Mori, the cloth banner seems to provide a not-so-subtle nod to pressing local issues and provides a symbolic message of reassurance to the city. The Madonna is depicted at the top of the banner protecting the city from meteors raining down from above, quite clearly referencing the city's challenging economic times right now. The coldness of the blue sky above likewise transitions lower on the banner to the warm glow of a sunset. A silhouetted skyline represents the familiar city landmarks, punctuated prominently by the recognizable Torre del Mangia. The Madonna's cloak protects the city while providing its people with comforting warmth. Perhaps most intriguing is what is missing: no horses are depicted, seemingly rare for a *drappellone*. This is my interpretation, in any case, based on what I have seen and read.

Soon after communing with the *drappellone* as it trundles past, I turn my attention to the sensation of strange tapping on my feet. *What the ...* I think as I carefully look down. Suddenly a bottle of water magically appears through the bleachers next to my feet, and we all laugh as we realize that Dario is passing us gifts from below. The bottles are for his adopted family for the night, which we happily pass to them. Then another water appears between Linda and Helen, and we graciously accept it. Some of the heat and humidity continue to linger around us this evening, but fortunately we don't have to deal with the direct sun.

Linda and Helen are enjoying conversation about a plethora of topics. At some point my ears perk up, perhaps predictably, as their attention (finally) turns to the Palio. I am enjoying plentiful photographic opportunities as each of the seventeen contrade march and perform their intricate routines practically right in front of us. Still, one of my ears is tuned to Helen. Having spent her most recent career as planning director in several American cities, Helen is naturally thinking through her own scenarios for what Siena needs to do in the future.

"Look," she says to Linda with me listening in, "I just don't understand this lack of interest in offtrack betting and the hesitance to develop tourism here." To her credit, she has read nearly everything available about the Palio and has witnessed the communities of the contrade for the past month. Culturally uninformed she is not. But she wishes to propose a distinctly American, capitalist perspective here. *Okay, let's hear it*, I think.

"If the Palio is going to survive ten, fifteen years from now, they're going to need some serious tourism development," she says.

I jump in. "You don't think the Palio is going to survive here?" I say with some surprise.

"It just can't. There are no sponsors from the outside, and the city isn't allowing the event's promotion beyond those who happen to show up on their own. And for those who stumble into Siena during the Palio, it's pretty much *good luck* to them." She launches into one of her boisterous laughs.

"Well, I'm not sure about that." I can't help but egg her on. "Did you see the hundreds of kids in the bleachers during the trials? That's their future, right there. The parents are putting their kids in the bleachers."

By now Linda is turning her head back and forth between us as if watching a ping-pong match. Helen says, "Sure, there are kids involved now, but where is the money going to come from in the future? The Siena locals keep moving out to the suburbs as visitors take over. The ritual will likely go the way of others like it."

"That's definitely a challenge," I say. "But research over the past decades has shown a resurgence of interest among young people, and the contrada populations are generally growing, even if unevenly. How do you account for that? There are plenty of kids in the bleachers and in the Campo. They're coming from somewhere."

Unphased, she says, "I think there are three things they need to do here to assure this event's survival. First, allow offtrack betting. There is big money here, and horse racing is all about betting in the rest of the Western world. Second, they need to eliminate the backroom deals. The race needs to be honest without the impression and reality that some contenders are paying off others. Third, they need sponsors. The contrade need sponsors and promoters to sell their brands." Helen is on a roll now, and it's always fun to listen to her perspectives. I desperately try to hold in my laughter as I listen attentively to her three suggestions. I snap a few more photos—the Panther contingent is coming around the corner—and think in response to her suggestions, *No, no, and no.*

She continues, "Did you see that jewelry displayed for each contrada in the Palazzo Pubblico? My word, when I saw that jewelry, I thought, *My God, why aren't they replicating these things and making a fortune for the contrade?* They are absolutely stunning. People all over the world will want those designs. But they are trapped inside that building!" She points to the Palazzo.

"Well, I think those are all American approaches to development, and they may not go over well here," I diplomatically respond. "First, I'm convinced that the backroom dealing—the *partiti*—is part of the cultural process here."

"But it's not respected or understood outside of Siena," she responds. "It won't be taken seriously."

I shoot back, enjoying this debate, "Well, there's a fallacy with that kind of thinking, which assumes this whole ritual is designed for outsiders, which it's not. The deal-making is a fundamental part of the process here." She loves American football, so I attempt to find an analogy that might make sense to her. "It's like strategy, perhaps like the communication between a football coach on the field and the offensive and defensive coordinators up in the press box. They are strategizing too, behind the scenes."

And I can't help but add, "And the branding of jewelry by the contrade would completely dilute the local experience. As long as the locals show up, they can find their own way to pay for the Palio. I'm not concerned for the immediate or midterm future. I don't think it needs to be messed with through the capitalist approaches of Americans."

"Well, perhaps," she says. Then she drops the bombshell. "What they really need to do is abolish the lottery for the horses. Each contrada should choose its own horse, and they need jockeys that are loyal to the contrade," she says definitively. "This hiring of mercenaries makes no sense to me."

Well, of course it doesn't make sense, I think, *because we're not Senese*. I don't necessarily get it either, but so what? As shocked as I am, if equally amused, I am probably hearing the typical reaction of unsuspecting outsiders when they learn something about what really transpires here. None of this ritual is for the faint of heart or mind. Perhaps I am somewhat blinded by my own study of, and admitted fascination with, this remarkable place. Regardless, I just don't see a problem yet. As the saying goes, "If it's not broken, don't fix it." The most-prominent indicators that I have observed are pointing to a healthy future for the Palio and contrade system alike, even with local demographic changes. Rampant, overt commercialization of the event is the last thing the people here desire.

Still, it is instructive to note that we find ourselves in the midst of continued changes, visible to us even this summer. The Tuscan newspaper *La Nazione* printed a story recently that reviewed the new safety and security regulations now in place. Only last week I discovered new signage around the Campo that indicates what one can and cannot bring to Palio events.

Furthermore, there is a stronger police presence here. All of this reflects healthy change, from my perspective. The festival and its associated rituals are certainly evolving, and local authorities are changing with the times. That doesn't mean, however, that the Goose or the Wave need to be sponsored by the likes of Pepsi-Cola and Samsung to make this thing a success.

There are, quite literally, signs of change around the Campo, with one type of billboard providing a map of the bleachers and color-coded information about seating and—if I interpret it correctly—maximum prices that may be charged for the seats. The map strikes me as bringing the whole affair one step closer to the appearance of a stadium. According to the posters, the various business owners behind the bleachers have provided this information to the city administration. I have never seen this before, and it clearly represents one attempt to inject some central authority into the otherwise mysterious ticket sales. The information is only written in Italian, but this still provides a mountain of more information than what existed previously. I can imagine that local businesses may have finally grown weary of schmucks like me running from store to store to inquire about bleacher tickets. Guilty as charged.

Perhaps more important are new, seemingly permanent signs at the entrances to the Campo that provide locations of police stations, exit paths, medical staff, and information about what is allowed and not allowed in the Campo for the trials and Palio. There is even a schedule that provides the times after which the Campo will be blocked off. If that weren't enough, someone tried valiantly to translate all of this into English. The following sentence provides one cute example: "In order to watch the palio, it is **forbidden** to brings chairs,stools, prams,tables, benechs, boxes or any other kind of similar ibjects to piazza del campo." This quote is written precisely as viewed on the poster. Take a careful look. To the city's credit, this initial attempt would give way to more professionally written posters in future years.

The students had a lively discussion one night attempting to determine the accurate definition of a "pram." We decided by unanimous consent that a pram is indeed a stroller. The locals apparently don't know the rule, though, as a Cadillac-sized pram was parked along the inside of the barrier in front of me during an evening trial, with the hapless occupant repeatedly dropping his water bottle, which then rolled down the Campo into people's legs. As for me, it provided an unobstructed view as I commandeered its "air rights." But was it legal? Probably not. The police saw it during their cleaning of the track and even said hi to the parents, who hailed from the Shell contrada. But they made no effort to enforce the rule.

In any case, changes are afoot, and probably for the better. This is the first attempt that I have seen in three years to provide any public information in English, to map out the Campo and its bleacher availability, or to clarify what is and is not allowed inside the Campo (whether enforced or otherwise).

Dario provides one more amusing surprise before the *corteo storico* concludes. I realize once again that he is still missing, taking care of his Australian family and their various food and restroom needs—all from a rather challenging vantage point. He is now attempting to return to his temporary seating near us but in a slightly less-than-conventional way. First I see two boots emerge beside my own feet. The boots end up being attached to legs, and finally a full pair of blue jeans inches their way into the bleachers from *between* the rows. I slowly conclude that he will need more room to pull off this stunt. His head bumps up against my ankles, and it takes a moment for me to consciously understand that I need to move my feet if Dario is to fully make it through the slats from below. With my feet thus moved, his head gradually appears as if he is being born. *He's actually trying to do this*, I think, amazed. Finally his whole body appears, and he squirms around to iron out kinks in his joints and neck.

I congratulate his creative return. It is only later that I realize this was indeed his favored approach. It was likely more of a challenge for him to return through the veritable "door." If there is someone in Siena who purposely showboats to entertain his guests, it is not Dario. For him, the "normal" approach to return (on two feet) was simply too complicated. *Wow*, I think, *you can't find more local flavor than this*. Dario is personifying the local character of a place that just can't be replicated elsewhere. Hopefully some things here will never change.

❈ CHAPTER 18 ❈

Foul Play

THE *MORTARETTO* FIRES A BLAST ACROSS THE CAMPO. IT'S TIME TO MAKE history—Siena style. The horses and jockeys emerge one by one from Palazzo Pubblico for the latest version of this centuries-old festival in honor of the Virgin Mary of Provenzano. As each jockey emerges onto the track, he is handed a *nerbo*, the traditional whip. The trials are over; this is the real deal. They have one chance tonight to bring home glory and honor for one fortunate contrada. The competitors start their circling routine behind the *mossa*, as they have done religiously during the trials. If nothing else, this seems to serve as a cathartic exercise to quell the nerves of the horses if not the jockeys. As for the crowd, the nervous anticipation in the air is thicker than gelato.

Lineup of the Horses

Eventually we become aware that the noise level around us and throughout the Campo is gradually subsiding. The otherwise excitable voices of conversation are becoming softer, save for the two Australian girls who are playing behind us and whooping up all sorts of childlike glee. It's time to teach some manners, if the people in front of us have anything to say about it. Yet another contradiction emerges: expecting manners in the Campo. A couple of men in front of us shush the girls loudly, the universal sound that asks others to be quiet. Enough shushing takes place so that the parents eventually realize that something is up and that the girls need to calm down. Welcome to Siena! Theirs are the only voices we can really hear now and are probably audible across the Campo at Palazzo Pubblico. An ominous silence descends around us. The silence, as they say, is deafening and intense.

FOUL PLAY

Everyone in the know is awaiting the most important public announcement of the night, that of the lineup of the horses. Despite all the planning, dealing, gossiping, and speculations about which contestant might outdo another one, there is one more pivotal lottery to endure. The lineup order is not predetermined, as discussed in an earlier chapter, so there is no way for contrada leaders to plan for it—aside from various contingencies should a jockey find himself in this or that position (though I cannot imagine the voluminous playbooks a jockey must recall with so many possible combinations). The only chance for jockeys to react to the lineup order will come after the announcement, as they circle and fuss around one another at the *mossa*. This is where any final deals, likely only between the jockeys, might go down. I wonder what kind of schemes the jockeys are plotting with one another, either at the behest of their respective contrade or through their own free will. Which ones are friends or acquaintances? Which ones owe favors to another? Which will remain loyal to their employers' needs tonight, and which might betray?

The uncharacteristic silence throughout the Campo persists stubbornly while the *mossiere* calls out the lineup order for the first time. Each announcement leads to a brief but intense reaction from the crowd, either in favor, in frustration, or simply because they find it interesting for some reason. I find myself falling into this latter category, as long as my favored contrada don't end up in position ten, the *rincorsa*. After a minute, the order is finally made public, from positions one to ten: Wave, Ram, Turtle, Goose, Forest, Owl, Panther, Shell, Tower ... and Unicorn as *rincorsa*. Fascinating. My initial reaction is not much more profound than this expression of interest. The Goose is actually in the most successful position given the data since 1899. The Unicorn will have a shot at disrupting its rival, the Owl, if it wishes but is likely out of contention for the race. The Wave and Turtle are in decent spots, if history is any measure once again. However, the Panther, Shell, and Tower will need an extra bit of Senese luck to launch themselves successfully out of those higher positions on the outside. "Ah well, no matter," I say, playing it down to Linda and Helen. "It really means little at this point. Last year's winners, the Dragon and Owl, were in positions six and two, if I remember correctly. And position two is actually the worst."

Following several attempts to assemble all ten horses at the *mossa*, the crowd settles in for the long haul. I stop counting the repeated lineup efforts.

Actually, the crowd's collective version of "settling in" consists of intensifying levels of frustration that devolve into yelling at the jockeys each time the lineup attempt fails. It is helpful to recall—if not a bit amusing as well—that this expression of frustration remains a significant part of the ritual. Patience would not be as much fun, and it allows the tired, disgruntled crowd to let off some steam.

Dario's words with respect to the Unicorn's jockey, Turbine, still ring in my ears. Turbine's the novice here tonight. He has never run a race, and now he's been thrown into the testy, stressful position of *rincorsa*. Talk about getting thrown into the fire. Some thirty thousand people, seventeen contrade, and the city's entire leadership are waiting on a rookie to make the first move. "But he's not even facing our direction. His back is to us most of the time!" Helen observes, throwing up her hands in startled confusion. This is her first Palio as well. I respond with some sympathy, "I don't know what he's doing, and maybe he doesn't either." I presume (always dangerous, of course) that every jockey out there tonight has been coached somehow for the *rincorsa* position, including how they should behave if selected. Then again, maybe not. Nonetheless, Linda and I start questioning such assumptions again as we continue to stare at the back side of Turbine. Is he peeking over his shoulder? Hard to tell what's really going on—what is actually real and not real.

Eventually Turbine makes a jump when the lineup is as disciplined as it is likely to get, and there is a sense that he has a decent chance to launch. But he doesn't ultimately carry through with his initial stutter. He balks in place. Still, it is just enough of an indicator to the *mossiere* to drop the *canape* for safety. Horses take off, with Tittia, racing for the Shell, comfortably in the lead. But the *mortaretto* sounds the false start right away, as Turbine keeps his steed parked without moving. We enjoy watching the horses and jockeys trot around the track to bring down the tension a notch.

As the lineup attempts continue, we spy a few additional trends that defy our immediate explanation. The Goose jockey, Tremendo, is nearly refusing to line up where he was assigned—or so it appears from our vantage point. He is nearly behaving like a second *rincorsa*. "So he's supposed to be number four, right?" Linda asks.

"Yes, that's what I recall," I say. "That's strange; he's just hanging back. I wonder if he made a deal to throw the race. I would think he'd be concerned about the Tower, however, and he's not going to catch anyone from back there."

Linda observes correctly, "Well, if nothing else, the Palio certainly has prime appeal for speculation!" Indeed. For nearly an hour the Goose has made only a few halfhearted attempts to line up between positions three and five, and sometimes he saunters over to positions eight and nine to hang out with them. What's his game?

Then there's the mysterious Ram, led by the notorious Veleno. He's supposed to be lining up in position two but is instead happily spending most of his time on the other side of the lineup. He seems to be enjoying occasional conversations (or bribing attempts) with the *mossiere*. At least, that's what it looks like from here, as his horse is often parked right across from the fellow who announces the lineup and releases the *canape*. Helen clues in on this too. "So what's up with the guy in the pink jacket and the feather in his hat?" she asks us with a chuckle. "He's having some conversation with the starter, and he's not lining up. What's that all about?" The question is rhetorical, of course, as neither Linda nor I have a solid answer either. All I know is that bizarre things are transpiring behind the *mossa* this year, with a variety of antics displayed by the Goose, Ram, and Unicorn, for starters. The Ram should be in position two by now, and the Goose in position four. What are the repercussions for those who don't start in the proper position? Does it really matter if they choose other positions that are located farther from the inside of the track? Two years ago during our first summer here, Porcupine contradaioli beat up Brio on the track for precisely that offense, ultimately leading to a two-year Palio ban for the Porcupine. At the present, however, no one in authority seems to be taking these wandering jockeys seriously.

Something is happening, as a handful of men have emerged on the track to our left and are making their way toward the *mossa*. The men—all ten grooms for the horses, we soon realize—are now scurrying past our seats. "Wow, what's going on with these guys?" Helen asks. She's beside herself now with sheer amazement of the spectacle thus far, and the race hasn't even started. I am as perplexed as anyone, more so regarding how they materialized onto the track. I hadn't seen them emerge from the Palazzo, so were they stationed somewhere else? Seeing all ten grooms in one place provides both a rush of excitement and a sense of concern at the same time. Why are they all running toward the horses?

Upon arriving at the *mossa*, they climb over, under, or around the ropes and move efficiently to their respective horses. Various activities transpire at each mount, from actual grooming to conversations. We just watch this unexpected development in bewilderment, wondering what might come next. Just as quickly as the grooms arrived, they all leave their horses, jump under or around the two *canape*, and scurry in front of us to their original posts. "I guess the horses needed a break, like a seventh-inning stretch?" Linda says. Helen adds, "Seems like the horses are extremely nervous and probably needed some calming down." Whatever, it's back to the lineup ritual again. I can't help but liken it to an auto race pit crew, minus the sound of electric tools.

I look at the sky and get a feeling of déjà vu, sensing a possible repeat of two years ago. The intensity of daylight in the Campo is gradually softening as the muggy air around us transitions to dusk. "This was already going to be a challenge to photograph before it got dark," I say to Linda with some exasperation. "I need to change my camera settings again, probably going up to 1600 ISO," which is basically a last-ditch effort to make the camera think there is enough daylight. I need a shutter speed that is high enough in the low light to capture the moving horses without turning each photo into one fuzzy mess. Part of me is looking forward to this photographic experiment, and I welcome the challenge. But I do want to go home with some decent photos to frame.

I spy Dario a few seats down. He has returned to our area somehow and is intently watching the *mossa*. His focus is laser sharp; he is essentially staring down the horses without blinking an eye. I can't resist. "Dario!" I quietly call out to not arouse much attention. He hears me and looks my way. "How much more time do they have?"

He looks at his watch and replies with a look of concern, "Five to ten more minutes."

I relay this information to Linda and Helen, and we discuss possible implications. Helen asks, "Would they really cancel the race tonight? How will everyone plan to come back tomorrow if their travel plans are set?" Helen is thinking practically, as one might expect.

"It doesn't matter," I reply frankly. "If it gets too dark to race, they cancel." I personally hope they don't cancel, of course, and I can't imagine the political ramifications if everyone gets sent home without seeing the grand finale. *The crowd thinks they're irritated now. Just try to pull that one*, I think.

Helen observes with a levity that only she can convey, "Well, the Unicorn is just dinking around over there and not even looking in this direction. Does he know his time is running out? Maybe he needs some consulting. One of his people needs to go talk to him!" We enjoy a good laugh over that one.

C'mon, rookie, start this thing! I think, modifying a similar quote from, again, *Apollo 13*. I enjoy the suspenseful wait as much as anyone, but enough is enough. Let's get it on. History awaits, as does celebration for someone afterward—amazingly only some two minutes after the race finally begins.

The noise level in the Campo is now at fever pitch, growing increasingly elevated and tense. People sense that it's go time. I've got my camera ready to fire continuous frames at an ISO setting that is approaching the stratosphere. I take some consolation in recalling that digital ISO speeds create less graininess than their film predecessors. In any case, this is no time to look away from the *mossa* to fuss with the camera. The horses are generally behaving, and they're nearly standing where they should. The Goose is still hanging behind the first three horses, but who cares at this point? He's had an hour to consider his strategy, whatever that may be. And then …

The Race Begins

The rookie Turbine makes his move for real this time, accelerating to a gallop around the outside of the pack. The *canape* drops, and they collectively thunder toward our seats. Despite my official academic role in Siena, I am simply cheering for some contrade over others tonight. As my camera chugs through multiple frames a second, my heart already starts to sink just a bit. The Forest launches out ahead quickly, with the Turtle close behind; the Wave and Tower complete the front four. By the time they thunder past our position, the dynamics of this race are already well in motion, if not yet determining the final outcome. The Goose is taking up the rear of the pack as expected, even falling behind the *rincorsa*. The Panther suffered a poor start for some reason, and its ally the Owl isn't faring too well either. But it's early in the race. They haven't dealt with San Martino yet. One mistake can instantly mix everything up, depending on who gets through that place alive.

LIVING THE PALIO

Even before San Martino, the drama begins. Veleno, riding for the Ram, comes from behind and is closing in on Tittia, riding for the Shell. Rather than pushing ahead to compete, Veleno is making his way up to the Shell on some sort of obsessive, personal mission. Tittia is valiantly trying to race but has not yet punched into the front four. His nemesis is closing in fast as they thunder past our seats at Fonte Gaia. Veleno then pulls up beside Tittia and desperately reaches to grab his blue jacket from behind. They are neck and neck. The crowd just down the track from us howls a collective gasp. *What the hell is he doing?* I quickly process what is transpiring. Veleno has a hold of Tittia's jacket and is not letting go. He pulls violently, and Tittia falls precariously into Veleno's side. Inevitably, Tittia can't survive on his mount. He tumbles onto the track and scurries away, well before any of the competitors has enjoyed a run at San Martino.

The Shell is thus already *scosso*, but only because Veleno just yanked the star jockey off of his horse! *That didn't just happen*, I think in an instant, startled. His mission seemingly accomplished, Veleno seems content to remain within the back of the pack; he isn't bothering anyone else, so the rampage has ceased. The Shell is effectively out of the running, despite having a rock star jockey riding the prized Occolé, likely the strongest horse in the Campo tonight. Veleno hangs back with the Goose, Panther, and now the riderless Shell in the second pack of horses. He is likely assuring that Occolé doesn't make a run for it on his own volition.

Blazing into San Martino are the front five: Forest, Wave, Tower, Owl, and Turtle, in that order and nearly lined up single file. They cruise around the turn in front of the mattresses almost like a train, one after the other. Although they manage to survive San Martino, the Wave jockey makes a potentially crucial error as he takes a wide arc to the outside. The Tower takes advantage and moves past the Wave into the number two position by the time they shoot past the chapel. Farther back, the Goose's jockey, Tremendo, makes some kind of tremendous mistake as he plunges off of Oppio and hits the dirt, capping off an arguably disastrous beginning for the Goose. Oppio—who won valiantly for the Dragon one year ago tonight—is now *scosso* along with Occolé for the Shell. Two of the favored horses tonight are now enjoying a pleasant gallop in the rear of the pack.

Now the first five have entered the stretch in front of Palazzo Pubblico, and the Forest is clearly in control, easily a horse length ahead of the Tower.

FOUL PLAY

The Wave is hanging on the Tower's tail. The Unicorn rookie, Turbine, is doing amazingly well, having moved into fifth position ahead of the Owl. They are barreling toward us again as they approach and rapidly pass the *mossa*, completing the first lap. Woosh! There they go. I hope these photos turn out, as they've got the hammer down! There are four front-runners now, with the Forest in the lead, followed more closely by the Tower and Wave, and the Turtle coming up fast. The Owl has lost steam, and the Unicorn seems rather alone in the fifth position. Plodding behind the Owl is the *scosso* Shell horse, Occolé, as if to say, "Hey, wait for me!" But he won't be much of a threat tonight, thanks to some apparent foul play. Okay, I have to favor the Tower or Turtle here; that's as good as it's likely going to get for my personal interests. But the Forest still leads into the second lap.

They lean into San Martino again and safely pass the chapel, and the dynamics start to change. The Tower's Brio strategically fires his afterburners and takes off for the Forest. There are hints that the Forest's horse isn't quite prepared to keep up the intensity, as the Tower manages to take its first lead of the night! The Wave follows the Tower's lead and likewise has passed the Forest by the time they reach the end of the second lap. Seemingly in full control for nearly two laps, Trecciolino has now backed into third place, with the Turtle sensing his weakness as well. Dario may get his wish after all. It's the Tower and Wave now, but the Turtle isn't giving in just yet. As for the other six or seven in the rear of the pack, they can likely envision their fate by now, and two of them are *scosso* anyway.

Not much changes into the third attempt at San Martino, though the Wave's jockey, nicknamed Salasso, clearly wants to win this thing. He's the only one giving the Tower's Brio a run for his money now. But alas, Salasso then makes a dreadful error as he cuts inside too quickly for the final turn at the Casato. The right side of horse and jockey together plow into the sharp corner of barriers at the turn, stalling their momentum. Ouch! Amazingly, they both bounce off alive and somehow pick up momentum again to finish the race, but the fate of the Wave is now sealed. Brio's hand and *nerbo* are already punching the air, signaling victory well before the finish; he knows he has it won. He celebrates as he crosses the finish, while the Wave settles for an embarrassing second place. The Tower has just put to bed a troubling decade without a win.

LIVING THE PALIO

Linda, Helen and I have front-row seats to a combination of ecstasy and chaos developing in front of us. Soon enough the Tower faithful have Brio on top of their shoulders, carrying him in mob-like fashion to San Martino to begin their celebration. Another contingent of Tower contradaioli, mostly young and middle-aged men, are making their way to the bleachers under the judges' stand to prepare for an extraction of their own—that of the traditional human mountain reaching skyward to retrieve the *drappellone*. Men are crying, hugging, and congratulating friends in the midst of other chaos nearby. As a halfhearted attempt to display good sportsmanship—likely mandated by the city, but I'm not sure—a parade forms near the Casato of one banner waver from each contrada, and a colorful line of waving contrada flags makes its way toward the *mossa*. For the banner wavers' part, they are adding nicely to the festive atmosphere in the Campo. To our right the *drappellone* is being prepared for its lowering onto the track. To our left—well, there is a lot happening and evolving with the passing of every few seconds. Some horses and jockeys are in the midst of mobs as their grooms attempt to remove and protect them from the crowds.

Then suddenly a number of people, including women, are running fearfully in front of the bleachers, clearly attempting to remove themselves from a scuffle that has emerged down the track. I can't quite see what's happening, but I'm satisfied about my safety here in the stands. I'm actually not sure yet about my own immediate future tonight. For now, however, I am perfectly content to watch the action from my expensive perch before I give it up for good. Most others from this section of bleachers have since moved on. Likewise, Linda and Helen have agreed to reconvene for postrace refreshments across the street at Cavallino Bianco. I carefully watch Linda disappear toward the judges' stand to make sure they are well on their way out of the mayhem. Meanwhile clusters of men from the Ram and Shell appear to be facing off, and the consensus around me is that the *cazzotti*, or ritualized fistfights, have begun—and for good reason. The Ram literally ripped away any chance of winning for the favored Shell, which for all intents and purposes is the *nonna* out of the ten who were racing. This was the Shell's to lose, and Tittia was likely itching for his third win in three years.

The bizarre ritual of the *cazzotti* provides yet another opportunity for outsiders to misinterpret the Palio. Those who do not immediately warm up to the idea of this particular facet of Siena life would certainly have my sympathies. Generally the *cazzotti* refer to occasional fistfights that can spontaneously erupt between rival contrade during the days of the Palio. They typically last only a few minutes but can go longer. While traditional rivals are most likely to partake in these relatively violent events, occasional non-rivals can likewise face off, should one contrada feel that it has been wronged by another. As one might expect, it is mostly the younger and middle-aged men who participate, and only a portion of the men actually do the fighting.

So, what is so ritualistic about a group fistfight? Well, there are unwritten rules, which may not come as a surprise at this point. No objects are allowed for hitting; only one's arms and fists can throw blows, and fists need to be clenched mainly to hit their rivals atop their heads. Occasional bloody noses or equivalent injuries can occur, although the brawl tends to wind down as blood starts to appear. Recently an overzealous participant used his belt to enhance his own affect, only to have plenty of digital images circulate until the culprit was found and chastised by much of the city's population. One might recall that during the rest of the year most of these people are acquaintences, or even family members who generally care for one another. Nobody wants to permanently injure those with whom they will be socializing or doing business a week later. In the end, the fistfights consist of a "very realistic theatrical representation," according to a long-time contradaiolo I spoke with.

As I stand here in the bleachers witnessing the Shell-Ram *cazzotti* with my own eyes, I am trying to comfort myself that no serious harm should result. They are letting off steam now, as the local police—many of them also contradaioli—wisely stay out of their way. As rare as the *cazzotti* may be, however, such events are increasingly posted on the internet, causing angst and occasional outrage from befuddled outsiders. It is easy to understand how someone could conclude Siena is quite the violent, unsafe place to visit. And yet, precisely the opposite is true, as we have seen. Only during the past few years has this uninformed, public perception become yet another headache for the city.

As the fighting continues, the Ram's jockey, Veleno, is literally just hanging out on his horse right now, not far from my position. Some of the Ram's contradaioli are now clustering around Veleno and seem to be more perplexed than anything. Are they cheering, or are they angry? Mouths and arms are flying, almost as if in startled surprise and shock—what had their jockey done? "Holy cow, boy, what did you just do?" I imagine them saying. I'm not sure the Ram contradaioli were prepared for this rapid turn of events near the beginning of the race. Time will tell as the inevitable fallout emerges tonight and tomorrow. I am certain, however, that I would not want to be a Shell contradaiolo tonight. If there was any question at all about the sustenance of this particular rivalry, it has entirely dissipated. This contentious relationship has been energized quite masterfully once again.

My attention turns back to my own contingent, my small contrada of students, faculty, and spouses that has just witnessed the event from a variety of perspectives. Two of our students, perhaps those most enthralled with the contrade and the Palio, braved the Campo center tonight and may very well still be in there somewhere before it clears out. As for me, I think I'll let the Tower celebrate on its own without my presence for a while. The Cavallino idea sounds tempting, so I'll go check out the post-race action across the street. Moreover, there is gelato to be consumed.

A New Victor

About an hour later, Linda, Helen and I spill into the street with those still lingering around. We decide to head north to our respective apartments as I finish off Linda's gelato. It should be fairly quiet in the She-Wolf, given their lack of participation in this one—likewise for Helen's penalized Porcupine farther north. *Wow, it got dark while we were hidden in the bowels of Cavallino.* A familiar sound of drums greets our ears yet again as we make our way toward Banchi di Sopra, the city's prime social thoroughfare known locally as Il Corso. The drums are steadily approaching with their mesmerizing rhythm. "That must be the Tower, starting to march around the city," I say to the women, my voice raised to carry over the surrounding street noise. I can't resist. "I'm going to hold back and watch them march. See you at home." I instantly lose Linda and Helen in the throngs of people after announcing my intention to fall back.

The Tower contingent is approaching my position rapidly on Banchi di Sotto as I unleash my smartphone video camera one more time. It is pitch dark now, but I hold some hope that the constant glow of city lights and storefront windows will allow my camera to capture this part of the victory. The flags and drums move happily past me as I retreat to a typical doorway step. I'm well practiced with this trick, which doubly serves as a slightly better view while remaining out of the way. "Uh-oh," I say to myself as they hastily turn right onto Banchi di Sopra. This is no lumbering *corteo storico* in the Campo; these guys are moving! And they're heading for Helen and Linda, who tend to take their time. I humorously contemplate that the women are being chased by the Tower and will soon find themselves participating in the merriment whether they want to or not. What they envisioned as an uneventful stroll back home is about to get a whole lot busier. I might as well tag along, on yet one final contrada chase of my own.

Walking behind the last stragglers of the Tower, I spy where they are settling in for a spell: Piazza Salimbeni. *Of course!* I think. The logic of this location dawns on me. I scan the mingling crowd for the women with no success. *Oh well, they can take care of themselves.* The Tower contradaioli, or Torraioli, are now occupying the piazza in front of the headquarters for Banca Monte dei Paschi, providing a tribute to their city's incomparable benefactor. The imposing nineteenth-century statue of Sallustio Bandini near the piazza's center provides a central focus for the celebration tonight. A few seemingly startled pairs of tourists are sitting at the statue's base, and they are smiling at one another as the Tower engulfs their previously tranquil spot. Flags are waving madly, drums are pounding energetically, and the Torraioli are savoring their first victory in a decade. I have a feeling that we're going to see more of the Tower in upcoming days.

Finally it is time for me to depart their impromptu celebration here as well. I wonder if I will be physically present for similar festivities next year. For now I take my leave and make my way back to Via Vallerozzi and the She-Wolf. With a grin I remind myself, *The She-Wolf will be running next year.*

By Saturday, two days after the race, various news and local perspectives trickle in with respect to the craziness of July 2. It only required twenty-four hours for Veleno, the renegade jockey for the Ram, to be suspended yet again from at least the next Palio in August. This was an urgent and immediate matter, according to an article in *La Nazione*, as he clearly violated Palio regulations by grabbing the back of Tittia's jacket and pulling him off of his horse. Soon the public prosecutor's office in Siena will open a full investigation into the matter. Another news article commented that the Piazza del Campo has not seen such a blatant, violent act between jockeys in many years. It is possible that Veleno acted independently, as one article suggested. Still, many here seem to be wondering to what extent Veleno acted on his own accord. Even the most-informed Senesi may never know.

Buon Viaggio!

There is always a surprise lurking around the corner in Siena. Even the final morning of our program provides its own little wrinkle, almost as if to say, "Hey, you're still in Siena. Enjoy it while it lasts." I set my alarm for 5:15 a.m. so I would have plenty of time to get ready and see the students off on Sunday morning. Instead of waking to the alarm, however, my smartphone alerts me around 5:00 a.m. that I have a message from Brad. He says they are already waiting at Piazza Gramsci and that the shuttle driver has arrived. *Oh gosh.* I blink my eyes open with mixed feelings. *They're all early by a half hour this morning.* This has been a pleasantly timely group, though perhaps less impressively before sunrise. I quickly reply that I will be there in about ten minutes, not realizing this is overly optimistic. With only some five hours of sleep, I grab my shorts and shirt, hastily exit the apartment, tumble down eighty-seven stairs (Linda and I count them often), and emerge into the predawn light. I march as expeditiously as possible without actually running up our hill toward Savini, our comforting local *pasticceria* (bakery) perched at the top. Not just a landmark to help us locate our narrow street, Savini also provides scrumptious rewards during our return home or after climbing our hill.

Even Savini isn't open yet to provide scurrying locals with modest breakfast treats. I admit to myself that Piazza Gramsci is actually a bit farther from our apartment than I might like to think—especially just after five in the morning. I don't like the feeling that everyone is waiting for me, though the group is still technically on schedule for their one-way trip to Rome's Fiumicino Airport. At first sight of Piazza Gramsci I scan the predawn solitude of the bus platforms and see the students dutifully clustered at their meeting place. I need to pay the driver before he takes them all to Rome for their flight.

But my late arrival isn't the wrinkle. This is: rather than being met by a set of tired eyes and groggy heads waiting in the van, I am pummeled by a flurry of simultaneous comments. *Now what's going on?* I wonder suspiciously as I make my final approach. Last year's extraction of students from Siena was not the easiest of feats, given an apparently shady shuttle company that put all sorts of obstacles in our way, not to mention a hefty additional charge that had not been agreed upon. Lesson learned, I hired our favored company for this return transfer well prior to our arrival in Siena. I appreciate the promptness of this driver, who has temporarily departed to find an ATM machine. While we wait for his return, I listen to a story that collectively emerges from several mouths, one student filling in as another leaves off.

"Our driver today, he's from the Ram contrada!" one begins. A smile breaks across my face as I think about the implications of this news. No one here had paid much attention to the Ram until Palio night. "He speaks good English, and he told us, 'We're the contrada that throws jockeys from horses,'" another student says in apparent good humor.

"Really!" I say in response. *No way.* Way.

Another student continues, "He said that the jockey was planning to retire after this Palio anyway, so he wasn't worried about future suspensions. He is pretty sure that the contrada instructed him to 'disrupt' the Shell but not necessarily by pulling him off his horse!" They were laughing by now. You can't beat Palio gossip at five thirty in the morning, and by Americans, no less. "He said that there is suspicion within his contrada that Tittia fell off 'too easily.' Tittia may have known that he was already falling behind in the race, so he may have played a role in making the Ram look bad."

Wow, I think, *that's some positive spin*. That's definitely one way to fan the flames of a rivalry for another generation or longer! The Ram contradaioli's great-grandchildren will be talking about this decades from now, forming their own perspectives and embellishing personal stories, regardless of what the full truth might have been.

Eventually the driver returns. My curiosity is now piqued. I'm not letting on, however, that the students just retold his story. I satisfy our financial obligation and begin my groggy farewell process to see the group on its way. At this moment preceding their final departure, my sleepy mind is working more slowly than I might prefer, but I manage to utter some well-deserved accolades to all of them.

Time will tell what really happened (or perhaps not) on Palio night between the Ram and Shell. Regardless, regulations were clearly violated, and the city is already taking action. As for me, not even a promised return back to bed can prevent me from taking one last photo as I turn left onto Via Vallerozzi. The future sunrise is casting a deep orange glow over the medieval buildings, silhouetted on our street. I nearly expect to see a smiling Madonna looking down, protecting the city with the warmth of her cloak, as depicted so powerfully on the *drappellone*. In this way I will provide my own silent farewell once again, perhaps contemplating potential future returns to the most beautiful of cities. For now it's back to bed, with some rare self-congratulations on completing a successful third year in more ways than one.

PART V
STALLOREGGI NIGHTS

❈ CHAPTER 19 ❈

Extraction of the Contrade

"Ciao Carlo! Are you still planning to attend the extraction next week?" I write to my new friend from the Panther before our return to Siena in 2016. We had indeed managed to stay in touch.

"Tom, yes, the Panterini are very concerned because the Eagle will run this time. My family and I will be on the Campo. You can find us down around San Martino." *Right, amidst only a few thousand people*, I contemplate.

"If all goes well with my travel, I will arrive in Siena about three hours before it starts!" I respond hopefully.

"Great, contact me when you arrive in the Campo!"

"Ok, I am going to buy a SIM card for my phone when I arrive, so I will text you after it is activated." A SIM card is basically a smart card that provides data and cell service from the local provider. The modest price for a month of service has proven invaluable. I have further learned to reinstall my American SIM card on the plane prior to arriving back in the United States, if I remember to carry a small paperclip.

"Excellent," he concludes, "see you soon and happy travels!" he wraps up. Our correspondence to date has consisted of a fair mixture of emails and social media messages in combinations of English and Italian, allowing both of us to practice.

Poor Connections

Now, one week later, any number of unfortunate things could have thrown a proverbial wrench into my strategic schedule: flight delays, missed connections, lost luggage, non-existent landlord upon arrival in Siena, unexpected fire closing down an airport terminal (this actually happened not long ago in Rome), you name it. But somehow the planets have magically

EXTRACTION OF THE CONTRADE

aligned, quite thankfully placing me inside a Siena apartment for our fourth consecutive year. And precisely on schedule. It had to happen sometime, right? I am also happily benefitting from previous travel experience as one might hope. I managed a few hours of sleep last night on the flight and was nearly giddy on the bus to Siena, watching the rolling hills and high-speed trains go by. My immediate priority upon arrival would normally consist of initial unpacking and personal hygiene routines, followed by a much-needed nap. Not today, however. This is the evening of the extraction of the contrade, which generally occurs six weeks prior to the Palio. Staged like always in the Campo, a random drawing will determine which three lucky contrade will join the seven already slotted to run in July.

As readers might surmise, there is one particular contrada that will not enjoy a chance in this Palio. Not only has the jockey, Veleno II, been handed a 10-Palio ban for pulling Tittia off of his horse last year, but so has the entire Ram contrada for two *Palii*. In this city, all are held equally accountable.

With or without the Ram, I am patting myself on the back right now because, quite exceptionally, I have arrived on schedule to experience the extraction with my own eyes and ears for the first time. This is no accident, but a calculated effort to arrive a few days in advance of our student cohort—and ahead of Linda as well. She is currently escorting a young family member on a short trip elsewhere and will arrive in a matter of days. I am looking forward to adjusting to the Italian time zone while loading the fridge and apartment with essentials prior to everyone else's arrivals.

Consequently, the nap will need to take a back seat. I quickly throw some clothes into drawers and inspect the various amenities within the apartment. This time, we are a manageable three floors above street level along the main street of the Wave (Onda) Contrada, along the heart of Via Giovanni Duprè—and an easy five-minute walk to the Campo. I do manage to steal a few precious minutes to conduct our standard ritual, that of opening of shutters and windows to inspect our views. In older buildings like this, navigating the latches and layers of window coverings can be described as an adventure, perhaps even an event of its own. With the shutters finally breached, I notice that almost directly across the street is Bar a Onda, one of the typical streetside hangouts for Ondaioli.

My next goal is to connect my phone to the apartment's internet modem, which the property manager had reviewed with me during our walk-through. I can at least contact Carlo soon to inform him I am on my way to San Martino, the location of the Palio's most dangerous curve. Of course, I should know better when a property manager says confidently, "The internet works perfectly, just find this wireless address and type in the password. You'll be connected in no time! Let's go see the washing machine in the kitchen, shall we?" *Right. So, what is going on with my phone?* I think aloud, as I try to connect it with an incomprehensibly lengthy pass code that would be the envy of any security firm. Nothing. I hit the on-off button (*I think that's the one*) on the modem more times than I can count but remain flummoxed as to why both the orange and blue lights are blinking. One of them was supposed to be solid, I was told. The landlord had blown through that lesson somewhat hastily, to the point where I simply needed to trust that the unit would perform as promised. After fussing with the password again (*It says it's connected, so what's up with that?*), I am exhausting my list of obvious troubleshooting options. My tablet won't connect either. I could send messages from that device, if only it would recognize the Italian internet service. No luck. It's Sunday, so the property manager's office is naturally closed. I can't contact her again because, well, there's no internet. *Let's head up to the TIM store to get a new SIM card and all will be well,* I comfort myself.

    I peek out our street-side window again to find throngs of people headed to the Campo. It's time to get a move-on. I change into some suitable touristy summer garb, brush my teeth and hair, unleash my camera, and prepare to launch myself into Via Duprè below. As I double check my pockets for my wallet, phone, and keys, I gingerly lock the outside door behind me as I step into the busy street scene. It is as if I have instantly beamed down into the magical crowds of yet another Palio cycle. And in some surreal way, that is precisely what has happened.

    Walking toward the Campo, I soak in the urban ambiance once again as the climb steepens alongside of Palazzo Pubblico. Exiting our narrow street, I look around the Campo and remind myself why we love this place. The density of people lingering here is picking up, though not yet packed for the upcoming extraction. I don't linger myself, as time is of the essence. I plot a course directly across the shell-shaped public space and spy the tunneled alleyway opposite me. This route will lead directly to the angelic TIM store, where my precious SIM card awaits.

Upon climbing the steep alleyway stairs past the tourist stands, I see TIM where it has been located since our first year. Something is wrong, however. The single outside door seems to be closed, and my sense of frustration builds immediately. I realize the issue even before confirming the door is bolted shut. This is Sunday. *Ugh! Whose idea was it to arrive here on a Sunday?* I ask myself while my imaginary head beats against a Renaissance-era windowsill. No SIM card, and no communication with anyone until later Monday morning. Welcome back to Italy. Some things don't change much, not the least my travel planning skills. I would have liked to think otherwise.

Unexpected Encounter in the Campo

With my phone now useless and returned to my pocket, I decide to serpentine a bit through the growing crowd. Perhaps I can still find Carlo if I give it one chance. I am now on a mission, still fatigued from the voyage but with enough adrenaline to exhibit some enthusiasm. He is unaware of my connection issues, though I suspect he and his companions will successfully endure the extraction without my presence if necessary. I emerge from one of the tunneled alleys onto the Campo behind Fonte Gaia and launch myself down-slope toward San Martino. *Wow, there are already more people gathering,* I ponder as my path becomes increasingly erratic through the growing crowd.

At just over half-way down, my eyes are panning across faces to find someone familiar. Anyone. I take a few more steps, and then what to my wandering eyes does appear, but... Eddie? I am suddenly stopped in my tracks by none other than my old friend and colleague, Ed. I would recognize his hulking stature and graying beard anywhere, even several years after I last saw him. Ed is simply standing in my path, and I grind to a sudden halt with mouth hanging ajar in raw surprise.

"Tom!" he exclaims simply.

After taking in his face for a second, I respond in kind, "Eddie! What are you doing here?" I am clearly dumbfounded, though he probably expects no less. Ed and I had discussed possible joint study-abroad programs here and elsewhere in Europe, but neither of us had ever followed through. Actually, I am admittedly feeling somewhat perturbed at the moment, having been interrupted in my continued quest for Carlo—a quest which I now finally decide to abandon. I suppose some things aren't meant to be when so many obstacles present themselves. But it is neat to see Ed, quite out of context here.

He explains, "Well, I'm here taking a cooking class with Bruce. He's running a small program with some students here, and I'm tagging along to learn how to cook!"

"Wow, that's really cool," I respond genuinely. "So, are you teaching your own program this year? I know you devoted a good number of years teaching in northern Europe."

"No, not this year. I am enjoying what the university calls 'phased retirement'. So, I thought I'd check out Siena, since you and I talked about it quite a bit. We'll be here through the end of June if you want to get together for lunch or something." We thus make some initial plans to do just that.

Having ended my original quest, Ed will be my unwitting companion for the upcoming event, against all odds. *How do these encounters happen?* I ponder throughout our conversation. After some prompting, he is vaguely aware of Siena's 17 contrade, although he is curious about tonight's event as the crowd tightens around us.

"I just got here a couple of hours ago because I wanted to see the extraction. I haven't seen one in person yet," I begin my overview for him. "Oh, that must be a contrada marching in now!" I add, as we hear unified singing on the street leading toward San Martino. "I didn't know they organized themselves for this event; they normally march in as a large mass of people prior to the extraction of the horses on June 29." Either the Caterpillar or Shell is marching in, I gather, one of the larger contrade that can populate an event this early in the summer. We watch and listen as a few others find their way into the Campo, disbursing amidst the existing crowd. Other contrade are less organized for this event—the Panther, for instance, whose members like Carlo arrive in smaller groups of friends and family.

Then I detect the unmistakable drums of summer, as I call them, with the ever-familiar rhythm becoming more pronounced as it approaches the Campo. "I didn't know they bring in the community band for this," I tell Ed. "Oh, wait, that's no community band," as a very familiar pattern of flag waving erupts over the Campo. "That's the Dragon!" I say aloud to myself as much as to Ed.

Now I remember, today is also the patron saint holiday for the Dragon contrada, I explain—its annual *festa titolare*. Visitors often mistake their

• 235 •

EXTRACTION OF THE CONTRADE

roving parades to be directly related to the Palio, which they decidedly are not. "I guess the city allows them one final performance here prior to the extraction," I surmise. The crowd remains transfixed on the sizable contingent for the Dragon, dressed in their distinctive red, green, and yellow costumes. Their flags are waving to and fro above the crowd, occupying the entire lower part of the Campo in front of Palazzo Pubblico. I tell Ed, "We saw the Dragon march during our first year here, though we didn't know what it was all about at that time. This is the earliest I've been in Siena since then." Occasionally, when feeling discouraged at understanding so little about something, it helps to take comfort in how much has been learned already. For me, the tradition and general schedule of a contrada's *festa titolare* provides a pointed case, as I now accept this practice as common knowledge.

As the performance continues, I silently scan the façade of Palazzo Pubblico to review the contrada flags now flying—well, less impressively drooped or wrapped around their own poles. As expected, the seven flags represent those contrade guaranteed to run on July 2, namely those that did not do so last year. Lined up from left to right, I pick out the colors of the Caterpillar, She-Wolf, Dragon, Giraffe, Snail, Eagle, and Porcupine. I explain to Ed that the final three will be chosen by lottery tonight, though I have not done my research on YouTube to determine how this actually transpires. Sometimes it's more fun and unscripted that way.

A few minutes later, the Dragon contingent departs for their home *rione*, and one of the triple windows on the second floor of Palazzo Pubblico opens to briefly reveal the impressively long, silver bells of Siena's trumpets, known affectionately as the *chiarine* (singular: *chiarina*) while it is the *trombettiere* who play them. Every eye on the Campo is momentarily glued to this small contingent in their regal, blue costumes. They seem to be testing the waters, so to speak, as their instruments shuffle around a bit just inside the windows. Their owners are glancing out, as if to size up the crowd. They promptly back away and the windows close shut again. The episode resembles that of a cuckoo clock, where the little Gothic window opens for a peek outside before promptly shutting again. False alarm.

Eventually, the window opens once again, and the *trombettiere* look serious this time. It's a go. The melody and accompanying harmony of the Palio fanfare reverberate throughout the Campo, one which I have caught myself humming and whistling on any given day since 2013. I'm also starting to recognize the trumpeters themselves, a somewhat humorous, if telling acknowledgement of repeat visitations.

"So, how do they tell us which contrade are chosen?" asks Ed. "Is there a speaker system somewhere?"

"I'm not sure, but eventually all ten flags of those running the Palio will be hanging outside the windows, and there are only seven there now. Perhaps they add them later or something," I speculate. "All we know is that everyone here is facing Palazzo Pubblico with some expectation of an announcement."

The set of windows opens yet again, and the *trombettiere* are clearly preparing to play. The background noise around the Campo is quieting down, certainly guided by local Senesi who know the drill here. It's time to follow the lead of the crowd.

The same wonderful fanfare is played, after which they fumble with something other than their instruments. A flagpole suddenly emerges with its banner unfurling outside the window. I quickly recognize the blue and yellow insignia. "It's the Turtle!" I yell excitedly to Ed, who looks quizzically at me as if to say, "How do you know that, and what is the Turtle?" Suddenly, the whole crowd is abuzz with excited conversation, not the least being those contradaioli representing the Turtle. A group of maybe a hundred of them converges to our right, and fists are now punching the air in unison. They quickly ramp up into their own version of the Song of Verbena and are now the impromptu star performers within the Campo.

"Ok, so they just put the flag out, and that's it! Now we know how it's done," I confirm with Ed.

He responds, "Huh, so they don't need to put out the flags later. They're doing it right now as part of the announcement. That's pretty efficient!" *That it is, Edward, that it is indeed* (I am humorously recalling *National Lampoon's Christmas Vacation*).

Who says we can't learn quickly? The mystery has been put to bed. Right now there are two more contrade to be chosen, and I am personally hoping for the Red and Blue of the Panther to appear outside the window. The fanfare plays for a second time, and they fumble as expected with another flagpole. Then out comes the second banner: "Goose!" I yell. The Goose contradaioli proceed to go nuts as expected. "The Goose won during our first year here, but hasn't won since then," I explain. There's still one more chance for a lucky contrada tonight. However, there remains no more room for flags outside

EXTRACTION OF THE CONTRADE

that window, so another opens immediately to our right. The fanfare plays, and we all wait anxiously. Out it comes, and I try to identify the colors quickly, as if testing my own contrada knowledge. "Shell!" I yell at Ed, already deflated that the Panterini will not compete in July's "greatest show on turf." I am all but ignoring the instant celebration emanating from another part of the Campo.

I would later learn more about the process for selecting the final three contenders. From the perspective of those standing in the Campo as we are doing, it is easy to question the transparency of what is happening behind those windows. For all we know, the *trombettiere* could just as easily be playing "Eenie, meeny, miny, moe" with the flags up there. In contrast, the reality is more intentional, with a rather intricate approach. First, the mayor summons all 17 contrada captains to Palazzo Pubblico. From an urn, the mayor then randomly picks the names of three contrade. These are not necessarily the final three that will run in the Palio, however. That would be too easy. Instead, it is the captains of these three selected contrade who will pull the names from a second urn to determine which will run the Palio. The first of the three selected captains pulls a contrada name from the urn, determining the first contrada to run. This is followed by the second and the third captains doing the same in turn. It is even possible for captains to pick their own contrada! Of course, they could also end up choosing that of their rival. As each of the three captains pulls a name from the urn, the flag of the chosen contrada is placed outside the windows for all of us to see.[94] Thus, while it may appear that the selection occurs behind closed doors, all seventeen captains and the mayor are up there overseeing the process. I suppose that's good enough for us!

"Well, this is an interesting development," I tell Ed, already dissecting the possible ramifications of the final ten that will run. We should probably have Dario here, but I am as good as it gets right now. "The Eagle is running, and they are the official rival of the Panther. But the Panther is out, so my guess is that they are not the happiest people right now." I am also thinking of a deflated Carlo and his contemporaries perched somewhere nearby. Looking at the ten flags as my crib notes, I continue my analysis: "Let's see, the She-Wolf and Porcupine are another rival pair, and they are both running," I say nonchalantly, adding, "gosh, the She-Wolf just can't catch a break—they are the *nonna*, or grandmother, which is the nickname for the contrada that has gone the longest without a win. They haven't won since 1989."

"Wow, no kidding," says Ed, shaking his head. "I was a new faculty member at that point," essentially going back to the beginning of his academic career.

"Yes, it's amazing," I acknowledge. "Just think, there are older high-school and college graduates from the She-Wolf who have never seen a win in their lifetimes." I then add pessimistically, "And they could have a difficult time this go-around as well if their rival, the Porcupine, has anything to say about it. The She-Wolf nearly pulled off a win with a great horse and jockey during our first year here, but came in third place right at the end." I was, of course, referencing the still-infamous tumble of Brio and his steed, Indianos, near the finish line, thereby contributing to an unlikely win by a horse named Guess.

"As for the Shell," I continue with Ed bending in, "they had a tough break last year when the jockey for the Ram actually pulled the Shell's jockey off of his horse!" Ed is smiling in amazement, which I take as a sign to keep going. "Right there past the fountain! I still don't know if the Ram contrada sanctioned the plan or not, but that's why the Ram couldn't be selected tonight—they were disqualified. I suppose that it's karma that the Shell was chosen as the tenth contrada tonight." I laugh. "The Ram is likely gritting its collective teeth right now."

The saga of Veleno's fate would continue to unfold for nearly two years. His eventual ten-Palio ban by the city was not the end of the story. He was later charged with assault and taken to court by a local magistrate. This was the first time in known history that a violent act committed during the Palio was taken to trial as a criminal case. An uproar of local protest ensued, as such transgressions are traditionally enforced by the city's own penalties and Palio regulations—not by the common law. I have also been informed that even Giovanni Atzeni (Tittia) was not in favor of the trial. To adapt the ever-popular slogan for the City of Las Vegas, Nevada, *What happens in the Campo stays in the Campo*. Strangely enough, the judge would ultimately rule that Veleno would serve six months of community service with a local hippotherapy organization specializing in the use of horses to treat human neuromuscular disorders. This was nothing if not creative.

EXTRACTION OF THE CONTRADE

I turn my attention to other contrade. "As for the Dragon, they won fairly recently, two years ago when we were here, so they likely won't be trying hard in this one," I add. "But there's an interesting superstition playing out with the Caterpillar. Our main contact from that contrada, Dario, is hoping for mathematics to give them their next win."

Intrigued, Ed asks, "How do you figure?"

"Well, after not winning for decades, Dario has pointed out that they have won in '03, and '05, which adds up to 2008, when they won yet again. Doubling that brings us to their next logical win in 2016. And they *are* running," I say emphatically, with a slight grin as I point to their flag.

Of course, I contemplate with some amusement, if this trend continues into the later twenty-first century, sustaining the same pattern will mean fewer wins. It's going to be a rather lengthy wait between 2032 and 2064. I tell Ed facetiously, "Maybe it's just me, but this might not be the mathematical formula they want to get locked into!" I imagine the Brucaioli have already figured this out, but for now, the "doubling" philosophy provides a bit of inspiration. Let them have their fun. And beyond that, they have yet to be proven wrong!

"It's too bad I won't be here to see the race, as we're heading back in late June," Ed laments. "I never knew there was this much involved."

"Well, you'll be able to find the race all over YouTube on July 3," I comfort him a bit. "It happens so fast it's hard to really absorb all of the action, so I always need to watch it again anyway."

Looking around us, the crowd has dispersed as the evening turns to dusk. The Campo is now hosting only visitors like us, it seems, with a few children letting off steam through various chasing contests. Most others are lingering near the restaurants that ring the Campo, perhaps awaiting tables. Ed and I say our parting words for now, and I make a beeline for our apartment. Our lease is only hours old at this point. I am going to make one last-ditch effort to find internet service and contact Carlo. To accomplish that, I will predictably head to none other than our trusty hangout, Cavallino Bianco.

As expected, Enzo and two familiar employees are behind the food counter at Cavallino, essentially where I left them last year.

"Enzo, how are you?" I raise my voice over the din.

He looks up and recognizes me. "Thomas, ciao!" he responds in his characteristic accent.

I don't wish to delay their efficient serving efforts as customers are piling in. I make my way to an empty back table and get to work on my tablet. Enzo does sneak in a pasta plate for me, and he knows I'm good for it later. There is no surprise with my sudden return here; this establishment has become a welcome sanctuary.

Meet the Parents

My quest for the Holy Grail of internet service has finally succeeded. I send a few quick messages to family, followed by another to Carlo who may still be within walking distance. I apologize for my silence, but explain that it was out of my hands. *Bwoop*, a message returns almost instantly: "We are about to have dinner at Bar Il Palio. Come join us when you can!"

My first thought is one of surprise: *He wants me to interrupt their family dinner?* After coming to terms with this gracious invitation, I then reflect, *it's nice to see that local residents still frequent the restaurants around the Campo.* Even I tend to expect only tourists at these places, in their valiant effort to enjoy a romanticized Italian ambiance. Actually, plenty of locals frequent the Campo restaurants as well, as Carlo's family is demonstrating tonight. One significant factor for encouraging local patronage is, from my observations, close connections with family and friends who operate the restaurants. More than once have we been treated to an *aperitivo* or dinner because of a discount or table reservation provided by an acquaintance of an employee. And how does one distinguish between visitors and contradaioli at these establishments? Just listen for the singing. It is not uncommon to hear variations of the Song of Verbena emanating from any of the restaurant patios encircling the Campo, most frequently around Palio time.

Oh no, I tell myself, as a sense of dread overtakes my initial satisfaction with finding Carlo nearby. While Carlo actually speaks basic English and is improving, his parents and other relatives do not. I quickly coach myself that my limited Italian should be decent enough to handle standard greetings and introductions. I also keep one important excuse up my sleeve—that of my growing fatigue. An important new phrase in my Italian language playbook

EXTRACTION OF THE CONTRADE

may also be useful: *Non voglio imporre*—I do not want to impose. I do not intend to overstay my welcome by crashing their dinner party for too long.

Packing up my things, I now mentally prepare for my first Italian conversation of the year. Carlo has his phone, if we need to consult online translation apps, and he seems to enjoy speaking English for the practice. All of this aside, it will be fun to see him for the first time since last July.

I arrive at the outdoor tables of Bar Il Palio and scan around a bit. "Tom!" I hear from closer to the restaurant entrance. I head his way and find about 10 people enjoying their *aperitivo* prior to dinner, with some wine, water, cheese and meats, and probably prosecco scattered around. Let the party crashing begin! It is apparent, however, that they have already been briefed on Carlo's new friend, as they all say *ciao* and other greetings in near unison. I also recognize his girlfriend, Sofia, followed immediately by introductions to their respective parents and other family members. There are no extra seats, but Carlo gestures to pull up a chair from another table and chat for a bit. I proudly deploy my "I don't want to impose" phrase for the first time, to which they all wave it off and gesture for me to join them.

I have to wonder whether my own friends and family members in America would be equally welcoming of an unfamiliar outsider spontaneously joining them—especially without a scheduled appointment a month in advance. But this is Italy, and we are outdoors. The mood is relaxed and friendly. Indeed, they would almost be disappointed if their own friends within eyesight didn't at least stop to say hello.

With me now squeezed in and others returning to their conversations, I quickly discover that Carlo's Mom is a delight to chat with. I am already convinced that she and Linda will get along swimmingly. I learn that they have similar interests and educational backgrounds. As for Dad, he is practically a splitting image of Carlo with an identically infectious smile lighting up his face. As we have already seen in plenty of cases, Carlo's family does not claim generational roots within the Panther, or in any other contrada for that matter. After inquiring about their family history in Siena, Carlo and his father tag-team to explain their own background here. "I had been born in Siena, and lived briefly within the Panther," Carlo begins. "But we moved to another city when I was still young."

Carlo's Dad picks up the story, with Carlo helping to translate when necessary. "Our family is not from Siena, but because Carlo was born here, he became interested in his heritage. He discovered the Panther and went to high school with some Panterini his age, and it made sense for him to join the contrada."

This next part of the story piques my interest even more. Carlo adds, "After the victory in 2006, the contrada held a celebration dinner about a week later, and we all attended. My parents met some other people closer to their age, became friends, and thus decided to join the contrada as well." Thus, Carlo's parents ultimately forged their own friendships within the Panther, sparked in turn by their most recent victory a decade ago.

I now turn to Carlo. "I'm sorry about the extraction. It would have been fun to see the Panther run in July!"

Carlo shrugs and responds solemnly, "Yes, it is not a happy situation. We will not be in the Campo during the race to disrupt the Eagle," he explains.

"What else can be done? Can an alliance be formed?"

"Maybe, it depends on the Captain and his assistants, the *mangini*. We are a smaller contrada, with not as much power as some of the bigger ones. It also depends on the horse they extract. If they get a strong horse, a good jockey will likely follow. This is not a good thing." He calmly understates this last point with some nervous laughter attached. He turns to more pleasant matters: "Did you know that I have been selected for the *comparsa* this year as a drummer?"

"Oh wow, that's fantastic!" I respond with genuine surprise. Carlo has been teaching the Palio drum routine and cadence to young Panterini, most of them in elementary school.

"Are you going to wear the costume for the *corteo storico*?"

"Yes, and for other contrada functions this year."

"Congratulations! How did you get selected? Did you volunteer?"

"I was asked to do it. Every year they invite specific contradaioli, and it is cyclical. I also participated 11 years ago. It's a nice honor."

"So, do they choose people who have already been active in the contrada?" I try to clarify.

"Yes, generally, that is true. A leader of the contrada calls on the phone to ask if you can commit to it." He further explains that one can either be invited directly by the *priore* (contrada president) or the *addetto ai costumi* (manager of the costumes), or one can ask to participate and be accepted to join. Thus, selection occurs through one of various possible avenues. The

EXTRACTION OF THE CONTRADE

process of selecting individuals for the *comparsa* each year is, therefore, a rather informal one, though is principally carried out by the *addetto*. Whether or not phone calls are made to prospective participants like Carlo is partially dependent on the number of volunteers in a given year.

Shifting the topic a bit, I ask, "Ok, I have also heard that it is necessary to pay into the contrada if you are serving in some way. Do you have to pay?"

"Ah, not for the *comparsa*," he clarifies, speaking of his role in the *corteo storico* and *festa titolare* celebrations. Participants in any of the costumed events do not need to contribute funds to the contrada. He adds, "However, I do need to pay each year to teach the drums. I was asked to teach for two years because they knew I am a drummer, so I agreed," he chuckles.

"So, you have to pay to teach in the contrada? Why?" I ask, clearly puzzled once again with contrada logic.

"We all pay to participate in various roles, as a contrada leader or in another service. The higher your level of involvement or leadership role, the more you pay." His own annual contribution, he says, is several hundred euro.

"Oh, interesting, I didn't know that. I thought the expectation was only for the elected leaders." I am once again reminded of how much there remains to learn about the internal workings of the contrade. Foreigners may view this as twisted logic; volunteers and political figures in Siena are expected to pay into the contrada rather than the reverse because it is an honor to serve. One decides to do so for the intrinsic value of supporting the larger community.

Carlo then mentions, "I will be teaching the drums on Wednesday afternoons before the Palio. You can come and watch if you want."

"Where do you teach?" I ask, with growing enthusiasm.

"At the fountain, though sometimes we are up near the stable."

"I will definitely come to see that, and maybe I will drag some students along if we are not busy on Wednesday afternoons," I respond. We have enjoyed occasional discoveries of younger contradaioli practicing their flag and percussion skills in recent years, but now we have an invitation!

At this point, the group is ordering dinner, and I prepare to exit gracefully. I make some initial plans with Carlo for our group expedition to Monteriggioni on an upcoming Saturday. We will arrive by bus, and Carlo will walk us from the bus stop to the small walled village not far from Siena. After he leads us around the village, we are planning to take a hike back down to the nearby railway station and return to Siena by train.

A Rewarding Hike

Fast forward a couple of weeks, and our entire cohort has spent a wonderful morning exploring the walled hilltop village of Monteriggioni, having arrived by bus and led by the competent Carlo. Under nearly perfect skies, we had taken an early regional bus the 12 miles from Siena and hiked the steep, graveled road into the walled village. The one-way cost by bus is an affordable 3 euro, the equivalent of a mid-sized gelato cup. In his practiced English, Carlo provided some history to the group before "taking the hill." I assisted by filling in occasional English as necessary.

For its part, Monteriggioni was built and settled by the Senesi in the early 1200s as a buffer, or outer defense, against the more powerful Florence to the north. Throughout the first few centuries, the walled fortification had been attacked on numerous occasions by the Florentines and other regional powers whom we probably would not recognize today. For more than 300 years, the Senese outpost survived, until 1554 when control of the place was entrusted to one Giovannino Zeti. In an apparent bout of his own twisted logic, he attempted to befriend Florence by handing the village over to the Florentine troops. *Oops. Job opening.* Dubbed the "Great Betrayal" by the locals, the whole Siena republic would ultimately fall once and for all to Florence a year later.

Beyond this geopolitical context, the village and its circular wall and towers are considered among the best preserved in all of Italy. Moreover, the place's claim to fame is at least twofold: first, it was recognized by the famous poet, Dante Alighieri, who referenced the village's fourteen towers within his timeless *Inferno*. Multiple plaques and place names remind visitors of the town's association with the famed author. Secondly, and somewhat more recently, the online gaming community will be pleased to know that Monteriggioni serves as an important inspiration for *Assassin's Creed*.

Now following Carlo down below the walls, we eventually end up on a picturesque, mostly shaded walking trail on the way to the train station in Castellina in Chianti. This is one of the few times we have been able to enjoy the natural setting around Siena, so we are soaking in the tranquil if muggy

EXTRACTION OF THE CONTRADE

surroundings. The colorful greenery would already be the envy of Tuscan landscape painters, even without the lazy, sparkling stream just off the trail. Then without much warning, *Wooshhh! Screeeech, bang-bang, bang-bang!* A passenger train flies by on the other side of the stream, slamming the rail joints with steel on steel. In this way, the otherwise obscure railway is revealed amidst the nearby brush. *We are headed to the train station after all*, I remind myself. As the students collect their wits, I alert Carlo that it is now 12:30 p.m. On any other day, I would think little about the time out here, but this is no ordinary day. We have a call to make.

Readers may recall another new friend, Matteo, whom I had met by chance during the Panther's *Cena della Prova Generale*. After collecting his contact information, I shared my "moon shot" photos and happily continued our correspondence. As my comfort level increased, I asked him several months later if there were any opportunities for our students to become more involved with the contrada, perhaps even to volunteer somehow. To my delight, he nonchalantly responded that he would talk to his counterparts in the leadership. I was finding that hundreds of the Panterini, in another impressive display of *interclassismo*, are further linked on social media, from the top leadership on down. Matteo eventually responded with a couple of wonderful options, including a special evening museum tour, followed by a dinner with the contrada across the street at Società Due Porte. Another dinner would follow as the Palio approached. This would all take place well prior to the Palio when few, if any, guests are typically invited. Matteo promised to consider additional options as well.

Back to today, I was instructed to call Matteo at 12:30 sharp to fine tune the schedule, even though we would probably find ourselves somewhere between Monteriggioni and Castellina in Chianti. Still, the conference call can proceed as scheduled, direct from the trail. Such is the confidence provided by an Italian SIM card. The catch—there's usually a catch, as we have seen—Matteo speaks basic English at best, as one might expect. I will need to rely on Carlo to get me through the conversation.

As my phone speeds back and forth like ping pong between Carlo and me, we fumble through a friendly conversation with Matteo while standing in the shade. I manage to write some cryptic notes including dates, times, and events. As I thank Matteo profusely, it feels like Christmas has arrived in June. We are now scheduled for a personalized museum tour and contrada dinner, and one more dinner during the days of the Palio. The Panther may not be running in July, but this fact does not necessarily indicate a relaxed contrada schedule. In contrast, all contrade remain active with lunches, dinners, and other special events right up through the Palio.

Beyond these invitations, Matteo provides one further surprise that neither of us could have predicted. We thus conclude our phone call in the Tuscan countryside and excitedly race back to our group. Carlo is still staring at me in some sort of apparent shock.

"Guess what, everyone," I lead into it. "Carlo and I were just speaking with a leader of the Panther contrada. We have been invited to two contrada dinners and a museum tour!" This news is enough to encourage some whooping of celebration among our already enthusiastic cohort, along what is normally a peaceful nature trail. Any birds or squirrels nearby have long since vanished. "But wait, there's more..." I pause to add a bit of suspense. "You will all be serving dinner to the contrada on June 30."

CHAPTER 20

West Side Story

AT THIS NEWS, THE STUDENTS REACT WITH SURPRISE, CHEERS, AND CLAPS. In marked contrast, Carlo is puzzled. One student seems to speak for the group with a cheery, "Yay, we get to work!"

Carlo looks at me and says in English, "I have never seen students so excited to work before." The group responds with a collective chuckle. What Carlo had not seen was the students' preparation months in advance to learn the basics of Senese culture, history, and the Palio-contrada system. I am pleased that they understand the honor of serving the contrada and that they are enthused to give back to the larger community in a modest way.

That said, I am personally astonished. I wonder if it is unprecedented for outsiders to serve dinner for a contrada, whether in the Panther or elsewhere. As we continue our hike, I silently ask myself a barrage of questions: *How many people might attend the dinner? Will the students need any training? What will the Panther youth think about being temporarily removed from their volunteer positions? What of the contrada old-timers who may not get the "memo"? Would there be a "memo"? How will our presence be announced, along with our purpose for being in Siena? Will I have to give an introductory speech to thank everyone?* (After frightening myself, I quickly answer *no* to this last question.) I can already imagine myself grabbing a microphone and fumbling through a thank-you speech in front of 500 hungry contradaioli, in the Italian language of course, followed by polite, if tepid, applause. Then after dinner would come the hastily arranged yet assured vote of no-confidence in their leadership.

A Senese Shortcut

About a week following our eventful hike from Monteriggioni, I am texting with Silvia. Readers might recall that Silvia had joined us for our dinner with college-age Panterini and their family members. She has since become a reliable friend who regularly interacts with our students, having wisely mastered English to better communicate with clientele. Her family's business is a stone's throw from the Panther's symbolic outdoor space at Piazza del Conte.

"Silvia, ciao! You told me I should contact you to assist with meeting Simone." I text. I had asked who is responsible for leading the Panther's *Gruppo Giovani* (Young People's Group) to inquire about the museum tour and other potential events. Silvia offered to introduce me to Simone, who only speaks Italian but is apparently happy to meet with me.

"Tom, yes, I will look down at the bar and see if he is there." I chuckle at yet another case of finding people the old-fashioned way.

"Thanks! I am willing to meet him there if he prefers." Nailing down meeting places and times with people here is not the easiest of processes. Still, the outcome is often elegantly simple. If you catch someone immediately available, it is sometimes possible to meet them at some designated public place soon thereafter. For the Panterini, this often means Piazza del Conte, which further hosts a sleek panther sculpture overlooking the contrada fountain.

Silvia responds, "He is there now, and he will come to my place so I can introduce you. When can you be here?"

"Excellent. I will be there in 15 minutes, is that ok?" I ask, thinking now that this meeting will actually happen.

"Yes, I will tell him."

Ok, it's go time! I think to myself, starting to plan my opening introduction in Italian. My future acquaintance remains a complete mystery, as I have virtually no "intel" on what or whom to expect. I have my phone with its instant access to Google Translate as necessary, along with my rather traditional, if trusty, English-Italian dictionary. With more preparation than a final exam might require, I step out to find my shortcut up the steep slopes of the Wave *rione*, literally straight up into the Eagle, and through a tunneled alley named Vicolo (Alley) del Tone. Only lightly winded, I bolt out into the bustling main street of Via di Città, which serves Siena's oldest and most western of the three districts, appropriately named Terzo di Città for that very reason.

My shortcut avoids the Campo entirely and provides for quite a reduction in travel time. The one, perhaps significant caveat is the aforementioned fact that much of it is steeply sloped and up-hill. If I want to reduce the chances of dripping sweat by the time I meet someone, I need to consciously slow myself down and take the hills at a reasonable pace. When given a directional choice of her own, Linda will—nine times out of ten—wisely request the longer yet more level and scenic route through the Campo.

This reminds me of a peculiar observation. If you wish to better imitate local residents who ply these hills daily, it is necessary to practice excessively long, deliberate strides that take one up the hill at a slightly slower pace. Drop a fast-paced visitor like me on the same hill, however, and it appears like race walking in comparison. My habit is to take short, quick strides in an effort to conquer the hill as quickly as possible. I still often catch myself race-walking up hills until I counsel myself to slow down and lengthen my strides. I may reach the summit a few seconds later, but much less winded and quite a bit drier. Once again, the Senesi know how to take life in stride, so to speak.

Proximate Rivals

Still uphill but with a gentler slope, Via di Città meets the equally chaotic cross street of Via San Pietro. This intersection is commonly referred to as the Quattro Cantoni because the four main roads of the Terzo di Città intersect here. A right turn takes one directly to the front of the Duomo. To the left, I now briefly spy Linda's favorite gelateria called La Vecchia Latteria. One can witness the tasty product being made through their internal window, and we are now acquainted with the staff due to our admittedly frequent patronage. The place is clearly popular with tourists and contradaioli alike, especially the youngsters from nearby contrade.

On one corner of the intersection sits the comfortably-sized Piazza di Postierla, one of the symbolic outdoor hubs for the Eagle (*Aquila*) contrada. The name of *Postierla* generally reflects the distant medieval past when a defensive city wall and gate were located here. Today a rather massive column capped with a traditional she-wolf statue stands in the piazza near the intersection. Though in remarkably excellent condition (likely refurbished or reconstructed), this feature apparently dates in some form to the 1400s. Like the contrada of the same name, the she-wolf generally represents the storied founding of Siena by the sons of Remus. According to legend—greatly simplified for purposes here—the brothers Romulus and Remus had been born from a she-wolf and had ultimately founded Rome. At some point thereafter, Romulus felt compelled to kill Remus and did precisely that. Fearing for their lives, the sons of Remus promptly fled Rome, but not before stealing the she-wolf statue from Apollo's temple (how they managed to carry it remains a mystery). Their journey northward concluded on this very hilltop where they founded the city of *Sena*, now the oldest of Siena's three *terzi*. In this way, the she-wolf became a timeless symbol of Siena's apparent origins and can be found on numerous statues and sculptures decorating the cityscape and its buildings.

In addition to this meaningful civic landmark, the Eagle's rather humble baptismal fountain completes the public space. A nearly obscure alley leads from the piazza's back corner to the Eagle's own attractive garden area, which I had once accidentally discovered while chasing down the source of a live music concert.

More to the point, this piazza is nearly within sight of its rival's counterpart just up the street at Piazza del Conte. It is not uncommon during an evening stroll to find the Eagle's *alfieri* and drummers practicing here, within clear earshot of the Panther doing similarly. Due to this geographic proximity, we are told (with visual confirmation in recent years) that the police provide additional personnel to patrol this very intersection during the days of the Palio. There exists a higher than average probability that the *cazzotti* (ritualized fist fights) could break out between the two neighborhoods at a moment's notice. This is mostly explained by contrada geography: the Panthers cannot easily avoid walking through the Eagle's *rione* on their way to the Campo or elsewhere. Even on more peaceful evenings, the Eagle's symbolic space is a place to avoid for uneasy Panterini. Having acquired our gelato recently with Carlo and Sofia, Linda naturally headed to the stone bench in Piazza di Postierla. Carlo politely declined, however, motioning for us to continue onwards to more comfortable territory.

Given the deep-seated animosity between these west-side rivals, imagine my shock upon learning that the Eagle and Panther were once allies—and not long ago by Siena standards. The contemporary rivalry was forged only around the time of World War II. After enjoying an alliance for more than a century, a series of Palio-related events caused their mutual friendship to unravel.[95] The first occurred during the August 1936 Palio when the Eagle jockey conspired with the Snail to disrupt the Panther's heavily favored horse. The conspiracy succeeded, as the Panther's anticipated victory was thwarted. The alliance was consequently annulled, but only until 1938 when it was formally re-established. Lasting peace was not to be, however, as the Panther still sought vengeance for the 1936 incident. After Siena suspended the Palio during the War years of 1939-1945, the August Palio of 1946 provided such an opportunity. At the direct order of the Panther's captain—the same captain who had presided during the 1936 infraction—the jockey fiercely whipped his counterpart for the Eagle.

Then during the Eagle's *festa titolare* (patron saint celebration) later that year, Eagle contradaioli taunted the Panther publicly with insults spewed through a loudspeaker, thereby reminding the Panterini why their prized horse had lost in 1936. Suitably provoked, a scuffle ensued, after which the Panther removed its contrada flags from the Eagle's chapel. (Each contrada typically displays one or more flags of its allies in recognition of their mutual friendship—both along its main street and inside the chapel during ceremonies or events.) A more official end to the alliance came following a series of Panther contrada meetings in December 1947, the result of which included a decision to first ask the Eagle for an apology. Receiving no such gesture, the Panther officially parted ways with the Eagle, and a new rivalry was born.

Beyond the rivalry's "creation story," Piazza di Postierla enjoys an intriguing backstory of its own.[96] It is first important to know that the Eagle had been practically non-existent for more than a century. That is, until 1717 when representatives of the dormant contrada asked to participate in the August Palio. Rather than welcoming back the Eagle with open arms, however, the bordering contrade of the Panther, Forest, Turtle, and Wave reacted with hostility at the news. These four neighbors had essentially divided the Eagle's territory and claimed it for themselves. For its part, Piazza di Postierla had essentially been annexed by the Panther while the Eagle remained inactive. During those years, each contrada would raise money for its community by assigning an *accattano*, essentially a beggar, who would stand outside and solicit donations from passersby. The Panther's own *accattano* was accustomed to standing near the column at Piazza di Postierla to access the lucrative Quattro Cantoni intersection. With the reemergence of the Eagle and its historic claim to that public space, however, the Panther naturally dreaded the loss of a prime source of income. Only adding to the Panther's angst was the Eagle's victory in the Palio only one year after the contrada's official reinstatement.

The lingering border disputes between the Eagle and its four neighbors played a significant role in the aforementioned 1729 boundary decree by Princess Violante of Bavaria. Along with permanently stabilizing the boundaries of the remaining 17 contrade, the decree unequivocally assigned Piazza di Postierla to the Eagle. Clearly seeing the writing on the wall, the Panther ultimately negotiated with the reborn contrada to allow its *accattano's* fund-raising efforts to continue apace. The result was a successful compromise on a number of matters, not the least being that the Panther's beggar would be allowed to linger near the piazza's column on weekdays, as long as the agreement was renewed every three years. The Panther's assembly ratified the agreement on September 28, 1730, thereby signaling the birth of their mutual alliance that would last for more than two centuries.

Today, the Eagle-Panther rivalry enjoys a reputation of being perhaps Siena's most bitter one, though I have yet to personally witness direct evidence of this. Quite frankly, it is nearly impossible to imagine. The contrada's printed materials sometimes feature the cutest cartoon panther kittens on earth, and our own acquaintances have proven to be the most welcoming and gracious hosts. Such outward appearances do not exactly arouse sentiments of fear and awe, making it that much more difficult to imagine these people locking fists in passionate rage against their adversary. That said, I have admittedly been privy to more recent accounts of intentional provocations between younger Panterini males and their Eagle counterparts. Furthermore, it is clear that the rivalry lurks not far beneath the surface, if Carlo's subtle avoidance of the Eagle's piazza is any indication.

Of course, even bitter rivals can take it with a grain of salt, as we have seen previously. One Panther contradaiolo recently shared a story about his grandfather, who in the 1970s found himself in the middle of a fight between these two rivals. Suddenly, his wristwatch came off and flew away amidst the mayhem. As told by his grandfather, a leader of the Eagle involved in the brawl yelled, "Everybody, stop! [Paolo] lost his watch!" At which point, everybody ceased fighting to search for it. Once found, his grandfather secured it in his pocket and the brawl continued, the interruption immediately forgotten.

A second anecdote points to rather cordial relations during much of the year. This one is found in the Panther's regular periodical, *Il Grattapassere*, its title honoring the nickname of a beloved former jockey. In an article marking the fiftieth anniversary of the Panther-Eagle rivalry, the author concluded with a gracious message to his Eagle counterparts: "So, now, back to our days, a month away from yet another Christmas, I want to take this occasion to send our adversaries and their families my best wishes for happy holidays in the hope of a peaceful 1998 for everything, with the exclusion, of course, of the Palio!" [97]

A Pleasant Introduction

Once past the Quattro Cantoni intersection, Via di Città transitions into Via di Stalloreggi. Like Fontebranda for the Goose, Stalloreggi occupies a special sentiment for the Panterini, as the main street continues to cut through the heart of the contrada's *rione* and finds itself mentioned prominently in the contrada anthem and other folk songs. Now in their home territory, I sneak into one corner of Piazza del Conte to collect my wits. No sooner do I get my bearings when two people emerge almost simultaneously from buildings across the street. Perplexed, I actually recognize both of them. One of them is Silvia, who must have seen me skulking around outside. (Remember, you can't get away with anything around here!) And almost next door appears Simone! *I know this guy!* I think to myself as I reveal a smile of recognition. I may also be shaking my head at yet another pleasant coincidence. Simone returns his own recognition of me just as quickly. Meanwhile, Silvia is witnessing all of this and concludes with "Good, you both know each other!" before retreating back inside. Simone gestures with his own welcoming smile for me to join him. He is already patronizing what is apparently the Panther's preferred hangout. Already holding a glass of wine, he appears perfectly at home as he lingers in front of the bar near the door. He enjoys a commanding view of the street and piazza from here, essentially the secondary hub of the Panther's social space.

WEST SIDE STORY

Simone is an instantly likable fellow, with a lanky build and short, dark hair with almost a buzz cut on top. He loves to talk it up with anyone, including me. I first met Simone immediately following my infamous Panther museum visit when I sought a combined dinner between their group and ours. Since then I have run into him a few times, and he is always smiling and enjoying the social scene. Even better, he patiently accepts my limited Italian, and he slowly walks me through whatever assistance I require. Now introduced more formally, I chat with Simone for some time, standing with his glass of wine and me with a safer glass of prosecco. (*This bar doesn't have Fanta; what's up with that?*)

"So, you are a leader of the *Gruppo Giovani*? What kind of activities are you planning?" I begin.

"We have a hike scheduled, which maybe your class could join. There is also a pizza dinner and another lunch. I'm not sure of the dates, so I can text you," he replies, before offering some Italian grammar instruction.

"How long have you lived in Siena?" I ask, trying to learn something more about his own background.

"My whole life! Siena is my home. I don't want to be anywhere else." He grins broadly.

"What do you find special about the contrada?" I am always curious about how native Senesi answer this question.

"Well, it's like a big family, and we have always been a smaller contrada because we don't have direct access to residents outside the walls," he explains, somewhat surprising me with his nonchalant confirmation of what I had learned previously. "We don't have a lot of money, like the bigger contrade," he continues. "But I prefer it this way. Some of the others are too big, and it is a challenge to become familiar with everyone."

"So, you prefer a smaller contrada even though you might not win the Palio as often?"

"Well, that's somewhat true, as it is difficult to attract the better jockeys sometimes. But I would not want to be a part of a larger contrada. The Shell, or Caterpillar, for instance, or Porcupine—they are growing in size. Sometimes that comes with problems. People move in from outside Siena and become members, and you don't really know much about who they are."

"So, you do not want the contrada to grow?" I prod.

"No, I am very happy. We have everything we need. It's at a perfect size right now," he confirms. I have no idea how prevalent this perspective might be or whether he is trying to sugarcoat it for this outsider. Still, it is instructive to apparently learn that not everyone is seeking growth at all cost. Further, Simone is the fourth contradaiolo who has expressed a similar sentiment about the Panther. There might be something to it.

Simone and I manage to comprehend one another pretty well. He purposely speaks slowly to accommodate my learning curve, and occasionally even offers praise for correctly assembling the appropriate grammatical mix ("Bravissimo, Tom!"). Our conversation ultimately lasts awhile if we count all of his helpful instruction, fumbling through our respective schedules, and various discussion about his perspectives on the contrada. I appreciate his willingness to spend time with me at his favorite social hangout. We are occasionally interrupted by other arrivals who greet Simone as if he owns the place, with any combination of hugs, back slaps, and handshakes. Business is starting to pick up here. Eventually, I confirm that he will contact me with dates for the upcoming youth events. I leave him be, continuing to nurse his glass of wine as he lingers near the open entrance to the street.

Silvia's place is only a few doors down, and I nearly run smack into her uncle, Edoardo as he returns to their family's home base. This is a rare sighting indeed, so I act quickly with little thought. I say hello and ask if he remembers me from the previous year, to which he responds positively. In fact, I am a bit taken aback when he tells me in English, "I need a break. Come in and sit with me for a little while." How could I refuse?

Together we enter their establishment and he casually sits down behind a computer desk. I naturally take a chair opposite him. After some initial remarks about our class and plans for the summer, I ask a general question about Siena's economic status.

"Well, Siena's economy is based on four pillars," he starts to explain. "The bank, university, tourism, and the hospital. You might know that the bank collapsed a couple of years ago and is still being sold off." He is referring of course to the venerable Banca Monte dei Paschi. "The University is suffering some challenges and is experiencing lower enrollments," he continues, referring to the still highly regarded Università di Siena. "And for tourism, the city leaders are just starting to realize that they need to attract more visitors, rather than simply waiting for people to discover Siena.

WEST SIDE STORY

Without the Bank's full support, we need to develop other areas of the economy." Edoardo puts his hands behind his head and pushes his chair back, now becoming more introspective. "You see all of these buses driving to Siena for walking tours every day, but where are they staying?" he quizzes me.

"I actually don't know where they go at night," I respond honestly, realizing that these groups just magically disappear around dinner time. Soon thereafter, the Senesi take back their streets.

"Well, they can't stay in Siena because there are few decent hotels. The City hasn't encouraged building here, because, 'well, we're Siena, and we don't need to develop tourism! We have the Palio and the Bank!' they say." At this, I laugh. "Well, now they are paying attention and looking at how other places attract visitors, like Florence and, say, Grosetto. I've talked to tour group leaders, and they would love to stay in Siena. Instead, they have to drive an hour away to Florence or back down to the coast at night. We are losing a lot of business because of this."

I can't help but think about last year's conversation with Helen as we sat in the bleachers. *Perhaps she had a point.* Likewise, I have been told a few times that a sizable portion of Siena's population would just as well close the city gates to all visitors during the days of the Palio. It is safe to say that current public sentiments are split with respect to opening Siena's doors more thoroughly. Not helping the case for tourism has been a recent rash of graffiti, vandalism, and thefts of Senese artifacts. Much of this activity has been attributed to visitors rather than locals. Such occurrences are regularly reported in the local news media, making it only more difficult to promote the potential benefits that outsiders can bring. This is all quite understandable. As of this writing, the Eagle's public announcement holders have been damaged, and the Caterpillar's baptismal fountain has been vandalized three times—the second instance having occurred only weeks after its initial repair. Apparently unaware of nearby security cameras, a foreign college student was eventually apprehended. He admitted his guilt surrounding the third, most recent incident, if not the others. Beyond the Caterpillar, the Snail contrada is scrubbing off some incendiary graffiti on the outside of its city gate as I write this very sentence. Consequently, along with an increasing frequency of such graffiti reports, the Senesi are unfortunately experiencing a rude awakening to the standard challenges associated with tourism and the influx of outsiders.

While I am certain that the vast majority of visitors like us are generally respectful and decent people, it only requires a small trend of poor behaviors to sour a city's taste for tourism development. One local news article expressed such frustration with the following conclusion to yet another report of theft:

> Both the municipal administration and the police should begin to think about the anarchy that reigns supreme among tourists on the days of the festival. Now there is no more respect for anything, ranging from [taking] 'selfies' near the horse or . . . even trying to touch the horses for a caress. Aspects that in the past were very rare [have] instead become the order of the day.[98]

On the flip side, Edoardo also sees room for Siena's citizens to consider the benefits that outsiders can bring. "Siena is a very passionate place. I found my wonderful wife here, we have our family, our business, so we are doing well. I would rather not be anywhere else. But I came from a larger city about 25 years ago. The attitudes of the people here are different. It's more difficult for Siena to accept change and newer ideas. It's great to hold onto our traditions of the past, but the city is starting to realize that we need to open up a bit and see what other places are doing."

He then relates to a personal experience. "Here's an example, Tom. I was talking with some good friends the other day. I've known them for more than two decades. They were discussing some local issue, and when I offered my opinion, one of them waved at me and said, 'Don't worry about it, Edoardo, you haven't been here long enough to understand these things.' I mean, how long do I need to be here? I don't think it will ever happen, as I will always be the new guy," he adds quietly and without drama. He adds a chuckle, though I sense some latent frustration.

I get the sense that Edoardo would be just as happy to continue our conversation, were it not for the increasingly persistent distraction now overpowering us. The drums of summer are arriving. Edoardo isn't really phased, of course. It's like having a busy railroad outside one's home; the residents don't think twice about the occasional rumble or horn blast. Still, we both move to the door and peak outside. The repeating rhythm is now at fever pitch as it bounces off the nearby buildings. While I enjoy the familiar cadence as much as anyone, there is no longer any hope of continuing a coherent conversation.

I step into the street with Edoardo to see... Carlo! He and his drum are surrounded by a small entourage of young Panterini attempting to mimic his style and tempo. Carlo is in teaching mode, and they are strolling casually toward us along Via Stalloreggi as if enjoying their own miniature parade. The youngsters consist of a wide variety of ages, heights, and hairstyles. As I watch their otherwise humble entrance into Piazza del Conte, Carlo sends me an enthusiastic wave and smile before quickly returning to concentrate on his students. Caught up in conversations, the fact that this was the weekly time for contrada practice had completely slipped my mind.

More quietly, two other contrada instructors are assisting another set of youngsters with flag maneuvers. I have seen similar sessions play out elsewhere in recent years if I happen to be at the right place and time. Most amazing, perhaps, is how the children reveal no emotion or embarrassment while practicing, especially on display in front of who-knows how many tourists capturing their obligatory photos and videos. Are the students prepped for such public behaviors in advance? Or, are they simply numb to the tourist experience now that they have become accustomed to the attention? Perhaps some trainers purposely make use of public venues to prepare young performers for the eventual crowds. One thing that visitors like us don't often realize, Carlo would later explain, is that the children actually practice throughout the year. It is only during Palio time when they are seen and heard in public.

However, not all practice sessions are held in busy public venues at this time of year. I have accidentally discovered other contingents practicing in less noticeable alleys and building nooks. From a precise angle during a walk one evening, I spied a single young drummer practicing for the Goose in the back corner of Fontebranda while some 200 feet above him on the hill was his counterpart practicing for the Dragon. They do not always make themselves obvious. Either way, this instructional time is one of personal concentration, deference to instructors, and is overall a generally modest affair. The visitor is not the audience for these occasions. While anyone is welcome to watch and take photos respectfully from a distance, it is important to consider what a privilege it is to enjoy community members practicing in their own outdoor rooms.

As for this location, Piazza del Conte is not prone to high levels of tourist activity, though it can certainly attract a modest crowd. Currently, a few stragglers have heard the commotion and have arrived to satisfy their curiosity. The four children with flags have claimed the necessary space to twirl and swoop their solid red practice banners. Meanwhile, Carlo's drummers are now parked in a corner near the fountain, attempting to maintain a precise rhythm. Occasionally, Carlo reaches down to gently correct the hold of a drumstick, or to emphasize a certain approach. Somewhat humorously, the size of each drum matches that of its player, allowing them to manage their instruments without being overwhelmed. In one respect, tonight, we are witnessing the future of the contrada with its young talent maturing before our eyes.

Carlo and his students take a break, and silence once again pervades the outdoors. I wave goodbye and start my return down Via Stalloreggi toward the Eagle, only to stop suddenly in my tracks. I have forgotten something I brought with me earlier. Water bottle? No. *It's my notebook! Oh, crud* (expletive deleted). That notebook includes the bulk of my Italian phrases and planning information. *The last I saw it was with Simone at the bar*, I recollect. I do an about-face and start marching back up to Piazza del Conte. Now on a personal mission, I bolt for the bar entrance, and happen to show up at a rare moment when Simone is elsewhere. The bartender recognizes me, however, as Simone had kindly introduced us earlier. She points to the corner of the bar, sensing what I am seeking. "Yes! Thank you. See you soon," I say in Italian, and back out into the street I go.

Feeling relieved, I naturally glance across to the piazza to find one more pleasant surprise. *It's Matteo!* I haven't seen him since last year, and we had only spoken on the phone with Carlo during our recent hike.

"Thomas!" he yells. *He is happy to see me—a very good sign*, I think. "How are you?" He grabs one of my hands in both of his.

"Great to see you! Thanks for your help with the class," I say quickly. We are both leaning on the thin railing that separates us from the fountain.

"It's nothing," he responds modestly. "We will see you at the museum, right?"

"Yes, it is on our calendar. I was speaking with Simone about other possible activities," I add. "Also, I am wondering if Linda and I might be able to attend a contrada lunch or dinner on our own." I have wondered if they are genuinely supportive of me hanging around their community, with or without our cohort. Also, the students have amassed a packed schedule of their own, leaving precious few opportunities for further contrada events.

Then he drops another small bombshell: "Yes, of course. You are a friend of the Panther. You have an open invitation to attend any of our events."

"Wow, this is a great honor, thank you so much," I gush, now comfortable with expressing appreciation in Italian. Other men are lingering nearby, presumably waiting patiently to grab Matteo's ear. I thus say my goodbyes, and he turns his attention elsewhere.

Walking away for the second time this evening, I inwardly reflect on how one thing can lead serendipitously to another. Had I not forgotten my notebook, I would not have doubled back to the piazza to discover Matteo with his gracious invitation. Whether the planets somehow lined up or—more rationally—I was simply at the hub of Panther activities this evening, I shake my head once more. *This is the magic of Siena*, I contemplate. We have often advised the students, "Just get outside of your apartments and walk around in the evenings. You will nearly always stumble across some form of activity, someone you have already met, or an opportunity to make a new acquaintance. Just be there, and things can magically happen." Those who heed our advice are invariably itching to tell us stories the next day. Once again, I am apparently the beneficiary tonight of our own counsel.

CHAPTER 21

A Legendary Race

"Oh wow, this is so excellent! This is what the soccer players wear?" asks Angelo in quite decent English while meeting him at Piazza del Conte.

"Yes, I asked at the university store for the official men's jersey and shorts," I proudly exclaim. "They are large in American sizes, so they should fit you. I have no idea who the 'number one' on the jersey represents, but you are likely the first Senese to wear one, so I guess it makes sense," I chuckle as I hold up the jersey to reveal the bold, single digit on a deep blue background.

"I will definitely enjoy wearing them. They will be great to practice with."

"Well, I fully expect to see you wearing that during an upcoming contrada dinner!" I joke.

"Ha, I will see about that. Maybe!" He waffles as I intended. I then turn to our upcoming plans to join the Panther for our next event.

"I also want to confirm that you and some friends can still show the museum to our group next week. Simone mentioned that you would be able to lead the tour," I say in English, with the hope of hearing a confirmation in return.

"Yes, he talked to me about it, and I don't know who can come that night, but I will plan to see you at that time. That should work well, as we can all go to the società afterwards for dinner," he encourages.

"Ok, I will text you the day before to confirm. Thanks for spending some time with our class. It will be great to have them meet some people closer to their own age."

We close the conversation, and he heads briskly up Via Stalloreggi, carrying his new soccer attire. Prior to our arrival, I had asked him if he wanted anything I could easily pack from the US and this was his choice.

Readers might recall Angelo from my initial visit to the Panther museum discussed earlier. Since then he has served as a welcoming host into his contrada, clearly one of its most dedicated, young community members. In addition, he has ventured away from Italy to master his English competency and to earn a college degree. Of course, he still returns home for the summer *Palii*. We are fortunate that he is clearing his schedule one night to join our cohort at the museum and for dinner afterward.

Panther Museum Sequel

On this humid evening just prior to the days of the Palio, our museum tour has finally arrived. Once again I am now winding my way toward the Panther's narrow main street of Via San Quirico. Our students are already hanging outside Società Due Porte, catty-corned from the museum entrance. Normally bubbling with enlightening conversation, I find them uncharacteristically reserved while lingering uncomfortably outside a contrada hub they have yet to see.

It is just past 7:00 p.m., our designated meeting time with Angelo. I had carefully confirmed that someone would indeed meet us tonight. After a few awkward minutes, I let out a breath of relief as Angelo and a good number of his younger counterparts stroll toward us from the top of the hill. I silently celebrate at the rather sizable contingent that will join us tonight. As one might expect, both groups convene to exchange a shy set of greetings as they interact for the first time.

Immediately, we are aware of a playful bantering between Angelo and his main partner for the tour, Alessio, with whom Angelo is already trading barbs. "This is Alessio. He wishes he were taller so he could play better basketball, but that's not going to happen." Angelo ribs his more muscular, stocky peer. Alessio reveals that he is likewise beginning to explore the world outside Siena, currently continuing his studies elsewhere in Italy. The myriad of educational opportunities contrada youth are discovering within and beyond the Gothic City is impressive. Still, they also seem to return home for their most cherished events of the year.

Not to be outdone, Alessio retorts, "Well, Angelo here wishes that he had my good looks, so he has to compensate with sports." These and related comments serve as a sort-of ice breaker, allowing our group to relax and get to know their Senese counterparts.

As we enter the museum, the students continue to warm up to Angelo and Alessio. They are an engaging pair of guides, with their unscripted mix of family-type bantering and instruction from one room to the next. The younger boys and girls tagging along with them are adding another dimension to our visit, and they are gradually warming up to our cohort. A *scarier thing*, I contemplate: I am starting to recognize some of these youths from prior years and contrada events, having become something of an annual "regular."

Like that of the Caterpillar discussed previously, the museums of all contrade are organized in a logical fashion, with each room or hall space devoted to a central theme. Still, many of these places have been pieced together over time as various rooms or floors become available for sale or renovation, usually in any number of medieval-era buildings. Like the various twentieth-century baptismal fountains, the museums are a more recent addition to contrada properties. Consequently, the interior layout of each museum provides its own unique character and sense of place. The very act of moving from room to room requires unpredictable routes through any combination of vaulted ceilings, ramped hallways connecting multi-level rooms, and serpentine stairways. Occasionally, one is prompted to duck under a beam or low arch. This particular museum serves as a textbook case in point, with its one-of-a-kind floorplan. In a way, this and other contrada museums can be thought of as "living legacies" of their own, constantly being adapted for successive generations.

Back here at the Panther, the first room we enter from the street is likely the most fun, the Hall of Victories (*Sala delle Vittorie*). Let's just cut to the chase, so to speak, and see the Palio banners! Angelo proudly shows the most recent *drappellone* won by the Panther in July 2006, one decade earlier. Additionally, all of the contrada's twentieth century banners are likewise displayed in protected cases around the room, totaling ten in all—an average of one win per decade during that century. Given the times we live in, readers can find images and captions for all of them on the contrada's web site. The Panther found itself rather flush with wins during a few of those decades, accruing a respectable six victories between 1963 and 1994. Since that run of good

A LEGENDARY RACE

fortune, however, the people of Stalloreggi have earned a *drappellone* only once, the 2006 race to which we will return later.

As our guides shift around the room, I quietly direct our group's attention to the floor nearby. One of my favorite attractions is beneath our feet: an inlaid mosaic of the "rampant Panther," the most common contemporary symbol of the contrada, created in 1958 by local artisan Giordano Bruno Berrettini. Call me a sucker for inlaid floor mosaics, but this was one of the first things I noticed during my initial visit. *I have to get me one of those!* I am dreaming—no different than the first time I saw this full-color piece.

Alas, this is similar in scope to the massive metal door knockers and porcelain wall tiles we see for purchase in Siena and elsewhere. Such Italian wares are made to last centuries but simply would not fit—visually or physically—into our relatively flimsy wood-frame American homes. This fact can really lead to some measure of disappointment. You really need heavy, stone construction with thick, tile floors and doors that even the Florentine army could not penetrate (which, incidentally, was often the general goal for this high standard of construction). In a sense, your structure needs to be built like a dam before you even start to think about adding all of this cool, heavy stuff that doesn't fit in your carry-on bag. And you're certainly not installing it anywhere without making your floorboards droop or causing your drywall to crumble more quickly than one might hope. Perhaps more to the point, such decorations would just look out of place in much of contemporary American suburbia.

That said, Linda and I persevered once to get a bronze lion-shaped door knocker home from San Gimignano. A professional in our hometown had to cut the massive bolt because our front door of heavy, solid wood was still much too thin for its intended installation. Then, whenever anyone tried to gently deploy the knocker, the front door and nearby windows shook like an earthquake, as did our nerves.

Contrada Costuming

Eventually, we make our way to another sizable room with thick, wooden tables for costume preparation and maintenance. Many of the costumes are still worn for the *corteo storico*, *festa titolare*, and other contrada-related events.

My ears really perk up when I realize Alessio is discussing the evolution of costume designs. I am thinking about the *myth of the republic* concept discussed earlier. Prior to the 1860s—that is, before Italy was unified under one kingdom—the costume designs were actually inspired by those of the Piedmontese army of today's northern Italy, which was supporting the Kingdom of Sardinia during its war with Austria in 1848. If I understand correctly, none of these original costumes survive in this particular museum, though they are described in the historical contrada archives.

Following the unification of Italy in the early 1860s, the Renaissance era inspired the replacement costumes for the historical procession. Senese leaders were more interested in creating the spectacle of a "Renaissance fashion show," according to the contrada's website devoted to the topic.[99] For its part, the Panther replaced its earlier costumes to align more with the Renaissance theme, including redesigns in 1879, 1904, and 1928. This latter renewal was funded entirely for the first time by the Monte dei Paschi, and it continued to fund all successive costume renewals in 1955, 1981, and most recently, in 2001. The Foundation was the majority shareholder in the bank, as we have seen previously, which meant that the bank was essentially owned by the Senesi. By Statute, it was expected that most of the profits were to be distributed within the city and province. Given the bank's recent change in ownership during the economic crisis, any future funds for costume renewals will need to be found elsewhere.

Continuing on, the inspiration for the 1955 costumes came from early Renaissance Senese art of the 1400s, inspired in part by specific frescoes found within the Santa Maria della Scala (once Siena's civic hospital). The Panther's own versions took on the appearance of a "noble procession," complete with silk, velvet dresses, and lavish embroideries. Their designer, Bruno Marzi, was not only still alive but was also respected enough to earn a second commission for the ensuing overhaul of 1981. He apparently made little change, however, focusing on imaginative representations of the late Renaissance. In turn, the continued popularity of the 1981 designs served as the inspiration and reference point for the latest 2001 costume renewal. Consequently, the evolution of costume designs enjoys its own history. If one knows what to look for—or is fortunate to accompany a knowledgeable guide like Alessio—one can see much of this historical evolution play out inside this or any other contrada museum.

A LEGENDARY RACE

Sweet Victory

Following a barrage of fun-filled group photos and collective rounds of appreciation, our guides lead us out of the museum and across Via San Quirico to Società Due Porte. The younger Panterini are scattering elsewhere. I imagine we'll see many of them later at dinner. As for the società, I feel rather comfortable with the interior of its front portion, though I am chomping at the bit (pun intended) to see the rest of the facility. I am also curious to see the extent of activities and attendance within a smaller contrada that is not racing in the Palio. The activity around the società entrance is already buzzing as we arrive, with people darting in and out or engaged in conversation. As we move through the foyer, our cohort is already clustering more tightly to make room for those we are displacing. The density of human activity is matched by its upbeat clamor, as the sounds of conversation and the efforts of volunteers are competing for our attention. An American sports bar on Saturday night would be a rather subdued affair compared to the energy currently bouncing off the walls, floor, and ceiling. Far from discouraged, however, Alessio calls us together to address our group, testing his own voice projection.

He first motions for us to turn around at the top of the entry area's wide staircase. Above our heads on the wall is an enormous framed photograph, the size of which is indicative of the significant meaning it holds for the contrada. Representing what the Panterini refer to as *"il palio piu' bello di sempre"* (the most beautiful Palio ever), it features the Panther jockey overtaking that of the Eagle at the finish line during the race of July 2, 2006. I silently contemplate that we are approaching the tenth anniversary of this event, now less than a week away. The Panther can't win this one to make it an even decade, so they will need to hold out for the August campaign. For now, Alessio is nostalgically summarizing the magic of that race, despite the competing sounds around us. I chuckle, observing that it matters little whether we can hear the whole story or not. Alessio has been mentally transported back to that race and is reimagining the excitement from a decade earlier.

I must admit to feeling some pangs of sympathy for the poor Eagle contradaioli. Compared to the lengthy wait time for the start of many other races, this one required only seven minutes to launch the competitors. The lineup of horses at the *canape* found the Tower in the first position and the Eagle next door in the second. Its nemesis, the Panther, was way down the line at number nine, with the Porcupine serving as the *rincorsa*. The already-famous Luigi "Gigi" Bruschelli (Trecciolino), was the Porcupine's jockey, so his challenging position all but eliminated his hope of winning again.

The jockey for the Eagle was the lesser-known Virginio Zedde riding Ellery, a six-year-old female with only one previous Palio race to her name. Nicknamed simply "Lo Zedde," Virginio emerged from a family of jockeys, including his father and perhaps better-known brother, Giuseppe Zedde (nicknamed Gingillo).

Neither brother had yet won a Palio in Siena as of 2006, though Giuseppe would go ahead to win for the Caterpillar atop Elisir in August, 2008—the outcome of which is excitedly detailed in Robert Rodi's aforementioned book, *Seven Seasons in Siena*. He would then win his very next Palio in July 2009 for the Turtle, followed by his hiring by a hopeful Panther contrada that August. Unfortunately, his victory for the Turtle would be his last for quite some time.

As for Virginio, he was angling for his first victory while employed by the Eagle on that fateful July day of 2006. When Trecciolino decided to start the race quickly, the Panther's jockey, Andrea Mari (Brio), had barely moseyed into the ninth position behind the *canape*. With all ten contenders off and running, Brio found himself in the rear of the pack as expected, essentially parallel with Trecciolino by the time they passed Fonte Gaia. By this time the Eagle's Lo Zedde had already shot out ahead of everyone by at least a horse length, followed by the Forest, Ram, and Tower. As if the Eagle needed even more of a boost, several horses piled up against the mattresses at San Martino, thereby shaking up the dynamics of the race. By the time San Martino was clearing out the mess, Lo Zedde was already on his own and taking the turn at the Casato. Now in a distant second place was the originally hapless Goose, followed in turn by... Brio, riding an eight-year-old gelding named Choci. Still, it was difficult to imagine a Palio with a more certain outcome than the Eagle would soon enjoy.

Much of the second lap continued similarly, with Lo Zedde out ahead and the Goose and Panther far behind. However, as the third lap began, Brio had wisely taken two inside curves to eventually pass the Goose into second place. The traditional rivals were now in positions one and two, still with the

A LEGENDARY RACE

Eagle comfortably ahead. But Brio was closing the gap, and he finally put away the Goose once and for all. By the time the threesome had survived San Martino for the last time, the two rivals were only a few horse lengths apart. Still, not even the race's TV commentators likely foresaw what would happen next. Lo Zedde apparently didn't know how close the Panther had come. He consequently slacked off a bit prior to hitting the finish line, confident the race was his. This was all the encouragement Brio needed to pull off the upset. Only one meter from the finish line, Brio pushed Choci past the Eagle by maybe a nose length and stole what had been a presumed victory for Lo Zedde. *Oops.*

As one might imagine, the Eagle contrada was despondent that their assured victory had flipped into perhaps the most embarrassing second-place finish possible. Even a similar comeback win by any other contrada may not have stung quite as badly. But its rival? As one news article grossly understated, the surprise loss "will certainly make for difficult relations between Lo Zedde and the contender for which he ran."[100] Adding insult to injury, the Panthers still recall how the Eagle contradaioli in the Campo had assumed they had won and consequently rushed onto the track in celebration. To their astonished horror, they soon realized their mistake and went scampering back. Unfortunately, their sudden reversal was not fast enough to avoid the ensuing penalty. A fine was soon levied on the contrada for celebrating prematurely.

Despite his epic loss, Virginio Zedde has managed to enjoy a relatively successful career, including victories in other races outside Siena. As of this writing, however, he has yet to win a Palio in Piazza del Campo.

As for the Panterini, the victory has achieved legendary status. If there exists a more emotionally charged event in their recent memory, I do not know what it is. Aside from printed posters and banners of the race and its celebratory aftermath, Panterini of all ages have shown us a variety of archived digital imagery and videos on their personal devices, ready to share at a moment's notice. Some regularly use photos of the race to replace otherwise standard face-shots on their social media profiles. For the people of Stalloreggi, the victory was one for the ages and has achieved a life of its own. From this outsider's perspective, the legendary race continues to play a significant role in their community's very fabric, providing yet another shared bond between its members.

The Americans are Coming!

Under the continued leadership of Angelo and Alessio, we make our way past a rather large, open sitting room with no walls separating it from the main entryway or bar area. A lone television is perched up in the corner. A few Panterini are sitting at small, round tables to socialize in advance of tonight's dinner. It is still unclear to me exactly where the dinner will be held. They are not setting up any tables on Via San Quirico. In any case, I contemplate quickly that I have now moved beyond my own personal "high water mark" inside Società Due Porte, having not seen the facility beyond the bar where I once borrowed a pen. Angelo provides a few more comments and arm waves as we now turn right into an unadorned corridor with windows on one side, followed by a door at its terminus that opens into another sort-of anteroom. I really don't know how else to describe this layout. From there, another door leads back outside, forming a bottleneck; we all hug the wall to allow various Panterini to dart in or out. *Where are they going?*

My question is answered as I smile broadly. We are stepping outside into a *cortile*, or inner courtyard, surrounded by the società and other attached two-story buildings adorned with impressive round-arched windows. Lengthy rows of tables are set up parallel to one another, providing a perfect fit within this nearly square-shaped space. Welcome to the contrada's own outdoor dining room. I estimate that the space can fit a few hundred people. The folding tables have yet to be adorned with place settings, as plenty of time remains before dinner. Still, some of the volunteer youth are already lugging around various necessities—some of which are being handed more efficiently through windows—including packs of water, wine bottles, stacks of plates, and rolls of paper table coverings. This latter material is inscribed with regularly spaced logos of the "rampant Panther," not unlike the coverings we saw in the Goose. There must be one company nearby that supplies various contrada goods such as the decorated, rolled paper. With the assistance of standardized products designed for all contrade, the dinner preparation and setup is down to a science.

Given the extra time before dinner, we discover some opportune activities to encourage involvement with our hosts. "How many of you like to play cards?" Alessio asks our group. He gestures for our cohort to sit at one of the tables on the far side of the courtyard. Some respond enthusiastically about various games they enjoy. *Who says young people don't play cards anymore?* I think to myself. Nearly every year the students teach us different card games while sitting in circles in the twilight of the Campo. Alessio mentions a few games which none of us claim to recognize. Eager to learn, at least half the students jump in immediately. At this point, some of our younger Panterini friends from the museum are now huddling over our shoulders in hopes of watching or playing. Without even trying, young people from America and Siena are enjoying time together in a completely unscripted way. Just throw your group into a società with bored youngsters lurking about, and there you go.

For those of us merely looking on, a new distraction catches our eye: basketball hoops. In one corner of the courtyard is an extension where two freestanding hoops are currently stored, with one of them positioned for half-court play. A few of the Panterini are already bouncing the Italian version of basketballs and making half-hearted attempts to land the occasional bucket. Now feeling more at home here, some of our students decide to join in. I am more encouraged about this development when I see our own group happily deferring to our younger hosts who already live here. We will not be remembered as those boisterous Americans who always hog the ball.

Predictably, it is only a matter of a few minutes before I am asked to join. Strangely, this request requires little encouragement, as I have been gradually learning to play the game myself, in what is most likely a much-delayed interest in team sports. Thanks to some patient colleagues back home, I can now claim to hold my own with mini-jumpers, layups, and defensive takeaways in weekly pickup games. Not long after the students pull me in, I am passing the ball and attempting layups, albeit with the predictable sweat enveloping my body. *I'm glad this is not a formal event tonight*, I comfort myself. We have somehow appropriated the courtyard of a contrada for the moment, though fortunately with a pleasant faction of younger Panterini to vouch for us.

Amongst the Panterini

As dinner preparation intensifies, the young women volunteering tonight are fully engaged with rolling out the paper table coverings. Linda has found her way to the courtyard and is taking her seat across from me to enjoy various updates from the group. Soon thereafter, another contingent is placing water and wine bottles at regular intervals, including both *naturale* and *frizzante* water options. Although we Americans tend to prefer the non-carbonated *naturale*, beggars can't be choosers. Once that disappears—and it always does, quickly—the bitter, carbonated option still does the trick. At restaurants, Linda and I have learned to distinguish between *acqua gassata* (carbonated water) or *non-gassata* (natural, no gas), usually with a chuckle shared between us. Even years later, it is not uncommon to quickly grab a water bottle without thinking, only to discover annoyingly that it is carbonated. *Rats!* Welcome back to Italy. Still, if quenching one's thirst is the primary objective, any of this stuff will work, pumped with gas or not.

As for the wine bottles decorating our table, they are sporting a design that I have not seen previously. I am already eyeballing one as a potential keepsake after it is emptied, though I admittedly am not personally willing to assist with the emptying part. Still, the wine will certainly disappear soon enough. As for the wine labels, they are unique to the contrada, with tonight's version including a red and blue background and a dominant "68" in the center—revealing the contrada's unique number once again. Angelo isn't quite sure about the history or meaning of 68, though he should not feel embarrassed by any means. Not even the experts have unlocked the mystery of contrada numbers to my knowledge, beyond the fact that every contrada has its own unique number within the range of 3 (Tower) and 90 (Ram). Such numerology is actually found throughout Italy, and thus is not unique to Siena. Still, the numbers serve as yet another identifier for each particular contrada. Aside from the wine labels, "68" can be seen boldly emblazoned across the t-shirts and sweatshirts of Panther youths during dinners like this one. I am also not immune to enjoying some fun with numerology myself, noting to Linda that my Mother's birth year plus our most recent anniversary add up to none other than 68. I receive the not-undeserved eye roll and wave-off in return. *But still!*

We have settled naturally in the corner of the courtyard nearest the basketball hoops and the impromptu children's playground. Various toys and playhouses are now decorating the paving stones nearby. The children are beginning to appear as well, with an occasional Mom or Dad in tow as deemed necessary. At our end of the table is a collection of probably 16 teenage girls, some of whom helped escort us earlier through the museum.

A LEGENDARY RACE

At one point, a student of ours reaches over to ask, "Why do you sing?" Though I might have phrased the question somewhat differently, I am certainly leaning in to hear their response. They are actually dumbstruck and for once tonight are speechless, not quite knowing how to reply. *Of course, they have been learning folk songs since they could talk, so it is simply a part of who they are*, I contemplate. Rather than tackle the question any further, one of them leads into a version of the Song of Verbena, a treat which we never turn down.

This initial vocal interlude seems to encourage additional singing on their part. Perhaps they are partially enjoying the novelty of an intrigued American audience nearby. As the evening progresses into the first two courses of the meal, our companions churn out a variety of songs, and other contradaioli around them catch the spirit and join in. We are unwittingly sitting at the center of a veritable Panther soundtrack. I am familiar with a couple of their songs, so I at least make an effort to hum along.

By this point, Linda has somehow befriended one of the girls sitting next to her. While conversation remains at fever pitch, the teen is now writing vigorously on the paper table covering, apparently at Linda's request. *What did Linda ask them to do?* I wonder. I had not been paying close attention. Friends nearby are now assisting with the task. Curiosity gets the better of me and I ask Linda what the girl is writing. Somewhat flummoxed, she responds, "I think the words to the song they just sung. I just asked her what the song meant," she replies with a shoulder shrug. It appears the project Linda inadvertently gave them is time-consuming, and they are kindly taking it more seriously than Linda had hoped.

I can tell they are having fun, however, and I can't wait to see what emerges on the tablecloth. This is a song I have heard repetitively at numerous contrada events and occasionally in the Campo. The sweet melody is always a welcome sound—the complete antithesis to a war chant. As written paragraphs emerge on the table catty-cornered from me, I briefly wonder how they will transfer this knowledge to Linda. No matter, though, as Linda simply passes her phone camera to easily capture the work. Concluding their task, I join Linda in praising their effort and thank them profusely. They think nothing of it and return to conversations. The lyrics and English translation are provided here:

LIVING THE PALIO

Suona suona campanina
Che per me non suoni mai
Ma stavolta suonerai
Suonerai soltanto per me (e din-don din-don)

Suona suona campanina
Suona e mai non ti stancare
Che ci s'ha da ripurgare
Tutta quanta la citta' (e din-don din-don)

Ring, ring, my little bell
Since you never ring for me
But this time you will ring
You will ring only for me (and ding-dong, ding-dong)

Ring, ring, my little bell
Ring and never get tired
That the time has come to purge
The whole city (and ding-dong, ding-dong)

As I would learn later, *campanina* translates as the "little bell" and serves as the folk song's central theme. It refers generally to the typically smaller bells found atop all contrada chapels. These are the very bells that Linda and I somehow managed to ring during the Goose victory several years ago, and they are expected to continue ringing all night after a contrada wins a Palio. One friend from the Panther fondly shared his own experience with me:

> People will alternate, and kids will pull the rope for hours. I remember doing it in 1978 but only for a little while because there were tens of kids wanting to do the same. It is indeed a small bell, and the sound is not too loud and often disappears among the noise of the winning contrada. But it will continue to ring for hours, and if you try hard enough, you will definitely hear it.

The song, therefore, expresses the hope of winning the next Palio, in turn allowing the bell to ring and "never get tired" through the night.

A LEGENDARY RACE

Meanwhile, the losing contrade proceed to (rhetorically, I am assured) purge themselves.

Here in the Panther's courtyard, the sun has finally set, giving way to even brighter artificial lighting from floodlights attached to the walls. Some of our youthful friends have departed for elsewhere as the first course (*primi piatti*) winds down. Had this been an actual restaurant, the point has been reached when adults settle in for lengthy conversations while the bored children become fidgety and cantankerous. However, this is no formal indoor restaurant where behaviors are seriously monitored. Rather, in this grand outdoor room, the children are sent to play with their counterparts on the periphery of the dinner scene, where their collective safety is assumed. It's a bit like a giant family barbecue in America.

Of course, elementary-school children can get creative on their own. Another kind of amazing race is developing near our end of the piazza where the children have room to run. "Wait a minute," I say with pleasant surprise. "They're holding their own Palio!" Soon enough, the boys and girls involved have calculated that they can run around the entire outer perimeter of the courtyard—albeit with a few obstacles to hurdle around. Most adults are preferring to remain focused on their internal conversations. Actually, this activity is probably nothing new to seasoned Panterini who have enjoyed friends and food here countless times. For us, however, the miniature Palio race is only becoming more humorous to watch between final bites of our *primi piatti*.

Eventually, the children organize themselves sufficiently to agree on their own starting line near our location. "We have prime seats near the *mossa*!" I joke to whomever is listening. Somehow, they start the race on cue and take off at speed. A few of them end up tripping over obstacles or their own feet, as at least two of them go down hard, disappearing from view. "Oohh, are they ok?!" I exclaim. But they reemerge just as quickly to chase after the others. Looking at my neighbor, I comment, "I bet whomever is assigned the Eagle has a slim chance of winning this one," I chuckle. That is, of course, if any of them have been assigned the Eagle at all.

Not unlike a miniature Piazza del Campo, we are following their bobbing heads around the perimeter. Eventually, they make the turn to our side and rush behind our chairs. Wooossshh! There they go! The race ends after one lap, although, eventually, many of them catch their breath and line up again. We witness four or five of these races before the participants eventually tire and split up for other activities. Those around me have been chuckling at the spectacle, though some of us notice a larger meaning.

Linda confirms, "This is like a giant outdoor family. The kids are having a blast, as long as they don't kill themselves. I mean, look at the basketball hoops! They are climbing the scaffolding."

I respond in kind, "This contrada really does have a relaxed atmosphere. The Panthers seem to be more informal and comfortable than some others." Perhaps Simone had made an important observation from our recent conversation; it may indeed be possible for a contrada's population to outgrow its ability to know everyone well enough.

As if to drive home this point, a lone toddler arrives near the far end of our group. We have no idea who she belongs to, but somehow she has commandeered a walker with wheels and is determined to drive it on her own. Staggering around with a contraption three times her size, she now insists on shoving it down the aisle between the tables. Given the proximity of chairs and people sitting back-to-back, however, this feat is daunting as she clangs into chair after chair. Who knows where the parents are? No matter, we're all laughing now and are taking turns, pulling in our chairs from both tables to widen her intricate path. *Let's see how far she can take that thing!* What is the message I take from this? She is everyone's child here tonight, and the parents clearly trust this is the case.

Speaking of which, at our end of the table, Linda has already made friends with the mother of two wayward toddlers sitting behind her. Dad comes and goes to assist with the kids, including bathroom runs and play time behind our table. Linda is in her element with children nearby, and eventually, she is joining Mom to assist in the makeshift playground in our corner of the courtyard. At one point, the Mom appears to be flustered, as her husband isn't immediately available. In a combination of Italian and English, Linda motions that she is happy to take the older one to the restroom if necessary. Mom is grateful, and thus Linda bids us farewell and leads the tyke into the società to find the restroom. Linda has not only made herself at home like the rest of us, but she is now assisting with other people's children. It was only a matter of time. We must seem friendly and trustworthy enough for Mom to hand over her child to a blond-haired stranger headed toward the door.

A LEGENDARY RACE

Eventually, Dad returns to his seat to find Linda and the rest of his family happily engaged in the playground area. His look of boredom while he scans the crowd encourages me to walk around our table and say hello—something particularly out of character for me, but so be it. I am likely comforted by the fact that both he and his wife have already seen me with Linda earlier this evening. Upon arrival I make my introduction. He speaks a little English, but I end up practicing my Italian through much of our ensuing conversation.

"My name is Pietro," he says with a smile, apparently pleased to have someone to chat with. After I explain our purpose here, he asks, "For how long are you in Siena?" This is the most common question directed to our group.

"We are here for five weeks, until after the Palio," I explain. "The students are learning about the Palio and contrade before they see the race," I add, letting him know that we have done our cultural homework.

"Yes, we are not running in this Palio, but our rival is running," he mentions with tightened lips and lowered eyebrows. He is not pleased.

"Are you or other contradaioli concerned about that?" I ask, curious as to the response I will hear.

"Yes, I would say we are concerned, though we won't really know until the extraction of the horses. If the Eagle draws a strong horse, we will be more nervous," he explains.

I follow up on this train of thought. "If the Eagle extracts a novice horse, they will not likely attract an experienced jockey, right?"

"Exactly, there is not much chance that a contrada will try hard to win and pay a lot of money if they are not in a strong position," Pietro explains. He then provides some personal perspective about the horses chosen to run the Palio: "When I was younger, we saw more famous horses chosen each year," he begins, followed by a litany of names of the four-legged heroes from a decade or two earlier. "But these days they don't often choose the best horses, or ones that have won the Palio. It's not that it's better or worse than what I remember, it's just different," he shrugs it off. I could still easily sense his frustration with how the Palio is run nowadays as he sees it. "My guess is that we won't see last year's winning horses. They will be in the *tratta* to get people's attention, but they will not likely be chosen to race. Nowadays, a horse wins one Palio, and it's out for good after that."

"Is that because the captains want a better chance of winning with a novice horse?"

"Yes, that's part of it, to select the horses in the middle—not the best or the worst. I think that some of the more influential people involved are also trying to control the race." He is referring to certain veteran jockeys who will remain unnamed here. They own a lot of horses and have trained a relatively large percentage of younger jockeys who also run the Palio.

The selection of horses has certainly shifted through time, like many other gradual changes to the Palio. Another long-time Panther contradaiolo had explained to me that horses actually once roamed the streets, mingling with the Senesi. It was from this pool of wandering steeds that the Palio horses were selected. These were typically slower horses owned by local residents. This practice actually continued up through the 1960s, after which the jockeys began to view the Palio more as a business. They consequently began to buy, own, and train horses specifically for the Palio. As the horses became more specialized through their breeding, they trended ever close to the *purosangue* (pure breed). These horses may have become faster, but they were increasingly prone to accidents and injuries. By the 1990s, this was being partially countered with the shift to selecting stronger, mixed breeds, albeit while sacrificing some speed.

Meanwhile, between the 1970s and 1990s, it was noticed that several faster horses were winning the lion's share of the *Palii* they raced (with venerated names including Rimini, Panezio, Urbino, Topolone, and Benito). This provided more of an incentive for captains to choose horses more in the middle of the field. In recent decades, the mix would generally consist of 3-4 very good horses, 3-4 moderate ones, and a couple of novices. Lately, the shift seems to have moved to more novices and fewer veterans. But every so often one or two previous Palio winners can be found in the final field of ten.

I am intrigued now because Pietro is discussing changes he has witnessed in recent decades. An opening presents itself: "Has the Panther remained the same size since you were younger?"

"Oh, no, it was much smaller 20 or 30 years ago," he says definitively. "It was even smaller before that, like prior to the 1970s."

"Really? Wow," I exclaim with visible surprise. I had expected him to claim it was either the same size or larger.

A LEGENDARY RACE

"Yes, my father remembers better and has mentioned the changes in the Panther," he continues. "I don't remember much before the 1980s, but before about 1978, the entire contrada could fit within this courtyard," he says while gesturing around the rest of the space. "For instance, the contrada has grown in membership since then, to the point where the *cena della prova generale* had to be moved to its current street location to accommodate our larger numbers. Prior to 1986, I think, everyone could fit into this courtyard for that event." Pietro is, of course, referring to the massive outdoor dinner scene that we had enjoyed the previous year. I reflect that even the Panther must have benefitted from the expanding interest in the contrade and Palio documented by other writers.

I am enjoying our conversation, though reality is beginning to collapse on us. Gelato is being served, and his children are returning to hopefully eat with Dad. Linda and Mom are wrapping up their impromptu play date nearby. Somehow I explain that we attended this dinner tonight because of past acquaintances I have made, including an assistant with the young people's group, Simone. With this knowledge, he throws me one more Senese surprise for the night:

"You know Simone? He is my cousin!"

No way. Way. There are a few hundred Panterini here tonight, and I am by chance speaking to Simone's cousin. My mouth opens once again and utters a genuine comment of surprise. I then feel the urge to compliment his cousin, Simone more rigorously.

"Simone has been a big help, and he is very friendly to work with. We have met at the bar near Piazza del Conte."

"Oh, yes, he loves to hang out there, and he has lived in Siena for a long time. I also like to tease him a lot, but he takes it," he adds. "He has a good sense of humor."

I respond, "Yes, he said that he could not be here with us tonight. I should text him and say I am talking to his cousin!" This thought just comes to me spontaneously.

"Yes, let's take a photo with both of us, and send it to show him what he is missing," he continues along my line of thinking with a smile. At which point, we take a selfie on my phone, and I send the photo as a message to him with a brief greeting from both of us. *This SIM card is paying off in more ways than one*, I silently realize.

LIVING THE PALIO

As Pietro and I part ways for the night, I catch myself grinning, shaking my head, and thinking once again to myself, *only in Siena.*

CHAPTER 22

Pushing the Envelope

"CARLO, CAN YOU STILL ATTEND THE DINNER WITH US TONIGHT?" I TEXT AS A confirmation.

"Tom, yes, Sofia and I will be there to spend time with your group!" he responds quickly.

"Ok, great! I need to coordinate with everyone to meet after the trial," I explain.

He then adds, "We are going to watch the trial at Due Porte. If you want, you can join us! We will be there by 18:30." Like all Italians, Carlo is using the 24-hour clock, what we might call "military time," which can throw Americans off guard. I am now to the point where I rarely need to think about converting the hours.

"Thanks for the invitation, I would enjoy watching it with you! I will check with Linda and will confirm," I write back reservedly, containing my enthusiasm. I have just been invited to my first società viewing event! I can easily forego lingering in the Campo to instead join Carlo, Sofia, and fellow Panterini in house.

Assignment of the Horses

It is mid-afternoon now, the hottest, most oppressive time of day when the outdoors are least appealing. Even in Siena, amidst the tourist throngs, a sizeable portion of stores and other businesses are closed for *pausa pranzo*, the traditional Italian afternoon break between 1:00 and 4:00 p.m. We were all present earlier for the emotional assignment of the horses, which occurred around 1:00 p.m. following the morning *tratta*. Held directly in front of Palazzo Pubblico, this pivotal event consists of a lottery to determine the match of horses with their respective contrade. During the hour prior to its start, each of the ten contrade competing in the Palio march into the Campo in an impressive display of solidarity, marked not only by their imposing front wall of determined men but also by unified singing or chanting as they arrive. If only for show, they present the variably intimidating appearance of a people prepared for war. In that vein, the "fighting" men take the lead into battle, thereby protecting the women and children who march behind. Eventually, all ten contrade take their place to stand in the Campo, amidst the rest of us onlookers.

Perhaps wisely, the assignment—also referred to as the drawing or extraction—is carried out with complete transparency, for all to witness in person or on television. The city's mayor personally announces the matches from a raised stage. The whole affair is elegantly simple, in marked contrast to the passion it evokes among the contradaioli. Upon drawing a printed slip marked with a number from one to ten, the slip is handed to the mayor who in turn proceeds to read it to the crowd. The numbers have already been matched with the final ten horses chosen to race in the Palio, displayed prominently on large score boards attached to the Palazzo Pubblico. To eliminate any suspicion of conspiracy, the mayor simultaneously holds the number at arm's length for all of us to see. Following his announcement of the number, the second slip of paper is drawn from a similar tumbler to select the horse's assigned contrada. As this second drawing takes place, the Campo turns eerily silent as the suspense rockets higher. Upon receiving the drawn slip, the mayor publically announces the contrada. The human reaction from the crowd is instant and passionate, though the particular emotion projected depends entirely on one's perspective. Emotions range from incomparable elation to utter disappointment. Their reactions can also be deceiving, as one contrada might celebrate because its rival extracted a less desirable horse.

Given Pietro's comments at the dinner last night, we did not expect to see previous Palio winners within the ten horses selected. This was precisely the case today, as no prior winners were included for the July 2 race. The most experienced horses are Mocambo and Porto Alabe, each having finished six races without a win. The Goose contradaioli were celebrating with fists in the air, yelling, and eventually singing as they led Porto Alabe out of the Campo toward Fontebranda. Likewise, the Turtle was moderately excited, though perhaps not to the level one might expect when landing the other veteran, Mocambo. Perhaps there is an inside story about Mocambo that I have yet to be told. In contrast, the Shell matched the level of ecstatic glee demonstrated by the Goose, having extracted Quadrivia, with only one Palio to its name. Another curiosity was the She-Wolf, which expressed mild enthusiasm for extracting Preziosa (Precious) Penelope. These are clearly the optimists of the day, as Preziosa has raced only once before. As the continuing *nonna* of Siena, however, I imagine the Lupaioli are willing to cling to any good news; they are essentially living on a prayer.

Most important for the Panterini, today's attendees from the Eagle were less than enthusiastic. They could practically be heard sulking as they departed the Campo. Renalzos is one of the five novice horses yet to attempt an actual race here. As we have seen in a previous chapter, he would be described as a *debuttante*, and his abilities remain a mystery. Of course, there is still reason for our friends from Stalloreggi to maintain slightly elevated nerves. Many of these horses are unknown quantities and will compete without any previous stars of the Palio to contend with. Sometimes a jockey from a particular stable knows these horses well and are keeping various secrets to themselves. They occasionally surprise the Senesi when they sign on with a contrada that supposedly has landed a novice. Others sometimes decide to sign on with a specific contrada well in advance of the Palio, regardless of what horse is extracted. This can occur when one or more of the contrada's allies agree to chip in a portion of the jockey's commission. For these reasons, the respective match of horse and jockey to a particular contrada can make little apparent sense on the surface.

Regardless, the question of the jockey-contrada assignments will become public this evening before they don their respective outfits for the first trial. Technically the jockey can shift to another contrada up until the morning of the Palio, though I have never seen such a thing occur during our time in Siena.

The Eagle has Landed

I decide to show up at Società Due Porte at around 6:45 p.m., hoping to find Carlo and Sofia already entrenched inside. Linda is waving this one off, content to enjoy her time elsewhere tonight. Upon arrival, I slip nearly unnoticed into the società where the decibel count is already at sports-bar level. Most others are either standing to socialize or have already taken seats in front of the raised television. I am feeling less self-conscious than in the past, which is quite frankly a relief and perhaps a personal milestone. In any case, there must be more dramatic issues for these people to ponder right now than seeing that gangly *Americano* lingering once again in their living room. At least, that is my wish. My tense shoulders still end up dropping a bit at the familiar sight of Carlo and Sofia, having already taken their seats. I approach their location and gravitate to the empty chair to Carlo's right.

"Ah, Tom! I saved a chair for you!" he says happily.

I say hello to Sofia on his opposite side. "I am surprised at how many people are here right now," I open. "Is this typical for a trial?"

"It depends. The younger contradaioli would tend to watch in the Campo if we were running. Tonight is our first look at the Eagle, and its jockey, Tremendo. There is a lot of interest in how the Eagle performs tonight," he explains, complete with this latest news of which I was unaware.

"You already know the jockeys?" I exclaim dumbly, somewhat aghast that I missed this latest development. I want to stay completely up to date and in the know! I realize now that I have not kept up with my news feeds online recently.

"Yes, Tremendo is the jockey for the Eagle," Carlo states matter-of-factly and without much outward expression of concern. "They did not get one of the better horses. This is a very good thing!" He laughs.

"Oh, I recognize Tremendo. Didn't he run for the Goose last year?"

"Maybe, I don't know. He has run 8 times but never won," he cites a statistic already committed to memory. He turns briefly to Sofia, something I applaud so as to avoid usurping all of his time here. I now undertake a personal mission to access local Siena news outlets on my phone to find a list of tonight's jockeys and their assigned contrade. I eventually hit pay dirt (no pun intended) and start to absorb the always-intriguing information.

"Oh wow, Trecciolino is running for the Dragon. I don't know why, because their horse is a novice," I say partially to myself. This may be a case, I consider, where Trecciolino could be holding inside information that gives him confidence. As for the Eagle's Tremendo, his real name is Francesco Caria and he is likely hoping to regain some respect after quickly being thrown from the Goose's prized Oppio last year. In related news, Enrico Bruschelli—Trecciolino's son—is assigned to the Giraffe, while the up-and-coming star,

Giovanni Atzeni (nicknamed Tittia), will make a second attempt with the Shell, likely hoping to finish the race this time atop his steed.

Also of note here is the Goose, which should be pleased with its jockey, Gingillo (Giuseppe Zedde), who is coming in with 21 *Palii* and two victories to his name. To recall, he is the more successful brother of Lo Zedde, who nearly won for the Eagle ten years ago. I would also be remiss to not mention another jockey of note, running for the ever-hopeful She-Wolf. Nicknamed Scompiglio, Jonatan Bartoletti is a veteran of 16 races with two victories of his own. One may recall that he ran for the Panther a year earlier but managed to secure a less than impressive outcome.

By the time I sort out the jockeys and their respective contrade, the chairs around us are filling in. The trial will apparently be "must-see TV." If we count everyone either sitting or standing, there are likely more than a hundred people here, and they are packing in around us. We are sitting about two-thirds back, so it is fun to watch the banter between everyone seated in front of us. If there was any lingering doubt about the intensity of the Panther-Eagle rivalry, this event is putting it to rest.

The track has been cleared and the city leaders and captains have strolled past the Casato to assume their positions on the judges' stand. As anticipated, we then catch our first glimpse of the ten selected horses and their assigned jockeys as they emerge one by one from Palazzo Pubblico. All remains calm until Tremendo comes into view for the Eagle. The place erupts around me with a sudden barrage of booing and likely other comments which I, fortunately, cannot understand. Carlo joins in with vigor. His smiles indicate that he is having fun more than spewing genuine vitriol, however. The main benefit of all the whooping against the Eagle, I interpret, is to let off some steam and nervous energy. A steady buzz of voices in the room continues for some time as the jockeys fall into their expected circling routine behind the *mossa*.

Following an expected, if lengthy, period of fidgeting, the contestants are lined up and ready to launch. Finally, the *canape* drops and the horses and jockeys leap forward, some faster than others. This is a trial, so most jockeys will be more conservative. Still, there is a general sense of racing, and our entire room is glued to see the results upon their arrival at San Martino. Somewhere in the middle of the pack, Tremendo enters the turn.

BOOM! Our room erupts instantly in celebration as if reacting to a final championship score. Some viewers jump to their feet and chairs fly backwards. Others have their arms raised in sheer joy and are high-fiving one another. Carlo is one of them. The whole incident catches me off guard. The Eagle's Tremendo has succumbed to San Martino and has fallen from Renalzos, now enjoying a pleasant gallop amidst his peers. While I actually did witness the fall, it required a split second longer for me to process what was happening. By then the room was on its feet. I find myself cheering and clapping along with them, but not because I carry a serious grudge against the Yellow and Black. I am merely sharing in their joy and supporting those around me. I can't help but celebrate as well, albeit with a little bit of levity. At least two thoughts are racing through my head. First: *This is unbelievable, and I'm here to be a part of it!* Second: *This is only one of six trials. What will their emotions be like during the actual race?* I can't even imagine.

Cultural Boundaries

Our group has arrived for dinner once again in the Panther's inner courtyard, and we are in the process of taking our seats. I wait only minutes before excitedly unleashing my story about the trial. Others share their own personal observations from the Campo. Carlo and Sofia have claimed their seats with us as well. More specifically, I am curious about whether we will serve at tomorrow night's dinner, and students are starting to inquire about it. I assure them all that I will find Matteo later and ask about the status.

As if responding telepathically, Matteo finds me first. He shuffles down to our table area to greet our group and to welcome everyone back to the Panther. Then he turns more serious and focuses on me. "Can you come with me for a minute? I want to talk to you about something," he begins, with a look of concern on his face.

"Sure, I will follow you," I say with a smile, getting up from my chair. We settle near the corner at the opposite end of the courtyard.

"I really want to apologize," he starts with genuine regret. "We had talked about having the students serve at an upcoming dinner. Unfortunately, we will not be able to allow the students to serve the food to the contrada."

"Oh, no problem at all," I say with a smile. I can see this is really bothering him. He feels bad about the news, so I want to comfort him as quickly as possible. I add, "We were only thinking of ideas for how the students might volunteer to help the contrada. We are honored to simply be here for dinner!"

"Ok, that's good. We spoke about this, and we originally thought it would be fun. Now we are hearing some concerns and decided to postpone it for now." He then offers an explanation: "The contrada is nervous about the upcoming Palio. Our rival, the Eagle, is running. Emotions are very high right now. If we do anything to disrupt traditional ways of doing things, there is a chance it will make things worse."

"Yes, that makes perfect sense. We do not want to impose. I really appreciate your effort to discuss the idea!" I say comfortingly. I am also relieved a bit, given the superstitions that can pervade these events. Should we defy tradition here and see the Eagle win two nights later, one can imagine how long it will be before we are ever invited to return. Something would have to freeze over. He seems to be satisfied that I am not irritated, so he emphasizes our standing invitation for upcoming dinners.

As I expected, my explanation to the group is well received, and I quickly find a larger meaning within this change of plans. "We were apparently pushing the envelope here by challenging their cultural comfort zone," I offer as the students lean in to hear me. I end on a high note by expressing what an honor it is to be here regardless, to which they readily agree. Truth be told, the collective nerves of our own group have also diminished; some were clearly having second thoughts as reality closed in.

With Carlo listening in, I turn to him and ask, "Has anyone other than contrada members ever served a meal here?"

He responds, "Never," adding an anxious laugh. Yes, we were definitely pushing boundaries.

Later, I realize once again that our tables have run out of water, including both varieties. I had learned where they keep their stash, so I confidently set off to acquire more. Upon arrival I encounter our young friend, Angelo, who is taking a quick break from his duties.

"Tom! How are you enjoying the dinner?"

"Oh, it is always wonderful to be here, we are having lots of fun." I then add, "You might remember that they were planning to have us serve, but they decided it would not be wise with the upcoming Palio." Then he surprises me further with his own response.

"Yes, that's really interesting. I don't think Siena is ready for that yet."

Siena? I quickly think. He is indicating that this issue goes beyond a contrada that is nervous about its rival. He continues to reflect, "This type of activity does not typically happen in Siena, and it may disrupt how things are done. I would really like to see this change with time, but it might be too fast right now."

Angelo had clearly heard about the idea, as he was already prepared to offer his own thoughts. As I haul water back to our table, I am only more impressed that a younger person is so in tune with the cultural norms of Siena. He definitely has the pulse of his larger community.

The following day I would further mention to our group what another acquaintance had explained upon hearing my tale. The Panther has apparently earned the status of Siena's most emotional contrada. Their emotions tend to run high, and—perhaps during the Palio, at least—you mess with those emotions at your own risk. I suppose there are much worse reputations to endure.

❁ CHAPTER 23 ❁

A Rebirth for the Ages

THE JULY 2 PALIO IS NOW HISTORY. AS THE FINAL HINTS OF WESTERN LIGHT transition to darkness over the Campo, the victorious contradaioli are marching around its periphery to cherish their prized *drappellone*. I am watching a completely disorganized, if jubilant, multitude of contrada members make their way around the race track. This is the first time I have seen the celebration here after a victory. The parade's ecstatic participants number in the hundreds if not hitting the thousand mark. Many are enjoying their blinking pacifiers and other infant-related accouterments symbolizing the contrada's rebirth. Experience tells me that a larger proportion of the membership is already engaged with the celebration on their home territory. The Palio banner which their horse and jockey earned earlier tonight is leading the contingent. They are vigorously singing variations of the Song of Verbena and any other melody or chant that comes to mind next. This is their piazza for the time being, as relatively few onlookers are here with me, save for those enjoying a dinner or wine on the Campo's periphery as it returns to some semblance of normalcy. Other families and children, mostly visitors, are enjoying the open expanse of the Campo itself, with the expected traveling salesmen hocking various lighted flying contraptions for the kids. The *drappellone* and its entourage will soon find their way back to the *rione* to celebrate further into the night.

Bombshell

At this point, I receive a text from Carlo, asking where I am right now. He and his family were not able to be in Siena for the spectacle earlier this evening. Upon informing him of my current location, I also ask why the Panthers are so quiet on social media. "I don't see many posts about the race. Do they post in more private groups?" I ask. Furthermore, Piazza del Conte was virtually deserted when I strolled up there earlier to take a look.

"You should go to the società. You will find them there. I am very sorry I cannot come," he replies.

"Oh, are they meeting there?" I write. A part of me is already feeling annoyed that I was not keeping up with the contrada's schedule following the Palio.

In Carlo's next message, he drops what may be the biggest bombshell I have sustained since watching Guess pull off his unlikely victory three years earlier. The realization is instant and hits me like a *nerbo* striking my thick skull. My mouth is open as I stand there looking dumbly at my phone. *Oh, my goodness, of course!! I hadn't even thought about that!* I allow myself a moment to absorb the surprise and mild shock. I also reflect that I had not yet done the math, or the follow-up research to discover this fact on my own. Within seconds, I am plotting a course for Via San Quirico and Società Due Porte. I suspect that the mystery of the disappearing Panthers will be solved momentarily.

Shower Caps and Wine

With Linda retired for the night and our cohort enjoying the celebration elsewhere, I am on my own as I make the final right turn onto Main Street Panther. Darkness may have fallen, but daytime here continues almost blindingly as I take stock of this peculiar scene. Wall sconces are blazing as if they had been running the Palio tonight, with contrada banners draped at similar intervals over the street. *What is going on?* I wonder as I cautiously approach with eyebrows furrowed in curiosity. Unlike past expeditions into this place, I really don't have a plan here. I probably don't need one, however, as a humble newcomer to this crazy scene is not likely a going concern right now.

My first impression is one of a street party, at a similar, if reduced, scale of a victorious contrada. The street is filled with a densely packed crowd of energetic people chatting with one another and drinking either water, beer or wine—apparently, plenty of wine. While approaching, I step around remnant streams of red wine dripping from side tables onto the street itself, with the omnipresent plastic cups littered everywhere. *These people have been here for a while already*, I gather. The crowd is thick enough that I could likely walk over the tops of their heads without falling onto the street, all the way up to their horseless stable at the other end. An even closer inspection reveals a single line of folding tables and chairs embedded within the crowd. The tables and remaining occupants come into view only when I am nearly on top of them. Plastic plates stained with red sauce indicate the remains of a frantically prepared dinner recently consumed. The scene is reminiscent of the Goose three years earlier—with one rather peculiar exception.

Nearly everyone here is wearing a shower cap. Not only the women's heads are covered in plastic, but also the men, boys and girls, young and old. Some are clear, others are yellow plastic or perhaps even knitted. *Are they trying not to contaminate the food? Is there some new health standard for which an outdoor dinner must comply?* Nobody was wearing them earlier this week. Obviously, some hidden meaning needs to be uncovered here, as I may have tapped into one of Siena's lesser-known traditions of some kind. *In any case, now I know where the Panthers have been hanging out.* Then I hear my name yelled quite boisterously without warning. I am standing adjacent to a dinner table at which a number of older men are pointing at one another over some story or joke.

"Tahhhmm!" I hear suddenly. As the crowd parts near the entrance of Due Porte, a somewhat inebriated Angelo is in front of me with his arms raised in continued celebration. "Can you believe it? This is the best! You know why we are celebrating, right?" he asks, probably wondering why I am even standing here right now.

"Yes, congratulations! I am very happy for you! This is really fun to see!" I yell back to the extent that I am able. Thanks to Carlo's earlier information, I am now suitably in the know—with the exception of the shower caps. Then he attempts to introduce me to some of the older gentlemen at the table nearby.

"Hey, this is Tom, he's a professor in the United States! He got to see history tonight!" he adds, still pounding the air. "Tom, there's still plenty of wine. Go get some!" he commands happily as he looks around for whatever bottles might be left outside. I am not certain as to whether he is searching on my behalf or his. Giving up quickly on that quest, he is distracted by an acquaintance more his age and is leaving me to offer his peer a high-five and bear hug. If nothing else, I am grateful that even a slightly tipsy Angelo has inadvertently informed those within earshot of my belonging here. With that initial greeting, I slowly move up the street to soak in the atmosphere. I am passing a small cluster of young women and, despite the ocean of shower caps, I pick out Carmina right away.

"Tom, how are you doing?" Carmina smiles and acknowledges me with a bit less bravado than Angelo. She is merely in conversation mode now with her friends. She knows I am always learning about this place and is therefore quite used to me by now.

After offering my congratulations, I ask, "Why is everyone wearing shower caps?" I point to their heads. This is the last piece of the puzzle that I need to click into place, after which it all comes together.

She answers matter-of-factly and with a slight grin, "Well, because the Eagle is the new *nonna*. We are making fun of them."

Shower caps. Grandmother. Eagle. Got it. As tradition would have it, cartoons and related media commonly depict a newly anointed *nonna* wearing a grandmother's bonnet known as a *cuffia*.[101] When the *nonna* does eventually win a Palio, its members take great delight with transferring the symbolic *cuffia* to the new *nonna*. Of course, the new *nonna's* rival does the same, which is precisely the celebration I have stumbled across tonight.

Nonna Rising

The bombshell dropped earlier by Carlo was, consequently, that the Eagle had inadvertently become the new *nonna*. The Panther is counting this as a consolation victory without even sending a horse into the arena. And why not? They are beside themselves with delight, given that their own rival will now serve as the new grandmother of Siena. The Eagle has not won a Palio since July 3, 1992, now 24 years and counting. So, how did this come to pass?

To recall, the four most accomplished jockeys competing earlier tonight did not necessarily follow the most experienced horses to their respective contrade. Scompiglio was riding Preziosa Penelope which had raced only once before, tonight representing the She-Wolf. Likewise, the rising star, Tittia, chose to ride an encore race for the Shell, also riding a one-Palio veteran in Quadrivia. Of course, Trecciolino returned to attempt a record-tying fourteenth victory. Still, he would have to accomplish it on a horse no one in the Campo had ever seen race, named Phatos de Ozieri. The pair of them would be riding for the Dragon. Perhaps the most potent duo would be Giuseppe Zedde (Gingillo) atop Porto Alabe, one of the two most veteran horses. For sure, the Goose had a decent shot at this one, four years following their last victory. I would not have been surprised to see them emerge with another win on our watch.

For this race, three of the four top jockeys managed to secure the inner three spots at the *mossa*: The Goose, She-Wolf, and Dragon, respectively. Tittia and the Shell found themselves at the unenviable eighth spot, while the poor Caterpillar served as the *rincorsa* at number ten. *So much for their formulaic win tonight. They will have to wait until August.* Tremendo and the Eagle drew the rather neutral sixth position.

At the drop of the *canape*, the She-Wolf cut off the Goose quickly in its number one spot, immediately pushing the Goose further back. More perplexing was Tittia who shot outward from his high starting position and took the lead by nearly a horse length as they passed Fonte Gaia. Tittia's mentor and nemesis, Trecciolino, had already secured second place for the Dragon. Competing for third position were the Turtle, She-Wolf, and Giraffe. With the leaders already angling for the first turn, Tremendo's Eagle was already securing an unimpressive tenth place behind the *rincorsa*. One could almost hear a collective sigh of relief coming from the direction of Via Stalloreggi.

Heading into the dreaded San Martino was the Shell, Dragon, and She-Wolf in that order, with Tittia's lead almost destroyed when Quadrivia slipped. Somehow, he recovered without falling, and the first five made it through the turn unscathed. Only the Giraffe failed to remain in the race as horse and jockey careened into the mattresses. Tailgating the Giraffe was the Porcupine, which amazingly avoided the same fate and continued in the rear of the pack with the Eagle. By this time, Tittia was already assuming a comfortable lead at the Casato, followed farther back by the Dragon and She-Wolf. At this point, the Shell contradaioli should have been tasting victory.

For the next full lap, the leading competitors lined up largely behind one another, in the order of Tittia's Shell followed by the Dragon, She-Wolf and now the Goose. Nearing the end of the second lap, Tittia was determined to hold back Trecciolino, who was gallantly trying to pass Tittia on the outside against the barriers near the Casato. Tittia smelled this easily, however, and simply moved to the left to cut him off. Trecciolino thus fell back a bit and likely lost some momentum. For whatever reason, Trecciolino stayed in the center of the track well into the third lap, as Tittia maintained his advantage on the inside. Behind both of them in third place was the steadfast She-Wolf. All three of them, together with the Goose, survived the third and final turn at San Martino. Something changed here, however. Scompiglio took the She-Wolf to the inside, probably a risky move on this turn. But the result hit pay dirt, as he now found himself outmaneuvering Trecciolino into second place. The order coming out of San Martino was now the Shell, She-Wolf, Dragon, and Goose.

Then Scompiglio took off. Staying on the inside, he used the straightaway in front of Palazzo Pubblico and gradually came up alongside Tittia. His price to pay for doing so was a serious and repeated beating on his left arm from Tittia's *nerbo*. Then, it was almost as if Tittia saw the writing on the wall as he watched the She-Wolf and Dragon assume the lead. As they all passed the sharp inside barrier at the Casato for the last time, Scompiglio took the She-Wolf into its first lead of the night. Still, on the outside, Trecciolino made a valiant attempt to pass while heading for the finish, but Scompiglio wisely pinned him against the barrier. By then, both Trecciolino and Tittia had all but given up the fight as the She-Wolf sped across the finish line to become the winner for the first time since 1989. The embarrassing second-place finish would actually go to the Goose—a serious loss on a favored horse.

With an extraordinary win tonight, it was sheer joy for all of us to witness the *nonna* finally shedding its status. From what I could gather from a variety of sources, almost everyone was at least moderately happy for the She-Wolf. The contrada was overdue and the general consensus was that they deserved it. On the flip side, there were actually two losing contrade tonight—three, if you count the Goose. We know the Porcupine is not celebrating, given its role as the traditional rival of the She-Wolf. Moreover, the Eagle is certainly mortified, as Carlo had brought to my attention well after the race. Now that the She-Wolf was no longer the *nonna*, the Eagle immediately assumed that designation. And one can imagine that the Panther will do everything in its power to keep its rival there as long as humanly possible.

Later, we would learn that the Panther's celebration had unwittingly intersected with Siena's ongoing challenges regarding delinquent tourist behaviors. Following the She-Wolf victory, a brazen, if careless, pair of visitors had intentionally managed to steal a piece of the *asta* (pole) which supports the *drappellone*. Thinking they had captured a priceless souvenir, they further managed to walk through the historic center without anyone noticing—that is, until they found themselves wading through a sea of Panthers already toasting to the change of the *nonna*. Some of the celebrants noticed what the interlopers were carrying and confronted them. Upon explaining the significance of what the pair had stolen, the Panthers took back the piece and sent them on their way. The conclusion of this story could not have replicated a fairy-tale ending any more effectively. The stolen piece was turned over to the Panther's *priore*, who in turn contacted his counterpart in the She-Wolf. In a joyous meeting between the two contrada leaders, the piece was thereby turned over to its rightful owner. The impromptu ceremony was billed as a gesture of gratitude from the Panther for causing its rival to become the new *nonna*.

Within days, the feel-good story was headlining at least one local news outlet.[102] With a smile as I read, I could not help but interpret the story as an indicator of Siena's unwavering sense of community. While once again faced with the challenge of disrespectful visitors, the story exemplifies the best qualities of the Senesi that make this such a special place. The contrade watch out for one another and serve as a serious buffer against various social ills. Despite (or in concert with) the timeless rivalries and explosive emotions that define the days of the Palio, the Senesi work together to maintain their unique and effective community through mutual kindness and support of one another. That Siena remains one of Europe's safest cities is testament to the continued vibrancy of the contrada system and the people who believe in it.

Cappotto

Today is August 16, going on 1:00 p.m.—or 7:00 p.m. in Italy. After struggling to focus my mind during a university meeting, the realities of home are giving way once again to the emotions surrounding the Palio. I am currently live streaming the Palio coverage, admittedly experiencing a microcosm of Senese excitement right now.

"Carlo, I am streaming the Palio, but I don't know if they will show the race," I text.

A REBIRTH FOR THE AGES

"Tom, do not worry, I will tell you who wins."

Although every detail of the *corteo storico* is broadcast, my suspicions, unfortunately, play out. The channel is blocked just before race time and is not allowing live viewing. I try desperately to find other sites online from which to stream, but absolutely nothing on the internet is allowing viewers to witness the event live. This travesty has occurred before, so I am more frustrated than shocked. Approximately 45 long minutes later, I receive a message from Carlo (ding!).

"Lupa!!" (She-Wolf). He adds a few smiling emojis.

No way! Way. "Wow, they won again? That's incredible. I suppose that's still a good thing for the Panther, right?" I write back. Within the hour I should be able to find several videos of the race on YouTube.

"Yes, it is fine. There is no problem with the win for us," he writes with little emotion. Then he adds, "It was the same horse and same jockey as July! This happens very rarely in the Palio."

Carlo is not kidding. The amazing exclamation point to the She-Wolf saga is that the Black and Orange just managed what is known in Siena as a *cappotto*, whereby one contrada wins both the July and August *Palii* in the same year. Think about the challenges of winning just one Palio, let alone two races back-to-back. Some basic statistics drive home this point. As of this writing, only 17 *cappotti* (plural) have occurred since as far back as 1761, the earliest *cappotto* reported.[103] Prior to the She-Wolf victories, this has not happened since the Giraffe accomplished the same feat in 1997, the year following the so-called peace treaty between that contrada and its former adversary, the Caterpillar. Then one needs to go as far back as 1933 to find the previous occurrence, with the Turtle's double victories that year.

Still, the She-Wolf does have one additional *cappotto* to its name, if one cares to look nostalgically to the two races of 1785. Six of Siena's 17 contrade have never enjoyed a *cappotto*, namely the Eagle, Forest, Goose, Panther, Porcupine, and Unicorn.

If this were not enough to rattle the brain, the She-Wolf managed to set an even higher standard. They won both races with the same horse, Preziosa Penelope, and the same jockey, Jonatan Bartoletti (Scompiglio), which has not occurred since the Turtle's *cappotto* of 1933. Somehow, the captains allowed Preziosa to race again in August, which was unexpected in itself. The probability of the She-Wolf extracting the same horse as it did in July was miniscule, and nobody could plan on something like that happening. This was a historic year indeed, even by Palio standards.

Parting Reflections

But then, what year isn't historic in Siena? If our own adventures in the Gothic City have taught us anything, it is that every year brings new stories to tell. Perhaps one paradox is that amidst the Palio's staunchly guarded traditions emerges an annual tapestry of unique and unexpected occurrences. Thus, a book like this could conceivably go on forever (although readers need not fret, with this being the third and final edition).

Beyond our early lessons from the Caterpillar, our adventures within the Goose, and our new friends within the Panther, stories of the She-Wolf contrada have occasionally bubbled up within my own narrative herein. Having finally closed the door on a troubling era of its own, the She-Wolf and its double victories provide an appropriate place to close out my own story of discovery and some hard-won personal accomplishments. It is almost as if I have been immersed within a study-abroad program of my own, requiring years of personal fortitude to make a dent in a pesky language divide.

While my reticence among the Senesi may be perceived as overly cautious, I believe this is the most appropriate approach to earn trust and respect in any foreign place. And if one is fortunate, perhaps even some lasting friendships can result. Many of the contradaioli I met eventually lowered their guard and welcomed my involvement, but only after they recognized my genuine interest and enthusiasm. From my experience, to earn some level of acceptance as an outsider requires a healthy dose of patience in oneself and others, a genuine respect for different ways of life, an unwavering sense of humility, and a willingness to place serendipity in the driver's seat. It is not necessary to be known or loved by everyone, and social acceptance should occur naturally. This is likely true for any community, whereby the biggest difference maker is one's quality of time and contributions within it.

As Dario Castagno implied within his Foreword, visitors can sometimes find the Senesi unwilling to share much of their world with people they do not know well. For this, however, they should be forgiven. They collectively find themselves pressured to defend or explain their traditions to outsiders who understand little, yet too often rush to judgment. This community challenge will only magnify with the ongoing proliferation of social media and increasing global interactions. Cultural traditions once relatively isolated are now easily available for public scrutiny on the world stage. Consequently the need to educate others while considering Siena's public image will intensify. Perhaps as a bookend to Castagno's earlier observation, one middle-aged acquaintance from the (recovering) Porcupine explained the situation to me during an impromptu conversation. She reflected:

> Siena has a history of inviting and welcoming visitors, and we are friendly to outsiders. People have been traveling the Via Francigena for centuries, and we were one of the designated "hospital cities" during the [World] Wars. But I think you will find that we are sort-of closed about the contrada and Palio, because we just assume people will come and go quickly. They don't understand who we are, and it would take a long time to explain it. You can't understand the Palio by visiting for only three or four days.

At some point during our sixth, most recent summer in Siena, it dawned on me that some of the Panther contradaioli have simply become comfortable with my presence in their domain. In addition to being asked to assist with contrada museum tours, a modest number of Panterini actually know me by name (or variations thereof). Even this level of acceptance is immensely heartwarming. The Senesi share a distinctive cultural background, society, and heritage—all woven together to forge a resilient community through generations of time. I certainly may have earned a peak into their way of life, but little more. And that's perfectly fine. To experience what Castagno refers to as the *trinity*—that is, Siena, Palio, and contrade—has proven to be an incalculable honor.

It may be fitting to leave the last words here to a once nationally famous Senese radio/TV personality.[104] Before the Palio was televised, Silvio Gigli would conclude his radio broadcasts of the races for more than four decades with the same inspirational line: *"In un tripudio di bandiere e di colori, Siena trionfa, come sempre immortale"*—In a blaze of flags and colors, Siena triumphs, as always immortal.

Postscript

The July 2017 Palio one year after the *cappotto* found the Panther celebrating yet again. The grateful people of Stalloreggi hosted a full celebratory dinner in their courtyard for the victorious Giraffe in appreciation for relegating the Eagle to another dispiriting second-place finish.

The tireless veteran of the Palio, Luigi Bruschelli (Trecciolino), continues to seek his fourteenth victory to tie the all-time record for Palio wins by a single jockey. With the recent 2018 Palio season now behind us, the record still belongs to Andrea Degortes who compiled 14 victories of his own between 1965 and 1992. Trecciolino's aspirational goal remains elusive, with no wins to his name since 2012. His protégé and rising star, Giovanni Atzeni (Tittia) managed to win his fifth Palio in August 2015 for the Forest, on the heels of the Tower's victory discussed earlier. Since then, however, Tittia has endured a dry spell of his own, thereby giving way to other contemporaries—including Brio and Scompiglio—who have enjoyed their own recent successes in Piazza del Campo.

And once more, we return to the She-Wolf, which—as it turns out—was not finished with its lucky streak. In August 2018 Giuseppe Zedde (Gingillo) rode the now-legendary Porto Alabe to an easy victory for the Black and Orange, only two years after its *cappotto*. More stunning was that they accomplished this from the tenth position—the *rincorsa*. As the saying goes, *when it rains, it pours.*

In closing, little did I know—of all things to ponder in the universe—that the one-hundredth anniversary of the end of World War I (the Great War) would soon be upon us. The Senesi have recently, and with little notice, decided to commemorate this solumn occasion in the way they know best. That is, with a rare *Palio Straordinario*, or Extraordinary Palio, to be held in October 2018. For me, the meaning of this development is already undeniable. I will be headed, once again, back into the Campo.

(Author's Note: A full account of the Straordinario can be found in my follow-up book, *Unbridled Spirit: The Untold Story of the 2018 Extraordinary Palio in Siena, Italy*.)

Photo Gallery

View of the Terzo di Città and the Duomo as seen from the Torre del Mangia, Siena's bell tower

The Palazzo Pubblico, Siena's city hall, at night

The Church of Santa Maria di Provenzano, with a tent being prepared for a Giraffe contrada event

City crews installing the bleachers and barriers in preparation for the Palio in Piazza del Campo

Assembly of the large mattresses at the Curve of San Martino

Members of the Wave contrada march through their *rione* (neighborhood) to celebrate their patron saint

An adult instructor marches alongside a contingent of youth from the Unicorn contrada, helping them stay on the beat

Local Tuscan author Dario Castagno discusses traditions of the Caterpillar inside the contrada chapel

A contrada basketball game in Piazza Tolomei, in this case between the Owl and the Wave

The unfinished extension of Siena's cathedral, construction of which was halted permanently after the tragic Black Death of 1348

View of the curve of San Martino during the *tratta*

Trying to stop a runaway horse after throwing its jockey during the *tratta*

City and contrada officials walk around the track before one of the six trials, with hundreds of children cheering in the background

Goose contradaioli gather around their stable during the days of the Palio

The *barbaresco* (caretaker) for the Goose contrada leads its horse, Guess, back to the stable after a trial

Tittia guides his horse, Guess, around the turn at the Casato, followed by the horse and jockey for the Ram

The Panther's jockey, nicknamed Voglia, rides Pestifero during a morning trial

A line of police officers clears the track prior to an evening trial

The mounted Carabinieri demonstrate their skills at full gallop prior to the final evening trial, known as the *prova generale*

Teenagers serve dinner to more than a thousand contradaioli and guests during their *cena della prova generale* (dress rehearsal dinner), held adjacent to their ancient water supply, Fontebranda

Caterpillar contradaioli enjoy an evening dinner in the garden of Società l'Alba

Tables take over the street scene as youth from the Panther contrada set up for that evening's *cena della prova generale*

Young women from the Panther contrada await their volunteering duties to set tables for the *cena della prova generale*

At the Panther's *cena della prova generale* on the night before the Palio, with more than 1,400 in attendance

LIVING THE PALIO

Panther contradaioli and visitors await the blessing of the horse inside the contrada chapel

Panther contradaioli walk to the Duomo behind the *comparsa* to prepare for the *corteo storico* (historical procession)

Determined Palio spectators stake their claims in the Campo at approximately ten in the morning on the day of the race

The *alfieri* for the Goose contrada demonstrate their flag-waving skills in front of the Duomo prior to the *corteo storico*

The *corteo storico* makes its way to the Campo

The victory celebration for the Goose begins here at the Church of Santa Maria di Provenzano, with its horse, Guess, as the center of attention

A jubilant scene along Via di Santa Caterina to celebrate victory for the Goose

Tightening the *canape* (rope) across the track prior to a trial

Musicians playing their *chiarine* (long-belled trumpets) to announce the beginning of the assignment (drawing) of the horses

Siena's mayor displays the contrada names and numbers during the assignment of the horses, with one of two score boards visible behind him

The jockey Giovanni Atzeni (Tittia) represents the Shell contrada during a morning trial

The jockey Luigi "Gigi" Bruschelli (Trecciolino) represents the Dragon contrada during a morning trial

LIVING THE PALIO

The *carroccio* (symbolic chariot of triumph) makes its way around the track prior to the Palio, with the *drappellone* displayed on top

The *alfieri* for the Tower contrada perform the *sbandierata*, a remarkable routine of flag throwing, during the *corteo storico* in Piazza del Campo

Panther contradaioli socialize around their contrada fountain during the days of the Palio

Beginning of the July 2015 Palio race, with competitors having just launched off the *mossa* (starting line)

Horses and jockeys begin their first lap of the 2015 Palio as they pass Fonte Gaia. Notice the Ram's jockey on the right, lunging to "disrupt" the Shell's jockey, Tittia.

Jockey Andrea Mari (Brio) celebrates as he crosses the finish line with a victory for the Tower contrada

Ecstatic Tower contradaioli climb the bleachers to receive the *drappellone* following their victory in Piazza del Campo

The official presentation of the *drappellone* in the courtyard of Palazzo Pubblico about one week prior to the race

Jockey Jonatan Bartoletti (Scompiglio) represents the She-Wolf contrada with Preziosa Penelope during a morning trial

Jockey Francesco Caria (Tremendo) rides Renalzos for the Eagle during a morning trial while in the crosshairs of a telephoto lens

A rare celebration of transferring the symbolic *cuffia* (grandmother's bonnet) to the new *nonna*. In this case the Panther is celebrating that its rival, the Eagle, has become the new *nonna*

The inner courtyard of the Panther contrada, hosting members of the Giraffe in appreciation for causing the Eagle to come in second place during the July 2017 Palio

Acknowledgments

Our educational programs in Siena involved numerous contributors who deserve recognition for their important roles. Our partner institution in Siena, the Siena School for Liberal Arts, was truly a godsend, providing their school facilities, orientations, and housing assistance during our first two seasons. Of course, our academic programs in Siena would not have transpired without our adventurous students, who deserve recognition for their willingness to step outside their own comfort zones to experience new places and people, an ongoing theme throughout this book. Without their participation and serious academic interests, none of the summer programs would have occurred. Likewise, numerous brave colleagues deserve accolades for partnering with me during one or more of our summer programs.

Within Siena, numerous local individuals and establishments supported our engagement with the community. Representatives of the Oca (Goose) *contrada* (neighborhood) and the Pantera (Panther) contrada deserve a general round of appreciation for their consistent friendliness and encouragement for us to learn about their neighborhoods and associated rituals.

I wish to recognize a few Senese individuals by name. Dario Castagno, proud member of the Bruco (Caterpillar) contrada and prolific author and Tuscan expert, provided an intriguing window into the Senese and contrada communities. He also subsequently reviewed portions of this book for accuracy and appropriateness. Later additions to the book were similarly reviewed by Andrea Colella-Albino, a lifetime member of the Panther contrada. The extent to which his insights, clarifications, and anecdotes contributed to this work is beyond measure and is much appreciated. We were likewise fortunate to befriend a Siena resident and college student, Filippo Baiano, who shared many of his own insights with our students and participated readily in various class discussions and tours. His family's pizzeria, Cavallino Bianco (White Horse), served as a welcoming respite for informal class discussions and refreshments, especially its quiet second floor, where tourists rarely venture. Equally hospitable was the tireless Gioia Pancino and her family, owners and operators of the B&B Siena in Centro. Her family and friends encouraged us to enjoy and learn more about their beloved Pantera contrada beyond what I had hoped to accomplish during our short visits.

Aside from my own stories of personal escapades, this work would not have been as complete or as educational without the tremendous body of literature that preceded it. Numerous academic scholars and local authors have devoted good parts of their lives to accurately study and portray the profound depths of history and culture found in Siena. I have provided a bibliography and set of endnotes to properly recognize their research contributions pertaining to Siena and elsewhere. I am happy and humbled to provide in this book one more outlet for this collective body of work, allowing for a wider readership than typically possible within academic circles.

Writing stories for a blog is one thing, but compiling them into a professionally published book requires extraordinary efforts. In this respect I am indebted to Sylvia Somerville, a university editor. She thoroughly reviewed initial drafts of this manuscript and provided significant suggestions and editorial comments for improvement. I was delighted with her own growing enthusiasm for Siena and the Palio as she made her way further into the story.

I cannot ignore the continuous role my parents, Ken and Dee, played behind the scenes. They encouraged me to complete this book, and their eager consumption of my earlier stories provided at least a faint notion that others might find them of interest as well. Just as they have done for decades, my parents continue to support my adventures and encourage the sharing of knowledge and perspectives that books like this can provide.

And most significant is my adventurous wife, Linda, who makes guest appearances rather often throughout this story. Being the more sociable and unreserved member of this partnership, Linda provided opportunities for my own learning and experience that I may not have pursued otherwise. Given her incessant interest in learning, experiencing, and traveling, she naturally plays the role of a true geographer.

Glossary

Contrada Names

In English	In Italian	The People
Caterpillar	Bruco	Brucaioli
Dragon	Drago	Dragaioli
Eagle	Aquila	Aquilini
Forest	Selva	Selvaioli
Giraffe	Giraffa	Giraffini
Goose	Oca	Ocaioli
Owl	Civetta	Civettini
Panther	Pantera	Panterini
Porcupine	Istrice	Istriciaioli
Ram	Montone	Montonaioli
She-Wolf	Lupa	Lupaioli
Shell	Nicchio	Nicchiaioli
Snail	Chiocciola	Chiocciolini
Tower	Torre	Torraioli
Turtle	Tartuca	Tartuchini
Unicorn	Leocorno	Lecaioli
Wave	Onda	Ondaioli

Palio and Contrada Terms

addetto ai costumi. The manager, or caretaker of the contrada costumes worn for the *corteo storico, festa titolare,* and other contrada events. The role is considered a crucial one and is typically held by a more senior and respected contradaiolo. The *addetto* also manages the selection of individuals who participate and wear the costumes each year.

alfiere. One of two flag wavers representing a *contrada* and its official delegation known as the *comparsa* (plural: *alfieri*).

asta. The pole or flagstaff that supports the Palio banner, known as the *drappellone.* Typically painted in alternating black and white stripes to represent the colors of Siena.

balzana. The coat of arms for the city of Siena, usually displayed on a flag or shield with its upper half white and its lower half black.

barbaresco. A *contrada*'s official caretaker, or groom, of the horse while it is in possession of the *contrada* for the Palio race.

bàrbero. The Senese term for racehorse, originally referring to horses from North Africa or, more specifically, the Barbary States. The term also refers to one of a set of wooden balls used in a children's game called *palio dei bàrberi.*

brenna. A racehorse perceived as relatively unpromising and not likely to win the Palio.

Campo. The main public square, or piazza, of Siena, where the Palio is raced in July and August. Its more official name is the Piazza del Campo. Locals and visitors alike learn to simply refer to this open space as the Campo.

campanina. The small bell or bells in each of the contrada chapels. Following a Palio victory, contrada members—often children—attempt to keep the bell ringing throughout the night.

Campanone. Known more informally as the *Sunto,* the large bell at the top of the Torre del Mangia that once summoned the Senesi to battle or to public meetings. Today it rings during the entire *corteo storico* prior to the Palio.

canape. The thick hemp rope that serves as the starting line for the Palio race.

Il Canto della Verbena. "The Song of Verbena," one of the more beloved and commonly heard folk songs sung by the Senesi during the Palio and other citywide events. *Verbena* refers to the grass or herb that has traditionally grown between the bricks of the Campo.

capitano. The captain is elected by each *contrada* to take control during the days of the Palio. The captain is entrusted with complete authority to run the contrada and its operations related to the Palio, especially with respect to making deals (*partiti*) with other *contrade*.

cappotto. The *contrada* that has won both the July and August Palio races in the same year.

Carabinieri. The Italian military police, charged with policing both military and civilian populations. They are so named for the carbine rifles they once carried. Since 2001 it has served as one of the four Italian armed forces. A contingent of mounted Carabinieri entertains the crowd in the Campo just prior to the final evening trial (the *Prova Generale*).

carroccio. Known in Siena as the "Chariot of Triumph." The ox-drawn cart carries the Palio banner, or *drappellone*, at the end of the historical procession as it makes its way around the Campo prior to the Palio race. The cart vaguely represents the war chariot of Florence that was captured by the Senesi during the battle of Montaperti in the year 1260.

Casato. One of eleven streets that leads into the Campo. The turn at Casato is one of the two most dangerous places on the Palio racetrack.

cavallo. A horse. A smaller horse or pony is known as a *cavallino*.

cazzotti. Ritualized group fistfights, traditionally with up to two hundred participating males between the ages of roughly eighteen and forty. Usually lasting a few minutes or more, the fights typically (but not always) occur within the Piazza del Campo during or surrounding the day of the Palio race, usually involving members of rival contrade.

Cena della Prova Generale. The *contrada* dinner that follows the final evening trial on the day prior to the Palio race. This is typically the only *contrada* event that guests are allowed to attend, if tickets are purchased from the *contrada* office (*segretaria*) or directly from the *società*. Viewed as a good-luck dinner for *contradaioli*, the dinner usually occurs on a main street of the *contrada* with a special head table for elected officials and the jockey who has been hired to race the next day. Hundreds or even thousands of *contradaioli* and guests will typically attend this important, pre-Palio social event.

centro. The downtown or historical center of an Italian town or city (*città*). Often this area corresponds to the historical city inside its medieval walls, exemplified by that of Siena.

chiarine (singular: *chiarina*). The long-belled trumpets used to play the fanfare prior to various Palio events. The players are known as the *trombettiere* or *musici*.

comparsa. A costumed contingent of *contrada* members (*contradaioli*) representing the *contrada* in the historical procession (*corteo storico*) and related events. Participants in the *comparsa* include a drummer (*tamburino*), flag wavers (*alfieri*), and various other medieval-themed positions.

contrada. One of seventeen wards or neighborhoods existing within the historical, walled city of Siena. Each *contrada* constitutes a social structure that inhabits a physical territory (*rione*) within the city walls.

contradaiolo/a. A generic term referencing a member of a *contrada* (male/female).

corteo storico. The historical procession, or parade, that marches from the cathedral (Duomo) to the Campo before the Palio race. Participants are dressed in elaborate costumes loosely representing the political, social, and military components of the Republic of Siena prior to the city-state's downfall in 1555. The parade marches around the Campo in the hours before the race, with each *comparsa* demonstrating its flag-throwing and percussion skills.

cuffia. A symbolic grandmother's bonnet. When the contrada designated as the *nonna* (grandmother) finally wins a Palio, its members transfer the symbolic *cuffia* to the new *nonna*.

debuttante In this context, a novice horse experiencing its first race in the Palio. Such horses are generally considered unpromising by contradaioli but can sometimes surprise the Senesi with an unexpected victory.

drappellone The large silk banner awarded to the *contrada* whose horse wins the Palio race. This is the only prize for winning the Palio. *Drappellone* can be used interchangeably with the term *palio*, which also refers directly to the banner itself.

estrazione An extraction or drawing. Two extractions occur before each Palio: (1) extraction of the *contrade* and (2) extraction, or assignment of the horses. The first determines the three additional *contrade* that will compete with the other seven *contrade* that did not race the previous year. The second matches the ten horses with each of the ten *contrade*.

fantino. In this context, the jockey hired by a *contrada* to race in the Palio. Jockeys (*fantini*) in the Palio generally come from outside Siena and are the equivalent of mercenaries paid for their services to the *contrada*. Jockeys can ride for different contrade throughout the trials (*prove*) until the morning of the Palio, after which the jockey for a particular *contrada* can no longer be changed.

fazzoletto. The square-shaped, silk scarf given to each individual baptized into a *contrada*, either as a baby or later in life. The *fazzoletto* serves as the primary symbol of identity for a *contradaiolo*.

mangino. An assistant to the captain in charge of a *contrada* during the Palio. Typically, two *mangini* assist the captain with deal making and related negotiations (*partiti*) to help realize a victory for the contrada.

mortaretto. Literally a "small mortar" or cannon-type device located near the starting line (*mossa*) that detonates as a signal to clear the track, to announce the appearance of horses as they emerge from the Palazzo Pubblico, to indicate a false start, and to recognize when the winning horse crosses the finish line.

mossa. The location where the race starts, indicated by the starting rope (*canape*) strung across the track. This location doubly serves as the finish line for the race.

mossiere. The individual assigned to start the race. This person is responsible for calling the order in which each horse lines up at the start (*mossa*), assuring their successful lineup prior to starting the race.

nerbo. The whip provided to each *fantino* as he enters the track from the Palazzo Pubblico to line up for the race. The *nerbo* is created from the dried, stretched phallus of a calf.

nonna. Literally the "grandmother," a derogatory title assigned to the *contrada* that has endured the longest time without a Palio win.

Palio. A horse race run by ten of the seventeen *contrade* in Siena, Italy, on July 2 and August 16 each year, both in honor of the Virgin Mary, or Madonna. The term *palio* further derives from the Latin word *pallium*, or piece of cloth, referring to the cloth banner earned by the winning *contrada*. The Palio banner is also known as the *drappellone*.

palco dei giudici. The judges' stand, or balcony, from which city officials and *contrada* captains observe the Palio race and its trials. Siena's mayor (*sindaco*) typically stands precisely in the middle of these observers.

palco dei priore. A similar though smaller balcony than the judges' stand (see above) overlooking the curve of San Martino, from where the *contrada* presidents (*priore*) watch the Palio.

palchi. The stands or bleachers erected around the outside of the Campo racetrack. Groups of *contrada* members and paying visitors can sit in these bleachers as an alternative to standing in the center of the Campo to view the Palio and its trials.

Palazzo Pubblico. Literally, the "public palace," or city hall, of Siena. The medieval, Gothic-style structure has served as the seat of city government since its completion in the first half of the fourteenth century.

partiti. Agreements or deals made secretively between the captains and *mangini* of two *contrade*, in a strategic effort to influence the outcome of the Palio race. Agreements typically involve promises from one *contrada* to pay another in the event of a Palio victory.

piatto. In this context, the round, silver plate attached to the pole above the Palio banner, or *drappellone*. The plate is owned by the city (*comune*), and is loaned to the winning contrada until after the Dinner of the Plate (*Cena del Piatto*) traditionally held in January.

prova. Trial race in which the horses assigned to the ten *contrade* are tested for various skills in advance of the actual Palio. A total of six morning and evening trials (*prove*) precede the Palio. Each trial closely simulates the Palio race, with a total of three laps around the track.

prova generale. The final evening trial on the day before the Palio. Translated as the "General Trial," the Prova Generale constitutes the fifth of six total trials and is treated as a dress rehearsal.

quattrogiornisti. Tourists or visitors referred to as "four-dayers," by contrada members (contradaioli) because they come to Siena only to participate in the four days of the Palio.

rincorsa. In this context, the *rincorsa* is the horse assigned to the tenth position for the starting lineup of the Palio. Together with the *mossiere*, the *rincorsa* jockey holds the power to start the race when he pleases, by rushing from behind the starting line at a full gallop.

LIVING THE PALIO

rione. The physical territory or built environment occupied by a *contrada*. The current-day boundaries were finalized in 1729.

San Martino. One of three districts (*terzi*) of Siena, comprising the southeastern third of the city. The corner of the Campo closest to the district is referred to as the curve of San Martino, infamous as the most hazardous turn on the Palio racetrack.

sbandierata. The performance of the *alfieri*, or flag throwers, during the *corteo storico* prior to the Palio.

scosso. Literally, "shaken." If a jockey falls off his horse during the Palio, the horse is said to be running *scosso*. The horse can still win the Palio without its jockey, as long as its head ornament, the *spennacchiera*, remains attached.

società. The social hub, or clubhouse, of a contrada. Typically, the facility includes various gathering halls, a bar, and an attached outdoor patio or garden area open for use by contrada members. Its primary purpose through the early twentieth century was to provide mutual aid to contradaioli, while it now primarily serves as the focus of social events and activities.

spandierata. The performance of the *alfieri*, or flag throwers, during the *coreteo storico* prior to the Palio.

spennacchiera. The head ornament attached to the horse, displaying its contrada colors. At its center is a small, circular mirror. The *spennacchiera* needs to remain intact if a riderless horse, known as running *scosso*, is to win the Palio.

Sunto. Nickname for the large bell on the Mangia tower (Torre del Mangia), known as the *Campanone*. The bell was once used to summon the local population to public meetings or to prepare for battle. More recently it is rung throughout the entire historical procession (*corteo storico*) leading up to the Palio race.

tratta. An event held in the Campo before the six Palio trials (*prove*). Approximately thirty-five horses are tested on the racetrack in groups of six or seven at a time, with each group running three laps around the track as they would during the Palio. Following the *tratta*, the ten *contrada* captains decide on the final ten horses to run in the Palio. The *tratta* is then followed at midday by the extraction (*estrazione*), or drawing, of the horses, at which time they are assigned by lottery to the *contrade* in a public ritual in front of the Palazzo Pubblico.

zucchetta. Also known as a *zucchino*, the round helmet worn by a jockey (*fantino*) during the Palio race. The metal helmet provides a jockey with some protection during the race, particularly from the blows of another jockey's whip (*nerbo*).

Notes

1. Drechsler, "The Contrada, the Palio, and the Ben Comune," 101.
2. Catoni and Piccinni, *An Illustrated History of Siena*, 31.
3. United Nations Educational, Scientific, and Cultural Organization, "Historic Centre of Siena."
4. Gilmour, *The Pursuit of Italy*. I highly recommend this book as a thorough accounting of attempts to unify the Italian peninsula.
5. Kostof, *The City Shaped*, 70.
6. Catoni and Piccinni, *An Illustrated History of Siena*.
7. Lewis, *The City of Florence*. This book is highly recommended for a thorough accounting of the historical geography and development of Florence, Italy.
8. Gilmour, *The Pursuit of Italy*.
9. Dundes and Falassi, *La Terra in Piazza*. Although published nearly four decades ago, this book still serves as the primary source of information related to the Palio and contrade social system in Siena.
10. Ryan, "Panem et Circenses."
11. Drechsler, "The Contrada, the Palio, and the Ben Comune."
12. Silverman, "The Palio of Siena," 236.
13. Drechsler, "The Contrada, the Palio, and the Ben Comune," 109.
14. Tulini, "The Race-Track."
15. For all sorts of statistics associated with the Palio through history, see the online index at http://www.ilpalio.org/index_english.htm.
16. Dundes and Falassi, *La Terra in Piazza*.
17. Ibid.
18. Ibid.
19. Ibid.
20. Ibid.
21. Simpson, "Siena Palio Tamed by Health and Safety Rules."
22. Silverman, "The Palio of Siena," 236.

23. Luppiand Rivetti, "Siena's Cultural Organizations Threatened by Banking Scandal." See also Martinuzzi, "Monte Paschi Fails Siena Race as Oldest Bank Loses Trust."
24. Silverman, "The Palio of Siena."
25. Aloisi, "Monte Paschi Shareholders Delay Cash Call, Top Executives May Quit."
26. Drechsler, "The Contrada, the Palio, and the Ben Comune."
27. Ibid.
28. Warner, *Die Contraden von Siena. Lokale Traditionen und Globaler Wandel.* See also Drechsler, "The Contrada, the Palio, and the Ben Comune."
29. Drechsler, "The Contrada, the Palio, and the Ben Comune."
30. Ibid. See also Silverman, "The Palio of Siena."
31. Drechsler, "The Contrada, the Palio, and the Ben Comune."
32. Rodi, *Seven Seasons in Siena.*
33. See Dario Castagno's website for a listing of his publications: http://www.dariocastagno.com/books.html.
34. Figliola, "Space, Society and Self in Siena, Italy," 51.
35. "Contrade," *La Voce della Piazza.*
36. Figliola, "Space, Society, and Self in Siena, Italy," 49.
37. "Contrade," *La Voce della Piazza.*
38. Figliola, "Space, Society and Self in Siena, Italy," 79.
39. Park, "Passion, Remembrance, and Identity,", 88.
40. Ibid.
41. Meichtry, "Siena's Centuries-Old Holy War Played Out on Horseback."
42. Facaros, and Pauls, *Tuscany.* For a more thorough account of the life of Santa Caterina in and beyond Siena, see Burckhardt, *Siena, City of the Virgin.*
43. Lennard and Lennard, *Genius of the European Square,* 207.
44. Kostof, *The City Shaped.*
45. Lennard and Lennard, *Genius of the European Square.*
46. Dundes and Falassi, *La Terra in Piazza*
47. Ibid.
48. Figliola, *Space, Society, and Self in Siena, Italy,* 33.
49. Ibid., 33.
50. Figliola, *Space, Society, and Self in Siena, Italy.*
51. Ibid., 69.
52. Figliola, *Space, Society, and Self in Siena, Italy.*

53. Ibid., 19.
54. Logan, "The Palio of Siena."
55. Ibid., 53.
56. Ibid., 49.
57. Dundes and Falassi, *La Terra in Piazza*.
58. Ibid.
59. Logan, "The Palio of Siena."
60. Ibid.
61. Figliola, *Space, Society, and Self in Siena, Italy*, 50.
62. ilpalio.org, "Palio Time Schedules."
63. Silverman, "The Palio of Siena," 232.
64. Dundes and Falassi, *La Terra in Piazza*.
65. Ibid.
66. Ibid.
67. Ibid.
68. Ibid.
69. Gilmour, *The Pursuit of Italy*.
70. Ibid.
71. Ibid.
72. Logan, "The Palio of Siena," 55–56.
73. Drechsler, "The Contrada, the Palio, and the Ben Comune," 110.
74. Falassi, "Siena's Festival."
75. Silverman, "The Palio of Siena."
76. ilpalio.org, "The Palio Horse Race."
77. Silverman, "The Palio of Siena."
78. ilpalio.org, "The Palio Horse Race."
79. Dundes and Falassi, *La Terra in Piazza*.
80. Silverman, "The Palio of Siena."
81. Dundes and Falassi, *La Terra in Piazza*.
82. Ibid.
83. Ibid.
84. ilpalio.org, "L'Ordine alla Mossa Dal 1899."
85. Dundes and Falassi, *La Terra in Piazza*.
86. This detailed account of the race was admittedly not possible during my original, live viewing. I therefore consulted various YouTube videos and local newspaper accounts of the race to ensure accurate descriptions.
87. Logan, "The Palio of Siena," 46.

88. Dundes and Falassi, *La Terra in Piazza*.
89. Ibid.
90. Park, "Passion, Remembrance, and Identity," 93.
91. Dundes and Falassi, *La Terra in Piazza*.
92. Logan, "The Palio of Siena," 58.
93. Figliola, *Space, Society, and Self in Siena, Italy*, 36.
94. Dundes and Falassi, *La Terra in Piazza*.
95. Nattoni, "Storia di una Rivalità."
96. Leoncini, "Le Nozze d'Oro della nostra Rivalità con L'Aquila."
97. Ibid.
98. Corrieredisiena.corr.it. "Alabarda rubata e anarchia nei giorni di Palio."
99. www.contradadellapantera.it, "Monture."
100. Repubblica.it, "Palio di Siena, vince la Pantera battuta di un soffio l'Aquila".
101. Dundes and Falassi, *La Terra in Piazza*.
102. Corrieredisiena.corr.it. "Alabarda rubata e anarchia nei giorni di Palio."
103. ilpalio.org, "I 17 Cappotti."
104. www.impegnopersiena.com, "Silvio Gigli… e Siena trionfa immortale!"

Bibliography

Aloisi, Silvia. "Monte Paschi Shareholders Delay Cash Call, Top Executives May Quit." *Reuters*, December 28, 2013. http://www.reuters.com.

Burckhardt, Titus. *Siena, City of the Virgin*. Bloomington, IN: World Wisdom, 2008.

Catoni, Giuliano, and Gabriella Piccinni. *An Illustrated History of Siena*. Pisa, Italy: Pacini Editore, 2008.

"Contrade." *La Voce della Piazza*. Accessed March 4, 2014. http://www.ilpaliodisiena.com/FAQ/contrade-eng.htm.

Contrada della Pantera. "Monture." Accessed 7 August, 2018. https://www.contradadellapantera.it/monture

Corriere di Siena. 2016. "Alabarda rubata e anarchia nei giorni di Palio." Accessed 19 July, 2018. 4 July.

Drechsler, Wolfgang. "The Contrada, the Palio, and the Ben Comune: Lessons from Siena," *TRAMES* 10 (2006): 99–125.

Dundes, Alan, and Alessandro Falassi. *La Terra in Piazza: An Interpretation of the Palio of Siena.* Berkeley: University of California Press, 1975.

Facaros, Dana, and Michael Pauls. *Tuscany.* 5th rev. ed. London: Cadogon Guides, 2010.

Falassi, Alessandro. "Siena's Festival." In *Palio*, edited by Alessandro Falassi and Guliano Catoni. Milan: Electa, 1983.

Figliola, Arthur. "Space, Society, and Self in Siena, Italy: A Study of Community, Identity, and Social Change in a Small, Southern European City." PhD diss., University of Massachusetts–Amherst, 2002.

Ghibellini, Senio. "Silvio Gigli... e Siena trionfa immortale!" *Impegno per Siena*. Accessed January 27, 2019. http://www.impegnopersiena.com.

Gilmour, David. *The Pursuit of Italy: A History of a Land, Its Regions and Their Peoples*. New York: Farrar, Straus and Giroux, 2011.

Il Palio di Siena. "Contrade." *La Voce della Piazza*. Accessed March 4, 2014. http://www.ilpalio.org

Il Palio di Siena. "I 17 Cappotti." Accessed July 25, 2018. https://www.ilpalio.org.

Il Palio di Siena. "L'Ordine alla Mossa Dal 1899." Accessed July 25, 2014. http://www.ilpalio.org.

Il Palio di Siena. "The Palio Horse Race." Accessed January 29, 2014. http://www.ilpalio.org.

Kostof, Spiro. *The City Shaped: Urban Patterns and Meanings Through History*. London: Thames and Hudson, 1991.

La Contrada della Pantera. "Monture". Accessed 15 July, 2018. https://www.contradadellapantera.it.

Lennard, Henry, and Suzanne Lennard. *Genius of the European Square*. International Making Cities Livable, 2008.

Leoncini, Alessandro. "Le Nozze d'Oro della nostra Rivalità con L'Aquila." *Il Grattapassere*, November, 1997.

Lewis, R. W. B. *The City of Florence: Historical Vistas and Personal Sightings*. New York: Henry Holt & Co., 1995.

Logan, Alice. "The Palio of Siena: Performance and Process." *Urban Anthropology* 7 (1978): 45–65.

Luppi, Stefano, and Ermanno Rivetti. "Siena's Cultural Organizations Threatened by Banking Scandal." *The Art Newspaper*, April 3, 2013. http://www.theartnewspaper.com

Martinuzzi, Elisa. "Monte Paschi Fails Siena Race as Oldest Bank Loses Trust." *Bloomberg News*, March 27, 2013. http://www.bloomberg.com.

Meichtry, Stacy. "Siena's Centuries-Old Holy War Played Out on Horseback." *National Catholic Reporter*, July 15, 2005, 4a(2).

Nattoni, Duccio. "Storia di una Rivalità." *Il Grattapassere*, December, 1996. Contrada della Pantera.

Park, Hamish. "Passion, Remembrance, and Identity: The Palio of Siena." *Journal of Mediterranean Studies* 2 (1992): 80–97.

Repubblica. "Palio di Siena, vince la Pantera battuta di un soffio l'Aquila". Accessed 15 July, 2018. http://www.repubblica.it.

Rodi, Robert. *Seven Seasons in Siena: My Quixotic Quest for Acceptance among Tuscany's Proudest People.* New York: Ballantine Books, 2011.

Ryan, Carrie. "Panem et Circenses." In *The Girl Who Was on Fire: Your Favorite Authors on Suzanne Collins' Hunger Games Trilogy*, edited by Leah Wilson. Dallas: BenBella Books, 2010.

Sadler, Helen. "Palio Questions and Answers." Accessed January 24, 2014. http://www.ilpalio.org.

Silverman, Sydel. "The Palio of Siena: Game, Ritual, or Politics?" In *Urban Life in the Renaissance*, edited by Susan Zimmerman and Ronald F. E. Weissman, 224–239. Newark: University of Delaware Press, 1989.

Simpson, Aislinn. "Siena Palio Tamed by Health and Safety Rules." *The Telegraph*, July 28, 2009. http://www.telegraph.co.uk.

Speck, Jeff. *Walkable City: How Downtown Can Save America, One Step at a Time.* New York: Farrar, Straus and Giroux, 2012.

Tulini, Rudi. "The Race-Track." Translated by Helen Elizabeth Sadler. Accessed January 24, 2014. http://www.ilpalio.org.

Warner, Anna Kathrin. *Die Contraden von Siena. Lokale Traditionen und Globaler Wandel.* Frankfurt/New York: Campus Verlag, 2004.

ABOUT THE AUTHOR

Thomas (Tom) Paradis is a professor of geography and community planning at Butler University in Indianapolis, Indiana, USA. He was previously a professor at Northern Arizona University where he was recognized as a President's Distinguished Teaching Fellow. In addition to his broad teaching experiences in human and physical geography, he taught and led study-abroad programs in Siena for five consecutive years. He has also authored and edited various books and articles related to architectural history, downtown redevelopment, tourism geography, history of the American home, and—about his latest research in Siena—*Unbridled Spirit: The Untold Story of the 2018 Extraordinary Palio in Siena, Italy* (2020).

www.ingramcontent.com/pod-product-compliance
Lightning Source LLC
Chambersburg PA
CBHW021052080526
44587CB00010B/220